Praise for "The Devil You Know"

2014 Silver Falchion Award Winner at Killer Nashville for
Best Nonfiction: True Crime

"Interesting ... brilliant ... amazing research and well-
written. One of the best true crime books I have read in a
long time."
- Edgar Winner True Crime Author Burl Baer

"(The perpetrator) was just a monster in waiting ... a
horrific crime. Young Brad deserves his story to be told."
- Blogtalk Radio, "The Missing & Exploited"

J. Yates

The Devil You Know

JUDITH A. YATES

Judith A. Yates, Publisher, 2013

Editor: Jessica Efird
academic.editing.nc@gmail.com

Copyright © 2013 by Judith Yates
First printing 2013

ISBN-13: 978-0615781891 (Judith Yates)
ISBN-10: 0615781896
Published by Judith A. Yates utilizing
createspace.com

www.truecrimebook.net
truecrimebook@yahoo.com

Special discounts are available on quantity purchases by
corporations, educators, and others. For details contact
truecrimebook@yahoo.com.
US Trade books & wholesalers:
Contact truecrimebook@yahoo.com

For Brad Maddux
&
In Memory of Jon Oldham

CONTENTS

1. Early Morning, March 10, 1990

2. Westport

3. Bradley

4. "Mushroom"

5. March 9, 1990 (Friday)

6. "Where is Brad?"

7. "This Boy's Dead, Isn't He?"

8. Mitigating & Aggravating Circumstances

9. How?

10. "I Don't Know"

11. Putting the Pieces Together

12. Afterwards

13. Help in Preventing Crimes Against Children

14. Acknowledgements

15. Appendix & Resources

Beware the devil you know more than the devil you don't know.
   - *Proverb*

"Evil is as necessary as good. We need one to measure the other. Sometimes it is obvious what is good and what is evil. Sometimes you will never tell them apart."

   - *J. Yates, lecture on "Causes of Crime"*

"Brad was an angel. He still is."
   - Ernest "Junior" Armstrong

Author's Note

The Devil You Know is not a fictionalized version of the murder of Bradley Maddux. The narrative is based on three years and thousands of hours of interviewing, researching, and reviewing documentation such as reports, legal transcripts, photographs, media, court reports, and proven resources. All persons mentioned are real, but in order to protect some persons' or business' privacy, some parties requested a change in name; a name that appears initially in italics informs the reader of that change. Although a work of nonfiction, the nature of the story necessitated the need to recreate some conversations, based on multiple interviews, because no verbatim record exists. These alterations are as minuscule as possible in order to remain true to the story. Some people refused to be, or could not be, involved; therefore, their involvement stems from the recollection of events of other sources and persons; the people involved and I researched and reevaluated this information for accuracy. All of the dates, places, and events are true.

A percentage of book sales will go to a nonprofit organization which funds cancer prevention, chosen by the Maddux family, in memory of Brad. The organization is Living Beyond Breast Cancer (LBBC).org)

It is hoped if one child can be saved, if one child killer can be stopped, Brad did not die in vain.

The Devil You Know

EARLY MORNING, MARCH 10, 1990

The patch of woods stood about four miles from the man's house. He pulled his truck off of the blacktop highway onto a gravel road called 1300 S., only about a half-mile from a little town called Alert, Indiana. Once a thriving railroad town, Alert now consisted of just a few streets. Something rattled in the truck as the tires hit the gravel. It was a shovel.

The truck rolled along and turned between two large, square pillars onto a smaller gravel road. A thick fog choked the night air and obscured his view. The truck crawled, and then it made a U-turn to come to a stop. The man sat in the cab for a moment, listening to his own breathing, then looked about, checking his surroundings, although he knew no one followed him. When he cut the headlights, stillness and darkness enveloped the truck. The slight rumble of the engine and the humming of the heater became distant in his ears as he inhaled. He looked at his hands. They looked no different. Shouldn't they? He looked at himself in the small rearview mirror. Shouldn't he look different? Perhaps a strange light of deception or guilt in his eyes?

The man looked back into the bed of his truck at the dark shape that lay there. He felt no emotion. He only felt as if he should get out and get to work. The task was simple: dig a hole, bury the bundle, throw some stuff away, and get back home.

The man sitting in the truck fit the profile of a child murderer, according to a study conducted by the Bureau of Justice entitled, "Child Victimizers: Violent Offenders and Their Victims." According to the study, the number of child murders per year grew rapidly between 1984 and 1993. The man who sat in the pickup truck in the woods that night did not know those statistics. Nor, others such as law enforcement, the courts, and the families and friends report later, did he seem to care.

Some time later, the man drove out of the woods. He experienced a problem leaving, the truck tires were bogged down in the mud, and needed to gas it and get away from the woods. He unwittingly left tire tracks in the mud. He did not know it at the time, but a shoe print also betrayed his presence, left behind in the dirt. One more thing remained behind him: the bundle in the back of his truck was gone. Now he needed to go somewhere to wash the blood out of the back of the truck. The fog swirled around the truck, and he could feel the tires hit the blacktop again. Now the gravel and dust did not mix with the fog and distort his vision.

Not too far away from where he rolled to a halt at a stop sign, a family slept. Only a few hours later, they would be frantically calling the police to find their missing little boy.

It took place all over America, but tonight it happened in a tiny town called Westport, Indiana, where things like that "just didn't happen."

2 WESTPORT

The United States Government eagerly acquired land in 1819 via treaties that they made with the Native Americans, whom they called "Indians." The Indians did not quite understand how one could "own" land, but they humored the pale-faced men who smelled strange and, at times, acted worse than their scent. In Indiana, "The Indian Treaty of St. Mary's" granted Indiana a tract of land known as *The New Purchase*. Two families settled in this region: the Fugits and the Griffiths. A populated area emerged from *The New Purchase* in 1821 and became known as Decatur County. Commodore Stephen Decatur was a Navy hero who led and survived many amazing battles, but who died from a gunshot wound inflicted in a dual. Eventually Decatur County would swell to a population of about 25,000, but that was in the distant future.

In the very south of Decatur County, Westport, nestled in the far southern tip of Decatur County, became an official town on March 23, 1836, when two enterprising men laid out a plat of twenty lots. Even their names sounded enterprising, like something out of a story by the author H. H. Munroe, or "Saki." Mr. Hockersmith Merryman and Mr. Simeon Sharp had a vision; people already lived around the area soon to be known as Westport, but it could become a successful town. Three log huts sprang up and a town, of sorts, emerged. The townspeople raised the first frame building, the pounding of a hammer was an unfamiliar sound to the deer, raccoons, and other creatures that previously lived on the land undisturbed by man. The second frame building followed and, according to Westport's own town history, owner Noah Merryman kept "a few groceries and plenty of whiskey."

The use and abuse of alcoholic drink would play a part in Decatur County's most heinous crime. But 1990 seemed an impossibly long way away—not even yet real, in young Westport's eyes.

3

Several years later, the town boasted a tannery, a blacksmith shop, a dry goods store, a drug store, a wagon shop, and several houses, and the inhabitants finally began to consider themselves to be part of a community. The people liked the sound of that: "community." Two churches, Methodist and Christian, rounded out the community. There was a school, and the business district stayed steady.

The United States found itself embroiled in the Civil War, and most of the men and older boys in Westport, like those in so many other towns in the area, went marching off, trying not to look back, trying so hard to appear brave. The times were grim, and most who left did not return. The ladies wept behind their handkerchiefs.

Disaster struck in Westport in August of 1872, when a fire, aided by a southerly wind, destroyed much of the town. It seemed as if the devil came to Westport, jumping from building to building and tossing flames wildly into the structures along Main Street. The flames destroyed the most prosperous businesses: a hotel, the drug store, and the dry goods store, even the new post office. Several homes also became victims of the flames. It made the front page of the nearby Greensburg paper, *The Daily News*. Days later, when the fire died and the embers turned to dark soot, some of the business owners jutted out their chins and wanted to rebuild on different streets, creating more space between businesses, lest another flame spark. Others, dejected, packed their bags. It put a dent in the population, cutting the number of inhabitants almost in half as the 1870's drew to a close. The community started to look anemic.

In the late 1880s, far away on the east coast, the first case on child abuse appeared in the courtroom, and it concluded successfully with justice delivered to the offenders. Church employee Etta Wheeler visited a New York tenement family to check on reports of a crying child when she found a starved, beaten, ten year old girl. Black and white photographs show a child covered in open gashes from head to foot. The case helped lead to the founding of the New York Society for the Prevention of Cruelty to Children (NYSPCC). Until then, children possessed no legal voice. Their lives consisted of hard work, low survival rates, biblical interpretations that gave

4

parental rights to beat their children ("spare the rod and spoil the child") and, in the beginning early years of the country, legalized marriages of adult men to girls as young as twelve. The average woman gave live birth at least seven times, and one in every three or four children born died before the age of fifteen. The average person lived to be forty years old. Financial necessity demanded that children work to help support the family. From industrialization to the farms of middle America, children worked machines as large as two-story homes without safety valves; they plowed fields from before sunrise to after dusk, or they picked cotton, toted buckets, looked after smaller siblings, herded animals, and if they did not catch a deadly disease, they survived. Poor conditions and lack of sanitation and modern medicine caused mortality rates to rise to incredible heights in both the cities and in rural America. Infant graves dotted landscapes and city gravesites. Because they did not expect children to survive, many adults did not form attachments to their children; without such emotional ties, the children could be seen as a commodity. Westport was no exception; however, the people of Westport did not consider the infant mortality rate to be the work of the devil, but rather as only a part of life.

1877 saw the birth of child protective legislation, including acts prohibiting the sale of intoxicants to minors. Alcoholism, according to the NYSPCC, figured greatly in the abuse and exploitation of children. In 1888, the NYSPCC began to pass acts "regulating obscene material with respect to children." Of course sexual abuse of children always plagued the nation, but now children possessed some legal refuge from their offenders. The Society did not just oversee the legal protection of children; from 1880 to 1950, the Society also worked with law enforcement to investigate missing children reports.

All of these things would come together in 1990 in Westport, but by then they were considered just a part of history.

1880 brought the V.G. & R. Railroad snorting, whistling, and chugging new life into a struggling Westport. The incoming rush of people helped restore the sense of community to the town as they arrived, seeking a safe society. The schools boasted a grand reputation.

5

Construction began, and Westport even acquired a newspaper in 1890. And then the devil appeared to visit again.

A second fire crept into the November night in 1911 and reduced eight buildings to kindling before the town tamed the devil's flames. Another hotel, several barns, a hardware store, and more businesses fell to their deaths. Fortunately modernization recently arrived in Westport, and fire fighters now possessed fire-fighting equipment that allowed them to save several buildings with this new technology. Modernization saved the community.

In fact, the world outside quickly caught up to and surpassed this community. Henry Ford introduced the first automobile to the world, and now in the streets, among the clip-clop of horse hooves and the jangle of bits and harnesses, folks heard "honk honk!" Service stations and garages went up quickly to accommodate these amazing machines. The puzzled horses probably eyed them from their feedbags, confused, the whites of their eyes showing as if to say, "What is this contraption?"

In 1889, the New York Society for the Prevention of Cruelty to Children assisted in "prohibiting the sale of tobacco to minors" (NYSPCC, 2000). Children slowly began to possess a legal voice.

It seemed as if the United States ground to a halt during the depression, from 1928 to almost 1940, and Westport felt the pinch along with everyone else. The community relied on one another more than ever. The blues spilled from radios, gardens sprang forth much-needed vegetables, and homeless families walked or rode or drove past, asking for – no work? Okay, thank you kindly.

Since the 1920s, business growth in Westport came to a standstill. A bakery, a restaurant, and a garage arose, but downtown Westport remained pretty much the same since. In the late 1940s, lots with homes began to spring up; like the tall stalks of corn so many relied on to survive, they grew on the outskirts of the community. Folks used State Highway 3 to get to those outskirts—a two-lane road built in 1937 that ran north to south.

Despite setbacks, Westport pulled along, always a community, and the construction of major highways eventually connected the little town to big cities. Interstate I65 cut north and south nearby. Soon they could travel to

6

Chicago or Milwaukee with ease; they were just hours from big cities like Nashville or Lexington. They could do all of this and yet still come home to their community. In all of Westport's advertisements, they still referred to themselves as a "community."

Today, downtown Westport is a pretty little area, with picturesque Victorian-style homes wedged between prairie-style one-story houses on the streets that lead to the main downtown area. Westport does not boast many restaurants; they have a store where you can order excellent home-made sandwiches, a pizza place with heaping portions and great service, but best of all, kids can ride their bicycles on the same main street where trucks and farm equipment rumble to and from town. Some of the original buildings that withstood the two fires still stand. A baseball diamond and basketball courts, reminiscent of a Norman Rockwell painting, stand in the middle of the town. A library, playground, and recreation center adjourn the fields and courts. Westport does not have any strings of fast-food restaurants or chain stores. It has a comfortable feel, like you can relax and slow to a stroll. Main Street, as you are driving away from downtown, is lined with ancient trees that create a canopy over the road, as if shading it from outside influences. It is as time stands still, and everyone says hello to each other by name. As the roads expand outside of the downtown area, homes become the more modern ranch-style and are made of brick. Old-fashioned names of streets like "Elizabeth" become "CR." People move a bit faster, and farmland replaces well-tended, small yards.

This is farming country, where stores that specialize in products like New Holland, Kubota, and Massey-Ferguson dot every other corner. Some folks decorate their kitchens in John Deere motifs, and flyers advertising tractor pulls hang in restaurant windows. When people give directions here, they do not name streets or give road numbers. "When you get to the second bend," they explain, "look for a big red barn, and then take that immediate right. Get to the second gravel road. It'll be the third house." Weather determines the success of livelihoods. Farmers know that if Wall Street has a bad day, hundreds of people can lose money, but they know far more importantly that if their farm has a bad month, millions of people may not eat. Because of this hard fact of life, the weather channel is monitored intently. "Farmers are truly the biggest gamblers in the United States," says one resident. They work long, hard hours in the field almost every day. A single piece of imperative farm equipment may cost more than a three-bedroom home, and it takes a lot of equipment to run a successful farm. Even with a zero dollar land investment, a farmer may invest $500 an acre, with fertilizer at $250 alone, in a place where they work anywhere from 500 to 7,000 acres per farm. If the weather agrees – not too much and not too little rain – the crops will pay off. When driving past the fields of Westport and seeing this equipment working in the fields, people will always wave, even if the farmer does not see them.

The drive on the outskirts of Westport is beautiful in any season, but fall produces colors that give the viewer a real treat. Mother Nature shows off her most brilliant hues of gold, emerald, yellow, russet, orange, and red. Huge leaves dance and twirl to land on the pavement of the two-lane highways, then whirl about madly as the eighteen-wheelers, cars, and farm trucks roll through the splendor. Cattle, horses, goats, and occasionally sheep dot the fields on either side, but it is mostly corn or beans. The crops that cover thousands of acres for miles serve to remind the driver that this is corn country. The air is crisp and clean, as if biting into a healthy, natural apple.

Westport's most notable landmark is a large covered bridge, built in 1880, located at the Southeast edge of Westport off of CR 1100S over Sand Creek. The signs that welcome visitors to town feature this beloved landmark. Everyone in Westport invites visitors to see their bridge before leaving, if they did not already get the chance to see it while visiting.

One resident can trace his roots to several hundred yards away from where he stands on his front porch. "My great-grandfather came from Ohio and built a two room sod house in that field," he says, pointing across the road at one of his acres. His great-grandmother refused to dwell in a sod home, so her husband selected the best wood around--oak and beech, which bugs could not penetrate-- and began building a large, white frame home several feet from the "soddy." His great-grandfather painted it white for practical reasons; white reflects heat. His great-

8

grandparents finally reunited when she took the train into town and joined her husband in 1867. Like the farmers around them, they kept an eye on the weather, first by "signs" and then by more sophisticated methods. Beans, corn, and wheat came up, quickly followed by cattle, as one relies on the other. The house still stands. The resident notes a church built in the 1800s nearby, still standing and still in use.

One resident is quick to talk about how Westport crime seemed to rise in the 1990s, but dissipated around 2000. Drug manufacturing, particularly methamphetamines, seems to be the current issue. The people manufacturing the "meth" steal chemicals from the farms and use the chemicals for "cooking" the drug. The Westport Police Department reported six registered sex offenders in 2010. There is a Police Chief, one Marshall, one Deputy Marshall, and one Reserve Officer in the department. All are white males.

Westport, like many small towns, seems to have its own unspoken but well-known set of norms. "People seem to get mad at you for doing well," says one ex-resident. People expect others to stay in a certain income, act a certain way, and remain in the Westport norm. "You have to stay mediocre." The resident grew up in Westport but says, "I got out as fast as I could" because the town "likes things a certain way. The schools had the typical groups: the athletes, the popular kids, the head bangers, the cowboys. Still, the social life of a young person is often limited to people their own age; "if you were out, you were out with everybody," explains the former Westport resident. There is not much attention paid on who "hangs out" with whom. This same philosophy affects the townspeople's lifestyles and behaviors. The community expects men to be rugged, strong, and intolerant of weakness or perceived gentleness in other men. Drinking at an early age is "a man thing" and a rite of passage. Young men are expected to sneak alcohol and imbibe in sex and smoking, or else to use smokeless tobacco known as "dip," to prove they are tough, strong, and heterosexual. By the 1990s, the NYSPCC offered free educational seminars on sexual abuse of minors. Federal and state laws attempt to protect children from sexual abuse, and

9

many agencies exist in an effort to assist victims. However, few small towns find this assistance necessary, or even important to know about. Everyone knows one another, and besides, they moved to the small town to escape city crime.

Indiana currently holds the twenty-ninth spot in the Violent Crime Rate National Ranking. In towns like Westport, violent crime seems to only exist far away in the big cities. In the last census, there were 1,374 people living in Westport. That is 540 households. The closest airport is a fifty-mile drive away. The town is 90% white. The majority of the residents are married. Most families have at least two children. It is not a gay-friendly town; when people say, "He's different," they say it as if it is not a good thing, and they mean homosexual, as if it is not a good thing. They mean homosexual, but they are too afraid to say the word. Everyone knows one another somehow, someway, either by marriage, birth, or friendship. Many people in Westport were born here and stayed here. Some folks were born in the area and moved away only to return. Most can trace their roots to a home down the road or across town. Almost everyone knows everyone else's business, be it divorce, marriage, how happy the other one is, or how dissatisfied someone is. Although the community has issues, no one expected the devil to return.

The devil did return. Despite the churches, from Life Aposolistic on State Road 3 to the Baptist Church on East Main, the devil came back. But he was not the devil the religions preached of. Growing up, the children of Westport learn that heaven is a place in the sky where fluffy white clouds and harps surround them, and angels sing choir songs and wear white robes. They learn that Hell is, well, hot. It consists of fire and brimstone, and it is where the devil reigns over misery, where Westport sinners fear to go. The devil in art is depicted as male and red; he spouts a pointed tail and red horns and carries a pitchfork. He always has an evil smile. You would recognize him anywhere so you could run away to safety. The devil the churches preach of is easy to spot and easier to avoid.

There is an old saying, "Beware the devil you know more than the devil you don't." It is a proverb meaning one should be more cautious of those they know than those they do not know. On March 10, 1990, in Westport, Indiana, this came true for a community, a family, some friends, and a little boy who trusted.

3 BRADLEY

BAM! BAM! BAM!
Tammy Hileman jumped, heart in her throat, hands instantly shaking as the adrenaline shot through her. One hand went to her throat in response to the noise at her back window. She peered at the hallway toward the rear of her home, wondering if she dared to go see ...
There was a knock at the front door.
Still slightly jumpy, Tammy hoisted herself up off the couch. Seven months pregnant, she moved slowly, and she used the edge of the couch to balance herself. She was a self-admitted "'fraidy cat" for no reason. She felt safe from burglars in her home, a cozy two bedroom she shared with her husband, *Jack*. No one had ever actually broken into their home and harmed her. She was a tall woman with sparkling blue eyes and flaxen hair. To a stranger, Tammy looked like she could take care of herself, but she would rather be baking in a sunny kitchen than a practicing pugilist.
When she opened the front door, she let out a breath of relief. There stood her nephew, twelve-year-old Bradley Maddux, a big grin showing the gap between his front teeth, blue eyes twinkling mischievously. "Brad!" she said loudly, opening the door to allow him in. "I was scared to death! There was a loud noise at the back of the house!"
Brad strutted in and Tammy failed to see the big grin on his face. "Don't worry, Aunt Tammy," he said gallantly. "I'll save you! I'm your white knight in shining armor!"
Tammy shut the door slowly and turned to look at her nephew, suspicion across her face. He was trying too hard to look casual. "I don't suppose you know anything about a noise, do you, Brad?" she asked.
His blue eyes became big and round, and he tried to bow his mouth into innocence. "What noise, Aunt Tammy? You mean someone hitting the back window?" Too late he realized he gave himself away, and they both broke into

12

laughter.

Tammy grabbed him by his husky shoulders and gave him a shake. "Boy, one of these days—" Then she pulled him close to hug him, and he hugged her back, tight.

"I'll always scare you with that one." He was waving her off, still chuckling. Brad loved a good prank and this was a particular favorite, like the time he asked a friend to scratch eerily on her back window and he then showed up on the porch innocently. "I'll save you! I'm your white knight in shining armor!" he told her from the porch, ready to "save" his "favorite aunt."

Tammy's husband, Jack, was Brad's maternal uncle, the brother of Brad's mother, Patti. Tammy could recall every detail of Brad's birth, and she instantly loved him. He spent a lot of time at her house. They watched television together, they played card games, and they listened to music and talked. Sometimes Brad, Tammy, and Jack would spend weekends on getaways to hotels where they would splash in the hotel pool, their laughter echoing off tiled walls. They would travel the few hours to Indianapolis, have a nice dinner somewhere, and giggle and talk and enjoy one another's company. Tammy loved Brad's siblings, Cody and Lindsay, who also spent time at her home, but she and Brad had a special bond. He doted on her and, when she became pregnant, he fussed over her, making sure she took care of herself.

"We still going swimming tonight?" Tammy asked him as they made their way to the couch. She moved to sit down carefully. He placed pillows around her for comfort.

"Of course!" Brad waited until she was comfortable before he sat. He loved swimming. He loved most sports. Brad began to softly rub Tammy's protruding belly and sing to it. "It's going to be a boy," he said knowingly.

"Now, how do you know that?"

Brad interrupted his little song to say, "I just know." He said to her stomach, "And his name is going to be Brandon."

Tammy leaned back on the couch, smiling at her nephew as he sang and softly patted her protruding tummy. "You'll feel silly when it's a girl."

Brad gave her one of his looks. ""I'll bet you a mushroom sauce pizza." He loved her mushroom pizzas. Once, when

13

she had run out of a certain ingredient, Tammy had improvised and used mushroom sauce for their homemade pizzas. Brad and Jack gobbled it up at dinner, raving it was the best they had ever had. Now it was a stock favorite.

"And if I win?" she asked him, ruffling his hair.

He pushed his short, dark hair back and said, "It's a boy," as if there was were no debating it. He leaned forward and talked to the baby in the womb. "I can't wait to meet you, Brandon," he whispered, patting Tammy's tummy softly. "I'm going to teach you to play football. Do you know what a football is? Don't worry. I'll show you how. We'll have fun. I love you!" He cooed into her stomach. "I loooove yooooouu, Brandon! Brandon the football player!"

Tammy shook her head at him. Brad, her white knight in shining armor.

Bradley Daryl Maddux was born on August 19, 1977 in Columbus, Indiana. His family called him "Brad." He had blonde, curly hair that darkened as he grew and had to be forced smooth for pictures. He had his mother's blue eyes, and freckles dotted his face. Brad's arrival excited Cody, who anxiously looked forward to being a big brother.

Brad's father, Daryl Maddux, hailed from Indianapolis. He graduated high school in Westport and then enlisted in the Navy in June of 1969. An early photograph of Daryl in uniform shows a serious young man, but there is a tiny bit of a smile trying to creep across his face. He looks proud to serve his country and excited, looking toward the adventures promised. In the military, Third Class Petty Officer Maddux was an E4. He was one of the 455 men who sailed on the USS Gridley DLG/CG-21, "The Grey Ghost of the South China Coast." To this day the guided missile ship, whose maximum speed was 30 knots, is still touted as, "The World's Greatest Cruiser."

The service took Daryl Maddux to Japan, and he did his duty while fighting from the decks of the USS Gridley in Viet Nam. His four years completed, Daryl left the Navy and returned to Westport to be with his family. His father, Richard, carved out a niche in town while Daryl served; the elder Maddux owned a pharmacy, Maddux Drug Store, in Westport.

Westport native Kenny Nugent's family grew up across the street from the Maddux family. He recalled going to

14

Maddux Drug Store and spending time at the old-fashioned soda shop that was part of the pharmacy. Kenny would spend much idle time there, talking to friends, eating, "hanging out with everyone." This included members of Daryl's family. Nugent recalls The Maddux Drug Store hosted many good times.

Daryl Maddux returned to the quiet town in 1973, after seeing the world. He obtained work in a mill, and in January of 1975, a family friend talked to him about working as an EMT. Daryl found his calling as an Emergency Management Technician, answering calls for help in Jennings County for anything from dog bites to fatal car crashes. Daryl was a big man, tall, with wide shoulders and big hands. He kept his hair military-short and neat. He looked like a football player, but he was more cerebral than muscular. He had a cool head and a way of talking to people that instantly put them at ease. He had an excellent sense of humor, but it was the quiet type; he would quip a one-liner or say something funny and you would have to be quick to catch on. He was a caregiver-type personality, a lifesaver. Daryl worked alongside law enforcement, including a young Indiana State Trooper he befriended named Jon Oldham. Oldham eventually moved through the ranks to become an investigator. When someone burglarized Richard Maddux's pharmacy, Jon Oldham took charge of the case. Daryl Maddux admired Oldham's tenacity and investigative skills. They remained friends and, many times, coworkers.

Daryl was also friends with a family named Compton. There were boys in the Compton family who were his age, and he spent a lot of his time with them. These boys had a cousin who was a pretty, dark-haired girl named Patti. Daryl knew her marginally because he knew her cousins, but he never really spoke to her. Finally, when he did, there was a spark. Daryl began spending more time talking to Patti, and the tall, handsome EMT and blue-eyed Patti fell in love.

They married and settled down in Westport to raise a family. Daryl continued his work as an EMT and Patti worked in a doctor's office. Daryl was a laid-back, quiet fellow, who was quiet and calm, who had a good heart—the kind of person that was good to have around in a pinch. Patti was tough, some even say difficult to get along

15

with initially, and could be abrasive; but she loved her family. Patti was the type of person who would call out a wrongdoing instantly, and if she felt something was not fair she would speak up. She was good to have around in an emergency and the type of person whom you would call on for solid advice. They lived on a street called West Kentucky Avenue, in a quiet neighborhood where neighbors watched out for one another, and everyone knew one another on a first name basis. Everyone looked out for one another's children, and if one child acted up, someone would call the child's parents. If one person needed help, another person assisted. It seemed idyllic, as if nothing bad could come to this community.

Cody Shane Maddux was born on February 2, 1974. February is bitterly cold in this part of Indiana, with incredibly cold temperatures and wind chills that can take your breath away. The winds sweep across the flat, barren fields, and power outages are normal due to the weather and winds. "The weather on my birthday always sucks," Cody, not a cold weather fan, says, ruthful.

Bradley Daryl Maddux came along in 1977. It seemed, looking back, as if he came out of the womb smiling. Everyone you talk to remembers Brad as a "happy" child. Every photo shows him not just smiling, but also enjoying a great laugh. "That's Brad," his best friend Ernest "Junior" Armstrong said later. "He was a happy-go-lucky kid. And he was funny! He was either laughing or he kept you laughing." One family snapshot pictures Brad, with his hands entwined in his curly hair, toddling to a stop. He is enjoying a good belly laugh. He is a safe, happy little boy. He is much-loved, and enjoying life. He is one year old.

Another picture, this time with Cody, as they celebrate Brad's first birthday, shows a very pleased-looking Brad with a new gift he received. Cody is evidently very happy for his little brother, as both are caught in mid-scream. It appears to have been a great celebration. With gaily-colored paper strewn about and both boys in high merriment, the celebration appears both fun and entertaining.

Patti snapped a proud "Mom moment" of her youngest son standing on the living room coffee table, doing some junior modeling of his new clothes. On the back of the picture she wrote in eloquent handwriting, "Brad, in new overalls his aunt got him, 1979." Brad is beaming. He is adorable, from his cotton curls to the rolled-up legs of his new attire. Destined to be a farmer.

When he was not quite two, Brad became a big brother himself. When Lindsay Ann was born on June 13, 1979, Brad was ecstatic. He was two years old, and he loved to climb up next to his new baby sister and coo to her. He would fall asleep protectively next to her. Lindsay was a pretty little baby, with eyes that inquisitively stared out at the world around her. Someone snuck up on Brad and ambushed him with a camera, snapping him while he tried to visit Lindsay in her crib. The result reveals a four-month-old Lindsay stretched out like a little starfish in her onesie and diaper. Brad is in his pajamas, his hand on his head and laughing hysterically. Lindsay's expression seems to say, "What's going on now?" Brad's expression reads, "Busted!"

As they grew, the three siblings grew fiercely supportive of one another, but they also were like polar magnets, as only siblings can be. "Lindsay got left out a lot," recalled a friend, "because she was a girl, and because she was little." Lindsay adored her big brothers and she toddled behind them, wanting to play with them. Occasionally she could sweet-talk Brad into joining her for a pretend tea party or at least humor her by playing "house" or some other girly endeavor. If she nagged him she may even get him to sit near while she played with her dolls. Cody, nearly five years her senior, she could never interest in a game, for he was ever practical, and stalwart in what boys were "supposed to do." Cody was a believer in what were 'boy games" and "girl games" per Westport standards. Brad would at least try.

For all his sweetness, Brad was also made of "snips and snails" as the old poem reads, and he was all boy. He was a blue jeans and t-shirts kind of kid, dressing up only if he had to do so. He enjoyed and preferred to spend his time fishing, spending times exploring the woods with his big brother, and racing about on farmland. Brad and Cody shared a room, and Lindsay had her own room. As brothers will, they played tricks on their sister. Lindsay would get furious and then laugh with them later. Like the time Cody tired of her going into his side of the room without his permission, so the boys devised a rubber band "rope" tied together, end to end. They rigged it to their doorknob so that when Lindsay snuck into the boy's room, the band would snap and whack her in the chest or face. Inevitably, she ran crying to mom, holding her cheek where the rubber band hit her.

"What happened?" Patti would ask. When Lindsay would admit that the boys contrived a way to stop her from trespassing again, and as a result she paid the price with a rubber band to the face, ever-practical Patti would say, "Well, you shouldn't have been in his room."

The house at 204 West Kentucky Avenue always seemed to have something going on, with two growing boys and a little girl chasing after them to catch up. "That girl," Cody Maddux says now, "Had more stitches growing up than..." he shakes his head. "I don't even remember how many times she was in the emergency room." Cody can account for three stitches in her head, but he adds immediately, "I didn't start it."

Circumstances necessitated the need for the Maddux parents to leave Cody in charge for the duration of one evening. Three-year-old Lindsay found herself alone, and, as always, she went searching for her brothers through the house. "Co-deee! Bwwwad!" She found them in Daryl and Patti's bedroom, sitting on the waterbed, imbibing in a tin of Sucrets cough drops where Patti had left them on the waterbed's headboard. Not wishing to be left out of anything resembling a treat, Lindsay also helped herself.

Crunch, crunch – Nasty! This was not candy! Disappointed, Lindsay placed the red and white tin back on the headboard, and Patti was none the wiser. This was about the time a new game began: jumping on the waterbed.

What fun it was, to jump off the side-rails onto the mattress that sloshed and rocked back and forth! Brad had naturally devolved into hysterics, laughing so hard that he could hardly stand, and Cody predictably tried to out-jump Brad. Then Cody would stumble and make Brad fall, and his shrieks filled the house. Both boys' faces were red, and their sweaty skin plastered their hair to their foreheads. Cody was rolling over on the bed, giggling and giggling, as Lindsay tried to keep her balance, doing a good job up until she lost her sea legs. When her skull connected with the headboard and the *crrrackk* resounded, it was Game Over.

Both boys were prepared for emergencies. When their parents came home, Cody and Brad explained they had been playing "cars," lining up two kitchen chairs side by side in the living room. Lindsay had the role of "Drunk Driver." When she had exited her vehicle, she fell and struck her head on the stone hearth. The Maddux parents packed her up, and it was off to the ER for Lindsay, their parents none the wiser.

Brad was wonderful at keeping secrets, and he always had your back. That is, until he got mad. When he got angry, and the freckles on his nose disappeared in a red, puffy face, his chunky body would swell up, his hands would double into fists, and he let fly all of the secrets that he kept stored in his mind. All of them; he tattled on his siblings, on his friends, and even on himself. This is how Daryl found out it was not a game of "cars" that led to little Lindsay cutting her head open. "I looked all over that bedroom for blood," Daryl Maddux said later. "White carpet! How those kids kept white carpet clean, I never figured it out. Then I found out: they had Lindsay stand in the bathtub while she bled so they could clean the comforter."

There was sibling upsets, but Brad hated rows and "he was very easy-going," Lindsay remembers. "We had the usual brother-sister things, but he didn't like to fight."

Brad's temper could flare on rare occasion—he would get angry about something, or at someone, and he would start to tattle. And the tattling kept going. His breath would come in short, fast spurts, he would shake, and his little fists would ball up. His usually happy face would turn red, and tears would fight to stay in his squinting eyes. Sometimes it was because of Cody, or a perceived injustice. But he was such a good boy, such a sweet kid, that it was difficult to stay angry with him. Besides, when he started the tattling, especially on himself, it was just so funny. Like the time he and his brother decided to take their grandfather's truck for a test-drive.

Brad and Cody's maternal step-grandfather, "Grandpa Dave" Giddings, asked the boys to move his truck from the yard. In the country, this is not a huge deal or even given a side glance; boys learn to drive and move farm equipment at an early age. It is safe when they drive a vehicle in a large field or backing out and pulling away from a barn. Both boys headed out the door. Grandpa Dave waited for their return ... and return...and waited. He waited for his keys to be returned He sat there, expecting the boys to return his keys at any moment... And he waited ... waited...

That is when the family discovered that the little boys decided that once they backed up the truck out of the drive, Brad and Cody might as well see what was going on downtown. They were not too far away; heck, they only needed to take a few turns, and downtown Westport would be theirs. One boy scooted the truck seat forward as far as it would go, sitting up tall to turn the steering wheel, peering under and around the wheel and dashboard. They puttered around town, up East Main Street, past Government Avenue, across South Poplar Street. Taking turns at the wheel, they took in the town, young gentlemen of leisure. They were two little boys, out for a drive in a pickup truck to see the sights, rolling along.

There was another time when Brad attempted to move a truck, but he was not as successful. Something happened in the scheme of things and the truck roared, and then it took on a life of its own. It lurched forward, through the yard, plowed through a bush, and stopped suddenly. Brad sat behind the wheel, his freckles appearing as dots on a blanche face for a few seconds, and then he fell over in the seat, laughing so hard that tears streamed down his cheeks.

"Grandpa Dave" was a big, barrel-chested man with a booming voice, tall, and who towered over most almost everyone in the town. He adored his grandchildren, and he was a pal to all of the boys in the area. He loved practical jokes and games as much as any of them and would play along as long as no one got hurt, and everyone had fun. He bantered back and forth with the kids, playing with them and joking. They loved him as much as he loved them back, and every youngster that grew up around him called him "Grandpa Dave." He stood up for those he cared about and could be mean if it came down to it, but his heart was huge—"bigger than he was" according to a neighbor—when it came down to Cody, Bradley, and

Lindsay. "He taught us all kinds of things," Cody Maddux says now. "Carpentry, building things."

Brad's best buddy, Junior Armstrong, remembers Grandpa Dave with great fondness. "He was so funny! He got into as much trouble as we did, and then he helped us hide."

Brad, as a little boy, often mimicked Dave, including the sometimes salty language. When Grandpa Dave was enjoying some particularly beautiful Christmas music, a family member recalls a tiny Brad sauntering in and asking, "Do you know the song, 'Ol' King Cole was a very merry soul with a big asshole?'" That's when Grandpa Dave knew little Brad picked up language like a parrot in a cage.

Brad kept Dave's cigarettes for him, partially in an effort to stop him from smoking, says a friend. Often Brad and Grandpa Dave would banter back and forth about the cigarettes, with Brad telling Dave to "catch him" to "come and get" a cigarette. "Brad!" Grandpa Dave called, grunting as he bent low to look under the house where Brad and his friends played in the small space. "Bring me a cigarette." He was puffing from his generous bulk.

"Come and get 'em!" Brad called out in merriment.

"Boy!" Grandpa Dave experienced trouble breathing due to the effort to lean so low; his belly was not as lean as it was back in the day. "Bring me a cigarette or I'll come under there to tan your hide!"

"Your butt won't even fit!"

Silence. Then all of them fell into hysterics. Grandpa Dave figured the boy was right. If he could not fit under the house to chase Brad, how could he possibly be fit to give a spanking?

One of Brad's friends recalls a water fight that started between Grandpa Dave, Brad, and some of his friends. The battle made its way into Main Street, until it seemed as if every kid in the neighborhood joined the fun. The fire department turned on the water plugs, and soon everyone was a part of it – and soaked—and laughing outrageously at one another and the fun.

Lynn Welch, a neighbor, lived near Grandpa Dave and his wife. She was older than Brad and remembers him as "a people pleaser. More like an adult pleaser. (Brad) was one of those kids who looks for approval," particularly from Grandpa Dave. She saw Brad as more inclined to hang

21

around the adults, looking for their attention. It was not in a bad way. Because of the personality of a small town, young boys seek out mentors and role models in order to obtain approval from them, or models to obtain approval from. The majority demands certain behaviors from each gender, and young people, who seek approval the most, want to be recognized for good behavior and need to know what "good behavior" means. "It's like a pat on the head for a puppy," Lynn Welch explains. "You know, 'you did well.'"

Later, people would wonder if Brad's need for acceptance led to the horror story.

Bradley Maddux did well in school. Westport proudly sported two schools, and Bradley attended Decatur Elementary School, "the Home of the Cougars." He would move to South Decatur Junior/Senior High School in 1991, for Decatur Elementary went from grades Preschool to sixth grade. He made above average grades; "Brad's grades were excellent," Cody remembers. "They passed me to get me the hell out of there. But Brad did a lot better than me in school." Their parents were strict about grades, particularly Patti. She wanted Brad to crack the books and take his education seriously. He did well, bringing home As and Bs to show his parents. His favorite class was Art, and he loved drawing. He would try to draw anything, concentrating carefully on the paper, blue eyes squinting and focused.

Despite taking his grades seriously, Brad was the class clown, always smiling and pleasant, always there when you needed to laugh. Student Summer Hobbs, a strikingly pretty little girl with dark hair and eyes, met Brad in kindergarten. The two went through school together, and Brad always had found a way to make Summer giggle. "He was the class clown," Summer says now. "He had the cutest little freckled smile." Sometimes a teacher would have to rap on a desk to get them to settle down. Summer would need to clamp a hand over her mouth to make herself hush, and she dared not sneak a look at her buddy, Brad, the source of the mirth.

Friends and family agree that even at a young age, Brad was quite a ladies man. "He was always telling girls, 'you look nice' and giving compliments," remembers Sheila

Padgett, who knew Brad from the time they were infants. Sheila's mother and Patti Maddux were good friends. Patti's sister, Judy, was also a good friend of Mrs. Padgett. Furthermore, the grandparents shared a property line: Grandpa Dave's backyard adjoined with the elder Padgett's yard. As a result, Sheila and Brad were toddlers together, and then they attended the same classes until the sixth grade. Even then, Sheila and Brad visited in the school lunchroom and on the playground, or at the city park. Little girls liked Brad because he was soft-spoken and sweet, with those pretty blue eyes and freckles on his nose. Brad also knew how to treat a lady; he smiled docilely at an age when other little boys pulled pigtails and made faces at the opposite sex.

Jill Bishop met Brad in the first grade and adored him instantly. Unlike Sheila, Jill and Brad were not in the same group; the classes of about ninety-four students were split into classroom groups numbering twenty-five to twenty-eight students each. Despite this setback, she met with him out on the playground and they played the usual games. "He was so happy, a great kid," Jill fondly reminisces. "Nice to everybody!" Even as a small boy, Brad "enjoyed life. He was always joking around, and you never saw him without a smile." Jill met Lindsay a little bit later when they passed in the hallway; she would meet Cody in Junior High.

In third grade, Brad's classroom seat was next to a cute little girl named Tasha Asher. Always the ladies' man, Brad and Tasha began talking to one another in class and shared giggles and secrets. "He was always sweet to me," Tasha recalls. Tasha's family also lived in Westport, and Brad, Tasha, and other friends lived close enough to each other that they could, as they grew, venture out together to play. At the time, Tasha Asher recalls, parents only gave the advice, "Be home before dark," and off the kids would go: to the park, to ride bicycles, or to whatever childhood adventure awaited them.

Brad earned a nickname from Tasha and another friend, *Lee*, a brother of Junior Armstrong. One day while sitting in class, the three students began discussing a popular movie starring Tom Cruise: "Top Gun," Lee told Tasha and Brad. Then one of them said, "Top *gum*," and the three burst into giggling. From then on, whenever they saw one another, they would call out, "Hey, Top Gum!" They walked to the playground, located in the center of town, and Brad would oblige pushing the merry-go-round for them, or swinging on the swing set, talking and laughing, being silly and enjoying the day.

Brad often asked Tasha if she would like to assist him on his paper route. "That made me feel special," she recalls, "He was a good friend to me, and I'll always cherish those memories."

Tasha often walked to a friend's house; and the best way to get there involved cutting through a large field. While walking through that field, she would make plans as to what she and her chums, usually including Brad, would do that evening, or on the weekend. Brad was "a rough and tumble" boy who loved sports and could play tough with his male friends, but when it came to Tasha or other little girls, he was sweet and took time out for them. This included, in play, his sister Lindsay.

On occasion, Brad and Cody allowed Lindsay to play "Army" with them, and she was a "soldier" in the pretend trenches. She also liked trooping along with them to the pond in her grandmother's backyard. Their paternal grandmother owned a home at the end of their street, and it held a marvelous pond, perfect for capturing frogs, turtles, and toads to bring home. Lindsay, Brad, and Cody sloshed about in the water, mud sucking at their shoes, as they scooped up the slimy creatures, shouting out their catch to one another. Light breezes ruffled their hair as the frogs and other amphibians leaped for safety. Brad's infectious laughter caught the others, and sometimes they laughed so hard, it was difficult to hunt.

Sheila Padgett found the carefully folded note slipped in her locker and read it in her third grade class. On the outside of the note was a hand drawn heart with an arrow through it, like on one of those old-fashioned valentines. "To Sheila from Brad" was printed painstakingly on .the note. It read:

I like you. Will you be my girl friend? Circle YES or NO

Of course, Sheila circled the YES and returned the note

shyly. And that was that. Their romance bloomed and they did what "couples" in third grade did: they sat together at lunch, and they played games on the playground during recess. Sheila cherished him. He was funny —he would say something off the cuff, make a funny comment, do practically anything, and it would make her double over laughing. He said "ma'am" and "sir" when appropriate and never tested his teachers' patience. They played "tag" at recess and saw each other in the town park, swinging on the swings and watching the older kids play sports.

One day Brad approached Sheila and opened up his hand. "I found this and I want to give it to you," he said, "Because you're my girlfriend." It was a delicate heart pendent made of rhinestones. The back was broken so she couldn't use it, but Sheila was so taken. She shyly accepted it and it sealed their elementary school romance. Brad was such a sweetie! And look what he gave her.

Later, Sheila discovered, Brad had "found" the pendent in Patti Maddux's jewelry box and snuck it out of their home. Later in the school year, Sheila Padgett was livid. It was third grade and she made the decision to tell her boyfriend just exactly what she thought of him, Mr. Brad Maddux, and rid herself of boy trouble for good. "I don't even remember what it was about," Sheila laughs now. But it was third grade, and he had broken her heart, and she was not about to let it show. Sheila marched up to Brad in the cafeteria. "You're a jerk!" she said loudly, lower lip trembling. "And I'm breaking up with you, so there!"

Brad regarded her with the cool disposition of a rooster who had plenty of chickies in the pen. "The feelings," he said calmly, "are mutual." He sounded more like a forty-year-old than a kid holding a lunch tray.

Oooh! How dare he! Sheila's anger reduced her to sputtering, but Brad's statement also took her by surprise. "The feelings are mutual?" What exactly did that mean? This was a first. Sheila was left red-faced and trying to figure out what exactly that meant (mutual?) when Brad started laughing. It was so Brad: say something crazy to take you off track when you were trying to be angry.

One evening Brad brought home a tiny puffball of a puppy, with a curly-q of a tail that rested across its haunches. Brad told his parents the most pitiful, heart-wrenching boy-meets-dog story: while riding his bicycle, he noticed a burlap sack on the roadside. He watched as this little black-and-brown pup bravely chewed its way to freedom while Brad rolled to a stop. As the tiny snout and round head popped out, two little black eyes met Brad's blue ones. "Isn't he cute?" Brad kept asking, pleading his case. "He's so cute!" The pup looked like a malamute-chow fence-jumping-Romeo mix, and it toddled about when not in Brad's protective arms. That was how Teddy found sanctuary with the Maddux family, and he was with them for thirteen long, happy, safe years.

Later, when Brad became angry over something and told on himself, Daryl found out about Teddy's true origin: A boy at school was telling classmates about the litter of pups his dog had, and Brad yearned for one. Brad arranged to peddle his bike several miles to the school chum's house to pick up a new puppy and bring it home, scheming the whole way.

Jean Hickey taught at South Decatur Elementary; she had spent her career teaching at this school, through kids who squirmed in their seats to children who sat at rapt attention. She embodied the quintessential teacher: she focused on children rather than numbers, she ensured each child received the education they deserved, and she had a knack for following and understanding her students' thought patterns, sometimes more than they did. She possessed a sweet disposition, but when she needed to, she could be a tough disciplinarian.

Brad was one of her students in her sixth grade Language Arts class. "He was a quiet, compassionate kid," she recalls. "A deep thinker." Each week Mrs. Hickey had assigned a creative writing exercise, picking a topic she knew would appeal to sixth graders. Looking over Brad's work, the teacher discovered "a very caring child." Despite his average grades, he could read and express his thoughts extremely well. "I knew his family," Mrs. Hickey explains. Brad's aunts sat in her classroom in their own time. One of his aunts lived across the street from her, and the Hickey back yard shared a border with the farm owned by Patti's parents. "We lived in Westport for thirty something years," she explains now. "We knew everyone." Brad was one of her more quiet students. When group discussions

26

went on in the classroom, he tended to appear shy. He was "laid back," which sometimes came off as lazy. But he did care about doing well in school, and he did his work as assigned.

Brad was growing up, about to be a teenager, and he idolized his older brother. At around this time, Cody entered what some of his friends dubbed "his wild stage," and Brad wanted to mimic him. In the cities, a "wild stage" might mean guns, sex, drugs, and serious crimes. In small towns, it would mean much less. "Brad knew Cody dipped (smokeless tobacco)," remembers a close friend. "So, Brad decided, well, if Cody did it, he would, too. So he took him a big ol' dip of snuff and put it in his lip." Brad's face registered disgust, shock, sickness, anything and everything but enjoyment. The young boy tried to roll the smokeless tobacco around in his mouth, all the while nodding about how much he was enjoying it. Brad turned green before he ran away to retch it up. He also tried to smoke, but he discovered immediately he did not like cigarettes. Brad did not go near drugs—none of his friends did. Some members of Brad's family, to this day, refuse to believe Brad ever put a beer bottle to his lips. Like many families, alcoholism hurt his relatives in the past, and from a young age Brad saw the results of the illness. Brad watched a grandmother suffer the throes of alcoholism, and he often called out family members who appeared to drink too much to his satisfaction. When he did drink, the alcohol hit him hard and fast, and he drank more for show than anything else. While his friends went through the stages of drinking to get intoxicated, as young people will do, Brad drank to fit in or to be part of the group.

Friends agreed on one thing for sure: Brad worshipped his older brother, Cody. He also looked up to an older cousin, who enjoyed the reputation of a badass, but who was, on the inside, nothing like his reputation. Brad wanted to mimic these older boys as much as he could. Cody was more of a daredevil personality, more of a wild-heart. Brad just tried.

Stephen, or "Steve," Rennekamp ended up in the class a year behind Brad, as the school decided to have Stephen repeat the fourth grade. Stephen saw Brad on the playground as their paths crossed, and "it was a small town

27

so everybody knew everybody." Steve saw Brad as "a good kid," meaning the Principal's office did not call him in often for some issue or another. Steve also saw Brad "acting like a punk" some days, meaning bullying or "running his mouth." Brad's general demeanor was hard to gauge for Steve. Once, Brad had invited Steve to play and Steve declined. "Some other time," he told Brad.

A close friend remembers a rare fight between Brad and Cody. They exchanged heated words until the boys stood nose to nose. Brad was red-faced, puffing, and his hands went into fists. Suddenly, Brad jumped at Cody. "But it was more of a bunny hop and a punch," recalls the friend. "Everyone fell out laughing!" Brad became angrier, which made everyone else laugh harder. Brad's ineffective fist-fighting methods became a source of mirth after this.

Everyone who knew him agrees: "Brad had a giggle you will never forget," as one of his best friends explains. It was significant and even contagious; you would start laughing just because Brad was chuckling!

"He was a jokester" Julie Ralston recalls, "He enjoyed making people laugh." Julie had a class with Brad in the sixth grade, and Brad would keep them all giggling so much that it could be difficult to concentrate on class work. Julie says, "I can still hear his laugh and voice." Brad had a unique, sweet laugh; his voice warbled indecisively on the edge of change, so it had a bit of a "scruffy" sound to it. Another one of Brad's friends recalls the same memory: Brad's laugh and voice, she says, will always stay with her. A few days prior to March 9, 1990, Julie recalls a "Milk Break" in school. "I always brought chocolate chip cookies for Milk Break," she explains now. That day, Brad asked if she would share. "I gave him two cookies. Two Chips Ahoy cookies." At the time, it meant nothing special.

A lot of Westport's adolescents knew they would stay in Westport and inherit their parent's property. Some knew exactly what there were going to do after graduation, while others dreamed of college or moving away to a big city like Chicago, but who had not yet figured out how to get there. Cody Maddux, for example, had an idea as to what he wanted. Brad was not like Cody; Cody considered being a farmer, which meant setting his sights early on to run a successful farm one day. Bradley was not sure what he wanted to be when he grew up. He was too busy concentrating on his grades, playing sports, and enjoying time with his friends.

Brad "was real easy-going in school," remembers a classmate. He was not the type of boy who particularly stood out because he was bad, or a sports star, or always in trouble. "It was a small school in a small town, so everyone knows one another, and he wasn't one to stick out for being a trouble-starter," explains the classmate. "He was just a nice kid." If a teacher asked for a volunteer, or needed assistance, Brad was there without asking twice. Sometimes it was hard to quit giggling and whispering in class, but compared to today's student behavior, Brad was not a problem. His parents taught him to respect his elders. So did Grandpa Dave.

Sports were a big item on boys' agendas in Westport, usually because they had little else to do. The ballpark in the center of town was usually busy, and Brad played little league baseball along with his other friends. Before that, it was T-ball. A man named Greg Allen coached Brad in both sports and remembers him fondly. "Brad was a docile kid," he says. "He came from a good family." He remembers Brad was always very respectful of his elders and his teammates, sort of reserved, and what he did not have by way of athletic skills or build, he had in heart and manners. Allen grew up with Daryl Maddux and knew him to be "a good man." At the time he was calling out directions to little boys on the ball field, Greg Allen also worked behind the wheel of an Indiana State Police patrol vehicle. He split his time between arresting bad guys, coaching the town youth, and working a small farm with his first love, animals. Brad was not one of those kids that, if he did not get to play or if the coach yelled at him, his parents came down from the bleachers to give Allen a tongue-lashing. Brad was not one to talk back if he was corrected. He followed the rules, he listened to adults, he used "Yes, sir" and "No, ma'am." Greg Allen respected Brad and his family. "Just a good kid," he remembers.

Brad played football, and Summer Hobbs, who began cheerleading in fourth grade, would cheer him and his team on. They would wave at one another from the

29

sidelines. If he wasn't in a game, Summer would join him, and they would climb to the top of the "monkey bars" in the city park to watch the games. They would buy bags of popcorn, giggle and cut up, and watch the others play sports. Summer found him to be sweet, funny, and a joy to be around. "He loved baseball," Summer recalls, years later; she can still feel the sun basking down on them, taste the salty popcorn, and hear Brad's infectious laugh.

School pictures show Brad's personality: a warm smile, an open persona, someone who looks like they would do anything for anyone: The kind of kid who aims to please and loves, and who is loved. There was a mischievous twinkle in his eye, but at the same time he is also the kind of kid you cannot stay angry at for too long. Friends and family echo this sentiment: he loved pranks, but he would also help people. He did things to test his mettle, like all boys will do, but he was also a boy who loved to fish and ride his motorcycle. He loved his paper route and could not wait to hop on his bicycle and go. He was a growing adolescent boy, so he tried his parent's patience. He was on the cusp of leaving childhood for his teen years, caught in the space between leaving toys for bigger things and stepping out into sixth grade, where life gets a bit rougher. Brad was not a leader-type personality, but he was a loyal sidekick and definitely a true pal. He was a bit soft around the middle, with a sunken chest and a roll of baby fat protruding at his tummy. He was sweet, and he was not a fighting type. He walked with a slight toddle. Tougher kids sometimes picked on him for these reasons. Life is not simple, and kids can be cruel. This can make a boy act out, or want to prove himself more than he has already. This can also get a boy into more trouble.

One young man who attended school with Brad remembers Brad as being "a bully. He hung out with bullies who liked to pick on other kids. He could be mean." Perhaps there was a reason for Brad's negative behavior, as another student discovered.

This classmate remembers Bradley Maddux as a bully, but at the same time, he saw a part of Brad that still haunts him today. Danny Kennedy was "an artsy person" at Decatur Elementary School. He was not good at sports and he did not care to play, preferring a book to a baseball.

"I wasn't the type to be picked for the team," he admits now. Thin, short, and sensitive, Danny was the typical "bookworm." Thus he was the brunt of jokes, of bullying, and in Indiana vernacular, "picking" from the bigger, tougher farm lads who walked the halls of the school. This included being pushed down on the playground to name-calling. "It made me feel alone, like I didn't belong," he admits. Brad Maddux was one of the boys who targeted Kennedy. "I saw him as a troubled guy, like he had things going on at home. He had a lot of anger and anxiety," and Brad allowed the pressures of measuring up to everyone else's standards "get to him." One day, Danny Kennedy decided he would take no more of the behavior and approached Brad. "Why," he asked the tougher boy, "Do you pick on me?"

Kennedy remembers Brad's answer clearly: "I don't want to, but everyone else does." That was when Danny Kennedy saw that Brad Maddux was trying to be the "tough guy," but it came with a price; "it wasn't who he really was." As a young boy, Danny Kennedy realized Brad was playing a role on the playground: tough bully, the pack mentality of ganging up on the weaker person to tease and taunt. Now he reflects, "It was how a boy was supposed to act" in Westport. Males had particular roles to play; they were supposed to be macho and "pick" on the boys who were more sensitive, or smaller, or less macho.

Danny confided in Brad how the teasing hurt him. After Danny and Brad talked, a strange thing happened: the teasing slowed down, and Danny Kennedy did not feel so alone. When the gang began to circle around Danny, Brad would tell them, "Let's go over here instead," and the group would disperse. Sometimes Brad told bullies outright, "Leave him alone," and the members of his pack would listen.

"He would redirect the bullying," Danny recalls. "So he protected me, in some ways." Danny did not play after school games with Brad or the others, as he lived away from Westport; "I always wished I'd have gotten to know (Brad) better," he says now.

Gretchen, Brad's cousin, saw Brad as a sweet boy who was always willing to help others. She remembers him as a friendly boy who did not see the bad in anyone, who

31

would go out of his way to run an errand, or assist, or volunteer. Sure, he was not perfect—he could be a prankster, and he was a growing boy—but it was difficult to find fault or be angry with him. He did not use drugs; she did not see him openly intoxicated or drinking alcohol, and he was respectful to his family. He had a wonderful sense of humor; he could just make you fall over at his one-liners and wry sense of wit. It wasn't nasty humor, like so many stand-up comics today. He loved hugs and he would give hugs freely. Brad loved people, and he was so trusting.

The Nugent family lived just a few houses down the street, on West Kentucky Avenue, from the Maddux family. They had a son named Robert, whom everyone called "Rob." Although he was a few years older than Brad, Rob knew Brad. Lindsay knew of Rob but was not familiar with him. Rob was closer in age to Cody than to Brad. Rob, or "Robby," as he was sometimes called, and Cody did all of the things young boys do. They loved Matchbox cars, the tiny replicas of real cars, "driving" the tiny cars in dirt piles and collecting them, trading them off and sharing the little cars together.

Robert Scott Nugent did not have a horrific childhood, but it was not particularly easy. He was three years old when his parents divorced. Growing up without a father figure can be difficult for young men, and studies have shown that boys growing up without strong male role models tend to commit petty crimes and experiment with drugs and alcohol at a young age. Luckily, Rob's life took some better turns.

Rob's mother remarried a man Rob describes as a "closet alcoholic." If an absent parent is not bad enough, an alcoholic parent can send a young child into a tailspin—particularly a parent who will refuse to seek treatment or admit there is a problem. In smaller communities, where people expect such problems to be ignored, and there are few resources to help families, children can be affected. Rob's mother ultimately divorced this man, and they moved away from Westport, Indiana. A family named Armstrong purchased the Nugent home.

Rob's biological father and his mother reunited; their relationship rekindled as some will do, and they remarried.

"My parents are the best," Rob says now. "They are good people. They were always there for me, no matter what. And our house was always clean and neat when I was growing up." The reunited Nugents moved to Rob's father's home in a little hamlet named Alert, "out in the sticks," Rob calls it. But it was a great place to be a boy, where you could climb, run, build, and pretend all day.

"My dad worked two jobs often," Rob reminisces. But somehow, Mr. Nugent was always there for his family. "He did a great job teaching me how a man is supposed to act." Rob adds ruefully, "I might not have always listened, but he was always there when I needed him."

Rob was sickly, and he was eventually diagnosed with Crohn's disease. It caused problems when Rob drank alcohol, causing him to retch and vomit. Crohn's disease is an inflammatory bowel disease without a known cause, but the condition is linked to problems with the immune system response.

To treat his condition, Rob was on Prednisone, a type of corticosteroid that helped his body adjust and function normally. Later, Rob would attribute the medication to saving his life in quite a different way.

The Nugent family was forced to tighten their budget, as Rob's medical bills were costly. He knew his family would not be able to assist him in paying for college in the future because of the hospital and doctor's costs. But his family was close-knit, and Rob's mom and dad assured him that they loved him. They instilled Christian values in Rob and ensured he was involved in healthy activities and had fun as a boy. His mother loved children, and Alert was a safe place to be—the kids could ride their bikes, walk, ride their go-carts and dirt bikes all over the neighborhood and in the surrounding woods, and everyone felt safe. Rob became involved in local sports and the youth groups in his church. All of the residents looked out for one another. If a kid did something dangerous or naughty, a parent's phone would ring with a detailed report. The reporting party would inevitably receive a "thank you," and the offender would always receive a severe reprimand.

The Armstrong family, who purchased the Nugent's Westport home, felt settled in by this time. The house rested near the corner of North Kathleen Drive and West

Kentucky, across from the Maddux home. The house did not have a fence, so they could cut through the yard from North Kathleen Drive to the back door, or from the Maddux home, they could walk across West Kentucky Avenue and knock on the front door. They had several children, including a son named Ernest, who went by the moniker "Junior." Junior and Brad became best friends, living across the street from one another and playing sports together. "Brad was sweet, innocent, giggling, and full of energy," Junior recalls. "He got along good with Cody and Lindsay. Lindsay got teased a little, but (the siblings) were very loving and caring." Lindsay remembers Junior visiting the Maddux home or Brad frequenting Junior's home quite often as she grew up. Lindsay also visited the Armstrong's quite often; she got along well with the family and was welcome there any time. Junior was a huge part of the Maddux clan as well.

When the Armstrong family moved to Westport, Junior's mom, *Mary*, had to find work out of town at a fast food restaurant to support her family. She worked hard, bussing tables and taking orders for little pay, coming home exhausted after working late and into the morning. When Junior was a baby, his parents got divorced. Mary's current significant other was a man almost fifteen years her junior, and Junior considered him to be a stepfather, even calling him "Dad." Junior's stepfather was a man who took no part in illegal drugs and rarely drank alcohol; Junior's mother was a social drinker and did not use drugs either.

"Junior's mom," says friend Lynn Welch "was a strange creature." Lynn knew Junior, Rob, and Cody, and she marginally knew Brad. "Junior's parents were never there," Lynn recalls. Lynn knew Patti Maddux and liked the family. Lynn was a few years older than Brad, but knew him the same way that "everyone in Westport knows everyone else." Lynn was one of the clusters of young people who gathered around the storefronts in downtown, or at the basketball courts, simply because, "There was nothing to do. Nothing."

The Armstrong adults worked a variety of jobs at various hours. This left a young boy home alone to do what he wanted, and for a boy as wild as Junior, the little town of Westport was open game.

Junior was younger than Rob Nugent by almost a year, but Junior was a tough kid who had to grow up quickly. To this day, he has few positive words for his biological father. He has even fewer positive words for his stepsiblings. He vacillates between calling his mother his "best friend" and other words. Junior Armstrong was a little boy who grew up craving love and needing attention from those he loved most. He has few memories of his childhood, and only a few of those are good memories. Most of the good ones involve his best friend, Brad Maddux.

"There is nothing in that area for a kid to do," Junior says now, "So you drink. You want to be like your older brother or sister. They get to run around, and back then, there weren't a lot of rules. So you do stupid kid things to be macho."

Rob met Junior as they both played sports; sports were one of the few healthy things to do for young boys in the area. Junior spent a lot of time at the Nugent's. Rob's mother and father welcomed him with open arms; Mrs. Nugent always had hugs, words of encouragement, and great, home-cooked dinners. The Nugent family was a family that sat down together to eat, and they truly took an interest in one another's lives. The boys often got together and played—and schemed.

They snuck cigarettes to smoke behind sheds, thinking they were clever. Little did they know their secret smoking sessions were not so secret —Rob's daddy was well aware of it. They snuck sips of liquor and, sometimes, got downright drunk. Rob had a go-cart, and the go-cart only had one way to stop—someone had to grab it, fall, and drag it until it slowed to a halt. Many a time found Rob racing behind the cart, hurtling himself in the air to catch it, and being dragged behind the driver until everyone finally came to a stop. Brad Maddux, who also played sports with the boys, often rode the go-cart with them. He was younger than Rob, but Rob enjoyed his company. Brad made Rob laugh, and Rob liked his fun-loving, easy-going personality. Both Rob and Brad loved motorcycles. "Brad was stoked when he finally got his motorcycle," Rob recalls. But the throttle cable needed repair, and when they cranked it up, Daryl Maddux found himself holding onto

35

the handlebars as the machine dragged him across the front lawn. Brad was stuck with the bicycle for a while.

"We were heathen boys," Junior grins at the few memories he does keep. "We were good mechanics—good at tearing things apart." He and Brad, sometimes with Cody or Rob at their side, managed to keep from breaking bones or losing eyes while adjusting motorcycle clutches and not using the brakes or other necessary safety equipment. Many times, Junior found himself saying, "I better lay this bike down or I'm going into the ditch face-first." All of them drank alcohol, but Brad drank "In a blue moon," according to Junior. "Make that the bluest of blue moons." When Brad drank, he favored a wine cooler called Purple Passion over beer or liquor. The wine cooler tasted more like a flavored punch than alcohol.

Teacher Jean Hickey also had Rob Nugent and Junior Armstrong sitting in her classroom. "They weren't as serious about their school as others," she says wryly. "But then, they were sixth grade boys." Rob and Junior "liked to have fun;" though never disrespectful, she often needed to redirect their attention to focus on class.

One of their favorite pastimes was to get their three-man dome tent and camp. They camped in backyards, in the woods nearby, or in someone's pasture, inhaling the spring aromas or looking out at a summer night of stars. They would sometimes bring beers, snuck out of the house or purchased via a friend. They talked about girls and sports and everything else young boys talked about. They were young, and they would live forever.

The boys found a special sport in killing and throwing possums on the awning of a local downtown business, so the next morning the proprietor would find twelve to fifteen dead possums on their awning. They soaped the windows of a local woman they found "scary." But for all of their pranks, they had a code: never steal. Never truly hurt anyone. No physical harm would ever come to anyone.

Cody, Bradley, and Lindsay Maddux grew up in a small town, where everyone knew one another, and most people had claims to everyone else by blood or by friendship. Some people moved to Westport to escape their problems, but most people had roots here that reached as deep as the aged oaks and ancient cedars planted around their great-grandparents' farm homes. It was, as so many people liked to say, a safe place to be.

4 "MUSHROOM"

Douglas Cecil Sims traveled down Indiana Highway 3 in Sardinia, on his way to a party. It was nothing formal, just a few folks getting together to drink and talk. Douglas sometimes went by "Doug" and sometimes people also called him "Mushroom." To some folks, he was like a shadow, barely speaking, unassuming. To a scant few, he had a somewhat questionable reputation around town, but no one could prove anything definitively. In a small town, folks will gossip; they talk until the story changes and until fiction becomes a fact. The facts at this time were: it was Friday, March 9, 1990; Douglas "Mushroom" Sims lived in an older manufactured home, or "trailer," in Sardinia; he worked at Mariah Foods; his parents, known to be strict religious people, lived across the road. And Mushroom intended on going to a party tonight to drink, talk, and hang out. Another fact was that his path would cross with Bradley Maddux, and this would end up being quite unfortunate.

Douglas Sims was related to Brad Maddux; Brad's maternal grandfather, Richard Maddux, was Doug's cousin. As Richard owned the Westport Pharmacy, many people knew Richard, and not just because of the small size of the town.

Sardinia is an unincorporated town not quite four miles southwest of Westport. Indiana Highway 3 is a straight shot highway that connects the two, and it is such an easy drive that little thought needs to be put into it. Sardinia is a smattering of houses and a lot of fields. The people are friendly here, and they wave at drivers whether they know the person or not. Tractors will often slow traffic on the two-lane Indiana 3 Highway that divides Sardinia in two. Sardinia is so small, it does not even have a stoplight. If you need gasoline, groceries, or even cigarettes, residents have to drive to Westport, the closest town, to buy anything. Besides Indiana 3, there are only three other

38

main streets. People in Sardinia, when giving directions, do not even use street names; they just ask whom the person seeks. "Turn left by that house with the boat, then go two roads over and turn left. Their house is the first house on your right." Not only does everyone know each other, they are also on a first name basis. If you ask for a street name, residents respond, "If you tell me who you're looking for it'd be easier to give directions. Bud and Cindy? Oh! They live..." Anyone standing outside suspiciously pays close attention to cars they do not recognize when vehicles enter the town from Highway 3.

As you drive down Indiana 3 South away from Sardinia, there is a cutoff to the tiny hamlet called Alert. It is easily within walking distance. It is easier to drive—not even five minutes on a nice day, and about ten minutes on a dark, foggy night.

Douglas Cecil Sims was born in Greensburg, Indiana on June 6, 1961. June is a hot, sultry time in Decatur County. Douglas had brown hair and brown eyes. His parents brought him home to Sardinia, to a quiet, suburban brick home with a roomy basement, located on a dead-end street, where it is safe for children to play. Turnover Creek, or "Crick" as it was pronounced in this area, ran meanderingly next to his backyard. His parents, *David* and *Betty*, had a reputation around town as "good people," meaning they worked hard at steady, honest jobs, attended church, were friendly, and took pride in their home. Their neighbors also thought of them as "religious" people; this meant they attended church on a regular basis, did not partake in alcohol, except for the little bit of homemade wine David and his brother brewed as a hobby, did not frequent bars or use bad language, and read the Bible as a norm, living by its rules and words. David was a tall, lanky man with short, neat hair, and Betty was short and slender. Douglas, or Doug as almost everyone called him, was the middle child of three. Everyone who knew the couple liked both David and Betty and, when questioned, always spoke highly of the two.

Betty Sims, Lynn Welch explains, "Was a lady. Very proper, formal, the kind of person who makes sure shirts are tucked in." One of Lynn's relatives worked with Betty at the meat market. It was not a glamorous job or one she

39

needed to dress-up for, but Betty always looked nice, her hair carefully coiffured, her lipstick just so, and her clothing ironed and clean. Betty Sims was proper and dignified without being cold or prudish.

David worked at a local factory, building and testing engines. He eventually retired from the company. Betty worked at Westport Meats. She wrapped and packaged the various meats for customers, including locally raised beef. She worked at the business for twenty years and she eventually went to work in retail. She liked to stay busy, despite David's chiding her to retire and take it easy.

As Doug grew old enough to play, Betty noticed he tended to be a loner. As a little boy, he had one friend who lived down the street from them. Otherwise, young Doug preferred his own company. Sometimes his older sibling would start bossing him about, as older siblings tend to do. Doug would get angry over this and they would squabble. A parent would intervene, and the issue would be settled.

As he grew old enough to venture out into the neighborhood, Doug met other boys who introduced him to the world of sports. The Sims have two professional sports players in their family lineage, so perhaps it is natural that Doug grew to love baseball and basketball. There was always a pickup game going on in the neighborhood right across the street, with both boys and girls jumping in and out of the game, baseballs and softballs flying. Or the kids would stroll down to Turnover Creek and use sticks as pretend guns, playing "war." They raced from tree to tree, rolling and dodging, shouting "Pow! Pow-Pow!" aiming and pretending to fire at one another. They gathered walnuts in their tanned arms and used them as missiles, throwing them at one another and laughing when they hit their target. There were several boys in the neighborhood, and they became fast friends. The Sims had a huge backyard in which to play. No one went near Highway 3, the double-laned highway, because they had enough space to play in and it was too dangerous to cross, particularly when dusk fell. It was a simple time. They had a creek and woods to explore. The neighbors kept an eye on you.

"Doug was a regular kid, just like any of us," says one of his closest friends. "We had a lot of fun! He liked sports. He would get in on neighborhood games. He was a regular kid growing up; nothing stands out in my mind that was different."

Doug joined the boy scouts. David Sims assisted, when he could, with the troop. Doug and his buddies were proud members of Troop 72. They learned how to camp, hike, fish, and did all the things scouts learned how to do. They qualified with .22 rifles. Doug seemed to enjoy it. They even got to go to camp over for a weekend, spending the night in their tents at a jamboree in Dupont, Indiana. "We slept near an old wood stove," remembers a fellow scout ruefully. "And the person who was supposed to watch it went to sleep. Boy, we woke up freezing!"

Doug did not like school, and he let it be known by sitting in the back of the classroom. "It's not that he can't do the work," teachers would tell Betty Sims when she went to parent-teacher conferences. "It's just he won't try." Doug simply hated school. Betty chalked it up to his being so shy.

Doug attended South Decatur Elementary. Jean Hickey was the teacher who taught his sixth-grade Language Arts class. Mrs. Hickey noted something about Doug, "He was very much a loner," she recalls. The kind-hearted teacher felt bad for the little boy who appeared so lonesome. She remarked that he always dressed well and in clean clothes. He came from a respectable family, and Mrs. Hickey knew Betty Sims to be industrious and pleasant. She also taught Doug's siblings in the past, one of whom was so incredibly outgoing and fun. "Maybe he's not well liked by other students," she wondered, but she could not fathom why that would be.

One of Doug's instructors in high school remembered him as a B and C student. He did not stand out from the crowd. He did not boast, like many adolescent boys are keen to do. School sports did not interest him, and he did not participate in any extracurricular activities like foreign language clubs, band, or other organizations. Perusing all four of his Yearbooks will only reveal the mandatory school photos and one casual photo of him playing checkers; his head is down, face bent to the board. He was slender and lanky, like his father. He liked animals, especially cats; the family always seemed to have a cat around the house, and Doug loved holding it and dangling

41

strings in front of its nose to bat at and jump after for play.

Outside of school, Doug and his father loved to shoot clay pigeons. They had several rifles and often went to the club to join others. They made their own loads, polished and cleaned their weapons to a shine, and went shooting on a regular basis. Doug was a very good shot. David still has their rifles they used. They also went mushroom hunting in the spring, when the dogwoods and the poplars came into bloom around the second or third week in April. They would walk through the woods, carefully seeking, then picking, the delicacy. This is how Doug Sims earned his moniker, "Mushroom."

Doug knew the slightly younger Kenny Nugent through their mutual attendance at South Decatur High, which happened to be their only option, and the two often exchanged a polite "Hello" as they crossed paths in the halls. Nugent found Doug to be polite and quiet; the sort of guy who did not fall prey to the pack mentality, act obnoxiously or loudly in the hallways, or do anything "unordinary."

The sun shining brightly in the lightly clouded sky made an excellent day for a game of basketball, and Jean Hickey claimed her seat on the bleachers. Her son was playing for the South Decatur Cougars, and excitement crackled in the air as the teams warmed up. Mrs. Hickey suddenly noticed Doug Sims moving toward her, purposely maneuvering in between others so he could get to her. When he arrived by her side, he said, "Hi, Mrs. Hickey."

"Hello, Doug!" She was glad to see him. Over the past few years, she enjoyed watching him grow into a fine-looking young man, and she smiled at the handsome youth shyly looking up at her, dressed in clothes he kept impeccably neat and clean.

"Can I sit by you?" he asked shyly. This took Mrs. Hickey by surprise; other kids his age congregated in groups, some even brought dates. Certainly no one wanted to be seen with a teacher.

"Sure." She moved over slightly, indicating a space on the bleachers. He sat down and thanked her. They launched into a polite discussion, inquiring after each other's well-being. From then on, each time there was some sort of sporting event, Doug would find his ex-teacher and ask to sit next to her. "We always sat on the bleachers," she remembers. "I always knew he'd come up and see me." Doug joined her for baseball games, too. Again, Doug seemed to be the loner, seeking a friend.

A student who is a few years younger than Doug remembers him as "someone who didn't have a lot of friends. I felt sorry for him, sometimes." Doug's sibling was popular, attractive, and when they walked into the room, all attention went toward them. The student noted this. "(They) got a lot of attention. (They) were involved in everything at school. Doug wasn't involved in anything."

Douglas Sims was a good-looking young man, with brown hair combed forward, neatly trimmed around his face, and a wisp of a mustache coming in. He was a tall, athletic boy with a deep voice. But as he grew into adolescence, his friends began to notice something else about Doug.

"Doug was different," some of his friends admit reluctantly; when pushed for further answers, they acknowledge that they do not just mean he was shy or he hated school. Unlike his peers, he did not partake in drinking. His dad and his uncle still sometimes brewed and kept homemade wine. Most teenaged boys would at least try to sneak a sip, but Doug did not even think of attempting it. However, the "different" label did not stem from that lack of common indulgence, but rather something else entirely. Friends noticed when the boys would start talking about girls, Doug would remain quiet. When his peers began dating, Doug stayed single. He did have one girlfriend in high school, but it did not last long and it boiled down to a date for the Senior Prom. Doug's parents had a pool table in their garage, and mixing teen boys and games of pool always led to talking about girls, but not with Doug. He always remained strangely silent on the subject of the opposite sex and what he would like to do with them. Then there were the wrestling matches.

The boys always liked to wrestle, pinning one another down and testing their strength. They especially liked to try to pin Doug because he was the "big guy" of the group. He was also good at wrestling would teach the other boys moves: grappling, handholds, foot positioning, and the like. Doug and another boy challenged each other to an impromptu match one Saturday while they hung out at someone's house, and the two boys eagerly assumed wrestling positions while the other boys watched them with excited eyes.

The boy, *Sam Sloan*, squared off across from Doug, and he and Doug took swipes at one another until they grappled. The other boys cheered them on, giving advice from the sidelines.

"Grab his, arm! His arm!"

"Go high, Sammy! Woo!"

Doug and Sam fell to the grassy lawn, fighting to get footholds. Sam thought he had Doug and was jubilant at the thought of finally beating the bigger, tougher opponent. Then Sam felt Doug's hand grasping for, and then wrapping around and squeezing, Sam's penis.

Sam released Doug as they rolled about on the lawn. Sam scrabbled to get away, crying out, "Give! Give!" He felt his face glow red-hot under his summer tan.

Doug, hair disheveled, panting, leaned back on the grass. Doug played it off. "We were just wrestlin'." He laughed loudly.

Sam managed to laugh and acted like it was an accident. "Man, what's wrong with you?" The other guys guffawed, realized what must have happened, and made a few cracks. No one was the wiser. Their friends were oblivious, truly believing it was merely a slip of the hand.

Sam stood away from the group, acting as if he needed to catch his breath, but his insides shook in shock and confusion. It wasn't an accident, he knew, and it was a grab and hold, not a mere brush of a palm. He knew Doug's grasp had been purposeful; he held it a little too long, and it could by no means be attributed to a mere brush of a palm. Two other boys already grappled with one another by the time he rejoined the group. Sam could distinguish no other unusual behavior from Doug. What was that all about?

Homosexuality was not discussed in Westport, unless it was to crack a crude joke or to make fun of someone. There was no one who was "out," meaning declared gay or lesbian, to his or her friends or family. People might harbor suspicions, but only because someone acted the stereotypical type: effeminate males or females who acted "different" towards women. Gay or lesbian was strictly taboo in this region. And if anyone did suspect, well, they

44

certainly did not ask. "Fag" and "homo" were insults they shouted in the hallways of school during a fight, or used derogatorily to put someone down in a conversation. "Playing like a girl" was definitely a slur in sports for boys. This was farm country, where people define gender by how tough a man acts and how well they play the roles expected of them. If a teenager did not go on dates with the opposite sex, kids often labeled them as homely or told them, "there is something wrong with you."

Sam made the decision then. "I wasn't going to do anymore wrestling with Doug."

As a young man, Doug began a part-time summer job with other Westport youth. They de-tasseled corn in the various fields that grew in the area. Farmers hired the youngsters, who were seeking quick spending money, to walk the rows and rows of corn in order to manually pull out the top part of the corn plant. After it is pulled out, the tassel is tossed to the earth for cross-pollination. It is hot, dirty, and sometimes boring. "Doug always could laugh as he worked," says a student who worked with him. "It is a hot, nasty job and it's in the hottest part of summer, so anyone that can make it fun, you want to be around. Doug made you laugh." During lunch break, the student remembered Doug as gregarious and a "regular member of the crew," except for "his mannerisms, and his voice. I always thought he was kind of feminine."

Doug graduated from high school with the same amount of fanfare as his peers. His high school pictures show a serious, unsmiling young man. His senior year came around, and it was time to decide what to do with his future. Some of his friends already reached the decision to stay in the area and take up their fathers' businesses or trades, while others focused on college. During his senior year, Doug decided he wanted to join the army. He talked to his parents and explained he liked to cook, and he wanted to join the armed forces to be a cook. Westport and Sardinia did not offer much in the way of a culinary arts future. David and Betty agreed bravely. They would miss him, but they wanted what was best for their son. David cleaned and put away their guns for when Doug returned and they could shoot clay pigeons, together, again.

Doug Sims became Food Service Specialist Sims in the

United States Army in 1980. His military service took him to Ft. Knox, Kentucky, then overseas to Germany. For a young man who previously never ventured from the cloistered streets of Westport, the world probably seemed huge and full of adventure. Suddenly, Doug experienced a barrage of races, architecture, skin colors, languages, foods, customs, and skills at a young man's front door.

A long-time resident in Decatur County now wonders about Doug's military service. "I didn't know he was homosexual until the murder. Maybe he turned gay in the military. You never know what those people do in there. I mean, gays fight the same as (straight) people… still."

In 1982, Doug Sims ran afoul of the law; this time it was in Kentucky, the "Bluegrass State." Doug was issued a citation for driving the wrong way down a one-way road on January 14. Other than two traffic warnings when he was younger, this was the only crime on his record … at the time.

The United States Army shipped Specialist 4 Sims overseas and stationed him at Ray Barracks, a U.S. Army installation in Friedberg, Germany. Ray Barracks enjoyed the distinction of having a famous draftee in its walls in 1958: Elvis A. Presley. Elvis filmed part of "GI Blues" near his actual station. Ray Barracks boasted an urban warfare training site, a firing range for personal weapons qualification, and vehicle maintenance facilities. It was eventually closed by the U.S. government in 2007 and returned to the German government.

Betty and David received a letter postmarked from Germany with the familiar return address on it. When they opened the letter, Betty had to sit down. The letter announced Doug's engagement! "He doesn't even know this girl!" Betty spewed.

"Now, now," David chuckled, patting her shoulder. "You know how it is. Those countries. They get those boys over there, and they think every girl over there is a pretty girl, or interesting, because they're away from home."

"Oh, how could he! We won't be able to attend! And I'm his mother!" Betty was not about to be placated. The nervous energy this letter produced caused her to quickly reduce the letter to a knot of paper in her small hands. "Oh!"

David continued smiling as Betty kept muttering to herself. She was, as he put it, "fit to be tied." He kept patting her shoulders and murmuring condolences.

David's prediction came true, and they heard no more about the wedding. Betty eventually calmed down. Probably some silly "wild hair" Doug concocted, they decided.

On October 20, 1982, Sims ran afoul of the law again, and this time it was on military paper. At the back gates of Ray Barracks of Gorbelheimer Hohl, he found himself in fisticuffs. To people in the Army, Doug violated Article 116, UCMJ; to civilians, he "got into it" with someone. On November 6, 1985, Sims' superiors demoted him down to an E-4, suspended him for two months, fined him one hundred dollars, placed him on barracks restriction for a week, and assigned him an extra week of duty.

Douglas Sims served his country without any other noted incident. When he returned home from the army, the family noticed a change in him immediately. According to Betty, Doug was intoxicated when he came off the airplane into the arms of his family. He began to drink, and he drank quite a bit. Doug moved in with his parents, back into his childhood home. He reunited with his childhood friends, but he did not seem to have time for social visits.

He did have time to volunteer to help with little league teams at the baseball diamond at the park in downtown Westport. "He had this big, booming voice," someone remembered. "So he was a good umpire."

The devil played games with Doug Sims' mind and soul, planting the seed of evil. Doug began to spend social time with young men who were much younger than he, but few thought it strange. It was a small town; everyone knew one another. Doug would pick up a game of basketball at the courts near the town baseball diamond. He befriended young boys on the court, and he loved to watch little league games. Later, Sims would take the young boys to the local fast food restaurant for frozen ice cream treats. "Everyone did that," a friend said. "It was the only place to go. We'd get a drink, a shake. An ice cream cone." Doug would treat them all to whatever they wanted.

"My mother knew Mrs. Sims well," Lynn Welch recalls. "I grew up hearing about how Doug took boys on fishing and camping trips."

Years later, after the crime, a law enforcement officer mused, "If we would have known the signs, paid attention, maybe we would have (known what to look for) and seen what Doug was doing. I don't know..."

As the years passed and Doug grew older, he began to keep company with boys at least ten years his junior, if not even younger. He had few adult friends. These few friends described Doug as slightly effeminate, and they mentioned that he was still very shy, especially for someone so well-traveled. They also noticed that he got along quite well with boys younger than himself, but not everyone thought of that as odd behavior. However, to an outsider looking in, it appears quite noticeably that the devil already began manipulating Doug's mind.

"Doug was like a big brother," insists *Mike Meadows*. Mike lived in Westport with his sister, *Linda*, and their mother. Mike and his friends from school spent the majority of their time on the basketball courts, located in downtown Westport. His friends included Cody Maddux. Shooting hoops and tossing a baseball were about the only things for young people to do at the time. Mike was a confessed "car nut." He loved classic vehicles and he already worked repairing and restoring cars at a family-owned garage in town. A man pulled up one day in a 1978 Buick Regal and Mike practically foamed at the mouth in his eagerness to talk to the owner. It was 1989, and Mike, like many teens his age, loved working and driving cars and having fun with his friends; his generation would live forever and did not need to think about serious issues. Mike met the Buick's owner, a man in his late twenties, named Doug Sims. Finally, the ecstatic Mike met someone who loved sports and cars as much as he did.

About six months later, Doug sold the Buick and purchased a brown, 1982 Ford F-100 pickup. After purchasing his new car, Doug added top lights to highlight the hood, installed a high-quality bed liner, and hung a suction-cupped stuffed animal in the rear window.

Later, this truck would be the most infamous vehicle in Decatur County.

"Doug ran with younger guys because the guys all his age thought he was 'funny,'" explains Mike Meadows. When pushed, Mike clarifies that the Westport community

48

"thought he was—you know—a homosexual." Doug never did anything to make Mike believe the rumors, and he certainly never "did anything" to Mike that would cause Mike to question Doug Sims' sexual orientation. "Nobody knew what (gay) was because of how we were raised," Mike laments today, "It's a small town." So Mike, his sister, and his friends would go to Doug's house in Sardinia to "hang out," a euphemism for drinking beers, watching television, playing cards, or just talking.

Doug still enjoyed cooking, and he obtained work in a restaurant near Sardinia. He met a girl there, and the Sims thought she might be "the one" to capture his shy heart. The girl was not married, but she had a little boy. Doug seemed to dote on the little boy, who in turn appeared to adore Doug. He even brought the boy over to his parents' house several times.

The relationship with the girl did not last.

Other than his time spent at the baseball diamond and basketball court, Doug's life was simple. He joined the Army Reserve on December 10, 1987. He quit the restaurant and worked the day shift at Mariah Foods—the same place that cut a check for Brad Maddux's relatives and their friends. Mariah Foods, once known as Standard Packing House, processed meats such as pork. Mariah employed anywhere from 100 to 200 employees at any given time. The drive to Mariah Foods, located in Columbus, Indiana, from Westport takes one on a thirty minute pleasure ride down a picturesque, sometimes windy road. The drive from Westport allowed the driver ample time to drink a large coffee while they gathered their thoughts for the day and woke up, roll down the window and take a deep breath and enjoy the earthy scent of the freshly plowed fields of the passing farmland. Groups of trees along the route made the ride both cool and a tad precarious; an occasional animal would meander into the road unsuspecting, so dead skunk, possum, and raccoon often dotted the road.

Doug Sims worked as a "pig sticker" for Mariah Foods. The process involved fatally shocking the huge hogs with electrical jolts, followed by the shackling of their hind legs. Machines with large chains and gears would then lift the bodies into the air and slowly swing them up to the second

49

floor. Pig stickers used a long, sharp knife to pierce the animal's neck, just at the jugular vein, slicing through the flesh quickly, making a neat, quick turn, and yanking it across and out, and slitting the jugular that allowed the animal to "bleed out." They left the animals in that position until all of the blood drained out before they moved on to the next step in the slaughtering process. "All of the blood has to be out before you can remove the meat for packaging," explains a former Mariah employee. "Or else you cannot use the meat." Every pig sticker needs to know one crucial task in order to perform their duty well; they must know the exact location of the jugular and how to pierce and slice the vein in the most efficient way possible. According to a former coworker, Doug Sims excelled at this task.

Later, people discussed this chilling afterthought with horror.

Doug worked the first shift. The clean-up crew came in on the second shift, and the maintenance took over the third shift. Doug would come home from work, eat his supper, and then knock back and watch television, sipping his favorite drink, iced tea. He often followed his meals with a bowl of his favorite ice cream. Most of the time, one or both of his parents joined him; if it was sports season they usually watched a game, cheering on their family members who were playing. Doug would get up and refill his glass and return to his favorite chair, let the family cat settle on his lap, and drink his iced tea while watching his favorite shows. "He loved his iced tea," his mother says with a smile.

Doug grew into a round-shouldered man, his arms and shoulders thick with muscles from sports and his macabre work at Mariah. He had a head full of thick, dark hair with a steadily receding hairline and an equally dark and bushy, but neatly trimmed, mustache. He had a thick mat of dark chest hair. Although not many people would find him particularly handsome, few would consider him aesthetically horrific. He was, as so many people said later, "An average looking guy."

Doug and his father still loved to shoot clay pigeons. On the way to the club they often stopped at McDonald's for coffee and egg McMuffins, the sandwiches made from English muffins, eggs, ham, and cheese. Doug easily wolfed down two of them in a sitting. They continued to make their own shooting loads, and Doug remained a very good shot.

A close friend of Doug knew his mother as a kindly woman, but they go on to explain that Doug's father could often "be mean." The friend confides, "I think David saw Mush as a failure. I suspected he was abusive." The friend wonders now "If his dad didn't think Mush was good enough." Still, Doug lived with his parents upon his return from the military.

In 1988, tragedy darkened Sardinia, the Sims family, and the Christmas holiday. One could easily believe that this travesty led to the opening of the devil's door. It could have been foreshadowing.

Glory, Doug's paternal grandmother, lived in Sardinia, across Highway 3 from David and Betty, on a road called 1270 S. Her husband died, and eventually her house had to be demolished. The family put an older manufactured home, or as some people called it, "a trailer," in place of her lost house. Upon entering, the kitchen expanded to the right, the living room to the left, and the bedroom resided in the back of the house. A bushy hedge grew on one side of the exterior of the house. It sported a nice awning over the front door, with two short steps leading up to a small deck on the porch, surrounded by a wooden trellis. It was nothing fancy, but it was nice, a white single-wide, one bedroom, and just the right size for Glory, who turned ninety in 1988. Glory still remained spry, and she habitually walked across Highway 3 to attend the church, built in the 1800s and still holding services, located just across the street. Sometime around Christmas, she decided she would like to attend a special children's Christmas presentation one evening. She dressed in her Sunday best and departed her home, turned right, and walked past two homes, walking down 1270 S. Then Glory prepared to cross Highway 3. Darkness already surrounded her, and a light mist seemed to emanate from the ground. Sardinian *Duff Leonard* and his hired help, student *Randy Piles*, just completed their work on Duff's farm when they saw the red and blue emergency lights illuminating the night skies of Sardinia on Highway 3 near the church. "We better go see what's going on," Duff told Randy, and they

51

jumped into his ancient pickup truck to rumble over. He threw the truck into park and leapt out; traffic clogged the road for miles in both directions. What he saw made him sick to his stomach. A driver stood near a stopped car, frantically explaining, "I never saw her; I swear, I never saw her!" One look around and Duff knew what happened. Human remains littered the road. Duff jumped out of his parked truck and rushed over to assist where he could. He pointed out to the arriving EMT paramedics where viscera lay. He soon found out it was Glory Sims. "I couldn't tell what was what," he explains now. "It was horrible. I'll never get it out of my mind. Glory had loved those Christmas pageants. She loved them! Especially the ones with the kids." He looks away. "It had to be a closed casket ceremony." After the horrific accident, the church put safety lights on the street, near their property, on Highway 3.

David and his brother kept the trailer home where Glory had lived. It sat dormant for about a year, and then Doug moved into it, making it his own. He carried the boxes in, cleaned it up, and hung his pictures. He kept a lot of his grandmother's belongings. Still, it was a typical bachelor pad. Now he had his own place, where he could be alone. He did not have anyone else around. It was just him. Well, him—and the Devil.

It was almost as if the stage were set for tragedy.

Doug Sims' young friends enjoyed going to the trailer home and riding around with him in his brown truck because, as one friend explains, "Doug was like a babysitter, really. He was a big teddy bear, a pushover. He wouldn't even argue with you." The group's two favorite pastimes were drinking beer and playing basketball. Doug supplied the beer and, at times, liquor; "whatever you wanted was there (at Doug's trailer)...I guess he figured it was better we were with him, safe, than out drinking and driving." Doug Sims, according to this friend, was not much of a drinking man. No one cared about the rumors or worried about Doug making any sexual advances. "He was never really alone with anyone," the friend explains. "There were always at least three guys with Doug." Drinking, according to this friend, was something you did in a small town, something expected of young men.

However, the festivities never involved drugs; Sims was not a drug user, and he did not let the boys use drugs around him. The young boys, ranging in age from fourteen to eighteen, drank for the experience of getting drunk. Doug Sims did not drink because, according to this pal, "He was watching out for us."

Still, very few people considered this strange behavior. Besides, Doug Sims did not fit the picture of a "dirty old man in a trench coat" as people imagine child predators.

"Doug Sims was so quiet," says one resident of Westport now. "I would see him around town, in the grocery store or wherever, and I'd wave and yell hello. He would just sort of wave; lift his hand up. He was so shy!" He was so quiet and unassuming that later, when his name came up as the primary suspect, and then the perpetrator, this resident refused to believe it. "He had the same pattern every day: he went to work, he went home. He never had visitors. Stayed in on the weekends." The town knew Sims as a hard worker, a quiet, albeit polite person, too shy to meet anyone and, even if he knew him or her, someone who would barely speak to those he encountered.

One of Sims' pals attributes Doug's shy nature to the rumors and name-calling. "Everyone said he was gay, and he got tired of hearing it." So Doug Sims stayed aloof, in a small town of less than 1,000 people.

But not all of the young people who encountered Doug found him harmless or fun. Summer Hobbs said flatly, "When you were around the guy—he scared me to death —there was so much evil around him. I know you're not supposed to judge, but he had an evil presence." Summer explains her father "saw it too," so much so that Mr. Hobbs warned his family, "I don't want to see you around the guy; he is not allowed around my kids. I don't even want to see him pulling up in my driveway!" If Doug Sims showed up while she spent time with friends, she "left the room because my dad said so." Summer Hobbs stayed as far away from Doug Sims as possible without trying to appear rude. "He always wore camouflage, and he reminded you of those crazy army men that sit in a dark corner, sharpening a knife. He was," she repeats, "just evil."

Prior to Brad's murder, people kept multiple incidents

53

secret and never discussed them, or they did not consider them unusual. After his death, people started to talk. Sometimes they shared gossip; sometimes they spread rumors. And sometimes, they even told the stone cold truth.

People recall seeing Doug Sims driving around town with several young boys in the back of his pickup, taking them to the fast food burger stand, *Dairy Stop*, for treats— particularly after a hot day of baseball. Sims would always buy. It seemed he constantly bought things for groups of young boys.

Sims would hang out at the local ballpark where the town youth gathered for games. He would talk to the young boys there, and buy them goodies from the snack bar. No one thought anything of it.

One of Sims' best friends states he heard stories of Doug being on medication, when he was younger, for Attention Deficit Disorder (ADD) or "some type of learning disability."

Someone told one law enforcement officer, before Brad's death, that Sims enticed young boys to his trailer with alcohol. One of Brad's friends confirms this as a fact, stating that said officer was aware of that information but did nothing about it.

Donnie Walker's parents belonged to the area club in his youth. According to several people, when Donnie stood innocently outside of the club one evening, a car slowed down and someone yanked Donnie into the vehicle. It was as if some sort of demonic force ambushed him. The perpetrator did not get away and Donnie's injuries sent him to the hospital. The man who unsuccessfully tried to grab Donnie had a father who promised to pay the entire hospital bill if the Walkers agreed to not press charges. All agreed. Donnie's would-be-kidnapper answered to the name of Douglas Sims.

To this day, Cody Maddux says he saw through Doug Sims' shy exterior and could plainly see Sims' obsession with young boys. "I would nod to him if I saw him in public, but I stayed away from him," Cody says now. "I told everyone to stay away from him." Already adamant that he correctly judged Sims' character, he grew even more serious about avoiding him. "I told everyone, but no

one would listen. I told him and told him—" he breaks off
and looks away, pained, at the thought of his little brother.
But because no one would believe bad things happened to
children in Westport, no one knew they should do
anything.

Westport is certainly not the only town where people
refuse to believe bad things happen to children. The
residents are not ignorant or uneducated. People all over
the world will refuse to believe horrible things occur in
their own backyard. People all over the planet "don't want
to talk about it" because the murder of a child is
frightening. They cannot understand, or do not want to
know, how a child predator operates. Like so many
neighborhoods, towns, and locations on the map,
Westport believed it was safe from evil.

Time and gossip changed the story of how Doug Sims
enticed Brad Maddux to go anywhere with him. One
rumor has Doug approaching Brad and two friends as they
went to make a purchase for Brad's aunt; Brad wanted to
buy her a soft drink, or a "pop," as they call it in this
region of the States. Sims lured the boys over to his house
with an offer to play a game of "army." He brought the
boys back some time later and kept Brad in his truck,
tricking Brad back for a longer game.

Another rumor sets the unwitting abduction at a basketball
game between Brad and two friends, to which Sims drives
up to and enjoys for a time. Sims watches the boys, like a
vulture circling his prey, then he approaches them with the
offer to go drink beer at his house. He arranges to meet
the boys downtown. The boys go with him and are later
dropped off at one of the boy's homes. Brad stays with
Sims.

Some remember hearing that Sims buried Brad in a
clearing in the woods, with only his head sticking out of
the earth, as if in some strange symbolic meaning. Others
said only his face remained exposed to the night air, in
some sort of Satanic ritual.

The "Satanic Ritual" rumor went around for some time.
To heighten it, people told others that Sims had removed
some of Brad's body parts prior to burial. There is no
evidence and no history of Doug Sims, Brad Maddux, or
any of their friends or family partaking in anything
remotely resembling satanic worship or interest.

Another rumor circulated that law enforcement officers beat a confession out of Sims. Because he would not admit guilt, they cut off the tape recorder and "made" him confess. Some people swear the arresting officers yanked Sims from his own doorway, shoved him into the side of his truck, and threatened him with his life if he did not talk.

Still another rumor, straight out of a horror movie, has Sims talking to coworkers at Mariah, holding a cattle prod, while his coworkers stood on a large metal plate. Sims laughs maniacally about what he "might have done" about Brad. Had he touched that metal plate with the electric prod, everyone would have received a jolt strong enough to kill a steer.

Some residents tell others that Brad's death resulted from a drug deal gone wrong. Sims left his body in a creek —a payment for an overdue debt involving illegal drugs.

Several of Sims' young friends insist that each time Sims would see Brad in public, Sims would become upset. "That boy doesn't need to live with his parents," Sims would fume; "He needs to be with my parents!" This is how the boys learned Sims and Brad were related, in some way. Sims would "go on and on" about how Brad's upbringing "was so wrong," and that the elder Sims could supply the loving home Brad deserved and needed. When Sims would go on what the boys called "a binge," imbibing in too much alcohol, he reportedly became overly emotional. "They need to get Brad out of that house," Sims would repeat. "They have to get that boy out of that house, let him stay with my parents!" It was strange; Cody was "outgoing," says one of Sims' friends, and "Brad was shy and backward." At one point, the boys assumed that Betty and David Sims took care of Brad at some point in his life, based on the way Doug carried on about the topic.

Still others insist Sims is innocent of all charges and the true killer lurks out there, somewhere. One family in particular, the Meadows, including Mike, initially refused to believe Doug Sims would harm anyone. They wondered if Sims confessed to a crime he did not do in order to protect someone else.

A rumor went around the youth of Westport: after Brad's death, the perpetrator removed Brad's penis and then

56

buried the body. Others told one another Brad's murderer tortured the boy and stabbed him multiple times.

Recent studies have shown that severe stress, including post traumatic stress disorder (PTSD) and childhood abuse, results in damage to the hippocampus, an area of the brain involved in memory. For example, combat veterans and childhood abuse survivors have shown, via testing (including Magnetic Resonance Imaging, or MRI), deficits on neuropsychological measures and a decline in the amount of the hippocampus. Therefore, it is highly possible that traumatic experiences will have long-term effects on the brain's function, including recall. A highly stressful event may create damage in memory, replacing the true event with a "pretend" or false memory, or it might wipe out a portion of that memory. The false memory is not an attempt to fib; the teller truly believes the false story as a truth. It is a story the brain has either concocted to keep the teller safe because the brain cannot process the emotions (such as in a rape case) or because of damage to the true memory due to the hippocampus. In a fascinating study entitled, *Chronic Stress Selectively Reduces Hippocampal Volume in Rats: A Longitudinal MRI Study:*

Stress is a biologically significant and pervasive factor that negatively impacts memory and hippocampal function in humans . . . results indicate that the hippocampus is particularly vulnerable to stress ... the present results clearly support the view that stress can alter the size o the hippocampus (Lee, Jarome, Li, Kim, and Helmstetter, Nov. 25, 2009).

The truth about the night Douglas Sims abducted Brad Maddux is quite frightening in its simplicity. The abduction occurred because Sims took advantage of a naïve young boy and manipulated some very simple factors: timing, trust, and a total lack of fear.

5 MARCH 10, 1990 (FRIDAY)

In the early part of Indiana March, the crispness of winter begins to dissolve as spring peeps around the corner. The night air still held a chill, but the days remained crisp and clear. Perfect camping weather, Rob Nugent and Junior Armstrong told their parents. To one another, they winked; the night also created a good atmosphere for drinking outdoors.

Rob and Junior planned the night out ahead of time. Stars filled the night sky and they felt like they owned the world. Nothing could harm them, and Westport, Indiana was their domain. They pitched the dome tent in the Armstrong's back yard on the cement porch. They filled it with sleeping bags, anticipating the sharp cold that came with March darkness. Mary Armstrong would not be home until later, as she was working a late shift at a fast food restaurant in Greensburg.

At the Maddux home, Brad cleaned up and then rummaged around his room, pulling on a pair of white jockey shorts, a pair of blue jeans, a yellow shirt with the Purdue logo, and white Voit brand sneakers. Because of the chilly night air, he carried a grey hooded sweatshirt "hoodie" and his blue jean jacket. It was about 4:30 p.m., and he scooped up some money to go skating with friends. He explained to his mother he was going to Greensburg with friends, including Summer Hobbs, and then planned to camp over at Junior's house with Junior and Rob. Patti agreed without concern. Westport was safe; the boys camped out often. Brad said his goodbyes and headed off to skate. Brad liked going to the skating rink and always enjoyed himself when he went. Greensburg, about fourteen miles away, was no metropolis, but it offered a lot more to do on the weekends than Westport.

Kiki Weston, Summer Hobbs, *Jeff Hommice*, a few other friends, and Brad headed for the Greensboro Roller Rink. Summer remembers that Rob Nugent and his friends aimlessly milled about as she and her friends prepared to leave. Rob saw Brad's yellow shirt and spouted, "Hey yellow belly!" Everyone laughed and Brad, looking down at his shirt, made a face at them. He vowed to show up his buddies once on skates.

Once they laced on their skates and hit the floor, however, Brad did not show up much of anyone. He got out onto the hardwood floor and tried to make the best of it, but he found it necessary to grab the rail or his behind met with the floor way too many times. Brad, his face red from trying, walked carefully back off the floor, unlaced his skates, and shook his head. He had no interest in breaking a bone or looking silly in front of those cute girls.

The Roller Rink featured one pool table, some video games, and a small dance floor. Summer and her friends danced to Michael Jackson songs and Brad watched; he did not care much for dancing, like a lot of boys his age. Summer danced happily on the dance floor, but Brad went to meander around the rink, talking to friends. He preferred the gridiron to the dance floor.

Finally the time came to load everyone into the car, and they returned to Westport. Jeff drove the boys home, and they dropped Brad off at the Maddux residence. They promised to see one another later, in school probably, and Brad waved to his pals as he went into the house.

By then, a chill laced the night air, so Brad donned his hoodie and jean jacket. He checked in with his parents, letting them know of his arrival and his pending departure to go camping with Junior and Rob across the street. Patti and Daryl gave their permission. Brad hopped on his bicycle and pedaled off.

That same night, Cody Maddux spent the night with a friend, *Tommy Stellar*, who happened to live in a house directly across the street from an apartment complex. Mike Meadows and his sister Linda lived with their mother in these apartments. "Sitting on his back porch, you could see the Meadows' apartment windows," says a friend of the boys.

Dollie Press was having a sleepover at Linda Meadows' home that night; Linda and Dollie walked across the street to join Cody and Tommy. Dollie was close friends with Rob Nugent; she loved him like a brother. She lived in Alert, the same little unincorporated town as Rob. She loved the Nugent family as well as her own, and today she calls Mrs. Nugent "a sweetheart." Although closer to Brad's age, Dollie knew Cody better—possibly because of Cody's popularity. The girls stood in the Stellar's front yard and chit-chatted with the boys. "I had begged and begged my mother to spend the night with Linda," Dollie says now. Mrs. Press was not fond of the more lenient Mrs. Meadows. "I had promised, and promised, I would obey all of my parents rules, I would not be out at dark, and I would stay at Linda's and not go anywhere else." So when Linda Meadows told Dollie she planned on visiting her boyfriend, Dollie felt stunned, and then a bit put out. Without Linda, there was not much to do. A bad case of the flu made Linda's brother bed-ridden, and Mrs. Meadows left a while ago. That left some friend of theirs, the guy named "Mush," who sat in the apartment drinking beer. Dollie did not know him, and she decided she did not want to stay alone in the apartment with him.

As Dollie, Cody, and Tommy talked and laughed, Brad came wheeling up on his bicycle. Dollie saw Brad as a bit immature for their group, of course he was younger, and, "He was the naive little brother that followed everyone around," she recalls today. "He was this bubbly little kid, always wanting to be in on everything his big brother was doing, or the older kids were doing. Sometimes it was like he'd have a story to brag about at school the next day if he hung out with the older kids."

"Get out of here," Cody told Brad. "We're talking."

As usual, Brad wanted to know what the older kids talked about and who said what about whom.

"Go on!" Cody told him. "It's none of your business."

Brad wheeled off, throwing a look at the three of them, but it did not last. "Brad was a happy kid," Dollie says now. "Always laughing." He often gave her a shy smile, showing the gap between his front teeth, or made her laugh. She described Brad as "the tagalong type, who'd pop up in places."

Brad took his bike home and parked it in preparation for his paper route the next morning, then headed for Junior's house, sleeping bag and blankets tucked under his arms. It was about 8:30 p.m. when Brad set up his sleeping bag and blankets in the dome tent with the other boys, and they discussed what to do with their evening. One of the boys remembered a party that a girl at school invited him to for tonight. Not really a party, per se, but a get together at the young lady's house. Maybe they could stop by her place. Her name was Linda Meadows.

Some of the parents in town found themselves raising an eyebrow at the quality of the Meadows family; Linda, her brother Mike, and their mom lived together. Rumors suggest Mrs. Meadows laps up quite a bit of alcohol, but her children deny the rumor's credence. Her attitude towards young people, like the ideas of some other parents in town, allowed the teenagers to drink alcohol, as long as they remained in a supervised location and did not drive home.

One of Linda's friends explains that none of Linda's personality strengths involved honesty; in fact, this friend called her "a habitual liar." To her credit, most teenagers do not necessarily practice 100% honesty, particularly when speaking to adults.

In the coolness of that March night, the three boys went walking through Westport, seeking mischief, something to do, and a way to kill adolescent time. They stopped at Highway 3, looking left and right for vehicles, before running across both lanes. They walked and jabbered, Brad cracking jokes, as usual, making them all laugh.

In small town America, despite the nostalgic lemonade stand ads that the media loves to portray, very few organized events for young people to partake in exist. "If there was more to do for young people during that time," Rob Nugent reflects now, "I don't think none of it would have happened. Brad would not have ever drank. Maybe Junior wouldn't be in the mess he's in. There was nothing to do for young people." The boys decided to walk to the apartment complex and call on Linda Meadows, or, if the party was lame, find something else.

Dollie, still in Tommy's yard, told Cody and Tommy, "I'd better check in." She still did not know where Linda went when she left earlier, and she wanted to make sure she followed her own mother's strict rules. Dollie made her way to the apartment building, took the stairs, and entered the apartment.

Mike still battled that horrible case of flu, and Dollie

doubted that Mrs. Meadows already returned from work. The eerily quiet apartment greeted her when she let herself in. That guy, Mush, still sat in the recliner, drinking a beer. Mush did not please the eyes when looked upon—a paunchy fellow who looked rough around the edges, balding, with haggard eyes. Just shy of two hundred pounds, he stood a little more than six feet tall. He parted his short and neat dark hair on the right side of his face. His high, receding hairline suggested he would begin balding soon. He wore a short mustache that emanated a slightly creepy vibe to Dollie. He looked like any other white male pushing thirty years old in the region; he did not stick out and he did not have any strange characteristics.

Dollie made small talk with Mush; her parents raised her to respect her elders and never act rudely. "If an adult told me to do something, I would do it, because they were the adult," she says now. She also knew of Mush but had never heard him speak, just recognized him as a friend of some of her friends. She discovered Mike had no chance for recovery anytime soon. "Well," she told Mush, "I'm going back outside."

Nothing about Mush made her wary or sent up warning signals. His attire was casual, in dark pants, a shirt, and a flannel shirt. He wore a cap, the type that had a mesh backing to keep your head cooler. Dollie knew several adults who drank beer, so Mush's drinking did not bother her. But as she passed by him in his recliner, he suddenly gripped her arm in his clammy hands. And Dollie Press' world changed.

"Come sit in my lap," he told her.

Dollie's heart went to her stomach. She felt Mush's grip tighten on her arm, pulling her slowly to him. *Maybe he's drunk*, she thought, but she did not smell alcohol. He did not slur his words, nor did he appear to sway unsteadily. Then she looked into his eyes. "His eyes," she says, years later, "Scared me to the bone."

"You're staying in the house with me." His voice was steady, quiet, soft. It was not a request, or a question. He made a demand, and it chilled the girl throughout her entire body. "You're not going to leave."

Dollie thought quickly as the terrifying man pulled her

towards him. Even this close, she still did not smell alcohol, and she did not recognize anything in his eyes except a coldness she had never before seen. "I left my jacket outside," she lied. "I have to go get it."

Mush sat there for what seemed like an eternity. Suddenly he released her arm. But his voice, like a cobra, made her stop in her tracks. "You will come," he told her quietly, "Directly back up to me."

It took every ounce of self-control that Dollie Press could muster for her to walk calmly out the door. Although already a teenager, she did not possess a shred of street-smarts or toughness. Throughout her entire, albeit somewhat short, life, no one ever spoke to her that way. She was shocked; her parents raised her to obey and respect grown-ups and to tell them the truth at all times. This was the first time in Dollie's young life that she lied to an adult, and something in her gut told her she acted correctly. Today she says, "I know now to trust your inner feeling," a sentiment she passes to her own children.

Cody and Tommy still stood in Tommy's yard, and Dollie joined them quickly. The boys noted a change in her. "I'm not going back in that house alone," she told them. "That guy freaks me out."

Linda came around the corner then, back from her visit with her boyfriend. She joined the trio on the front lawn. Tommy said something that made Cody laugh, but Cody calmed when he saw his brother, Junior, and Rob heading for the apartments. He walked over to them. The four paused to talk.

"You better get across the highway before it gets dark or Mom will have your ass," Cody told Brad. Highway 3 could be dangerous at night in that area, due to the darkness and speed of cars.

The boys chatted some more, and then Brad, Junior, and Rob headed for the apartments. Dollie and Linda led the way. Cody and Tommy stayed at the Stellar's house, as Cody planned to sleep over.

Later, Cody would recall seeing Doug Sims' truck parked at the apartments. Sims often hung out with Mike Meadows. Sometimes *Ben Frost* accompanied them. Ben and Mike, only half Sims' age, cared for each other like brothers. Ben was an only child, and the Frost family considered Mike to be "a second son," said Mike. Usually if someone saw Sims, they often found Mike and Ben alongside him. Sims bought alcohol for Ben and Mike, just like he did for the other kids. While Mike favored telling people exactly what he thought, Ben tended to be more passive and quiet. Sims, Mike explained later, "was a very quiet guy."

Summer Hobbs also thought highly of Ben. "Ben was like a brother," Summer explains. They talked about everything. Everything, for Ben Frost was carrying a secret, a monumental secret from the rest of the town.

Ben exuded an aura of seriousness about him, more so than his peers. Sure, he drank beer alongside them, joked and hung out in the same places. But Ben fought a lot with his own father, and he sought refuge at Summer Hobbs' home. He called Mr. and Mrs. Hobbs "Mom" and "Dad." Ben also called Mrs. Meadows "Mom."

"I knew something had happened to Ben," confides one of his closest friends. "Finally he admitted to me; he had been molested. But he never said who did it." His young friend did not know what to say, they only knew to keep the confidence and support Ben. Otherwise, Ben kept his secret.

Sims spent a lot of time with the Meadows' family, Cody Maddux remembers. In a little town, people get accustomed to seeing the same vehicles at the same places, the same faces at certain times or in certain locations. At the time it meant nothing.

Clusters of plain buildings with no security gates made up the apartment complex. One only needed to go through a main door to obtain entrance to the individual apartment units inside the buildings. They were two-story structures with a few windows for each unit. Although nothing fancy, maintenance kept the buildings from becoming derelict or unkempt.

The boys and girls went through the unlocked door into the building, turned left, and tromped up the stairs. Linda led them in. The apartment mirrored the building's outside in its lack of splendor, having only two bedrooms and an open floor plan with a small kitchen. In this particular home, the children and their parents drank alcohol, and Brad, Junior, and Rob followed suit. Rob noted that Brad spent more time "nursing" his beer rather than drinking it. He opened the beer and held it for lengthy periods of time, taking few sips. Junior and Rob, however, took complete advantage of the situation and helped themselves; the kids could not ignore the fact that the adults in the house allowed them to imbibe in alcohol. Linda and Dollie spoke to the boys about silly teenage chatter while Rob quickly grew quite intoxicated. As Rob made his way through the quickly filling apartment, someone introduced him to a man called "Mush," or "Mushroom."

Eventually, other friends showed up, and a few more people stopped by. It became a full-fledged party by Westport teen standards. A little over ten people crowded the two-bedroom apartment's living room and kitchen.

As Linda and Dollie meandered through the apartment, Mush talked to the boys. Dollie kept her head down. She would not make eye contact with Mush. The guys stood between them so she didn't have to look at him. She remained fearful of him, despite the seeming protection of the crowd.

Evidently Mush was a distant relative of Brad's—no big deal in Westport, as almost everyone had a relative nearby at all times, whether they be family by blood or by marriage. "We'd known him since the summer of 1989," Linda explained later. "He bought the kids alcohol." A few of her female friends did not like Mush. They found Mush weird and felt something wrong about him. Linda blew them off. "Why doesn't he have a girlfriend?" One would ask. Linda told him he was too shy to even approach a woman, much less ask her out. She did not give credence to the rumors of his homosexuality; "he wasn't 'girlie,'" she said later. "He would always wear camouflage. He didn't have any guns at his house."

"Hey!" Mike finally shouted from his bedroom, "Take it outside! I'm trying to sleep!" This drew giggles and mugged faces from the young people, but they shrugged it off. Grabbing a few to-go cups, they took the party outside.

One story surfaced about that night, and its validity varies depending on who tells the story.

Someone suggested a game of "tag," and everyone took it up. They decided to use Mush's two-toned brown truck as "base." Then Mush came outside and told them to stop slapping and hitting his truck. The game continued and the drinks flowed freely, until Cody Maddux spotted Brad in the fray.

"What the hell are you doing?" Cody demanded, crossing the road to his little brother. He pointed at Mush. "You're not supposed to be near this—this..."

Brad stopped playing the game and got into a heated argument with his brother. Cody then turned on Doug Sims. He began shouting at Sims, telling him to leave his brother alone, asking him just what the hell was a grown man doing, giving kids a bunch of alcohol?

Doug began arguing back, contrary to his usually quiet behavior. "Mush was not a strong person," says Linda Meadows. "He was quiet. He didn't do a lot of joking around, either. He was shy. I think that's why he hung out with people younger than him." Both voices became louder and louder.

The argument ended with both parties walking off in opposite directions. The group trooped back upstairs to the Meadows apartment.

Some people recall this incident, while others do not. It is difficult to discern the truth.

Cody does not recall any argument with Sims or Brad. Later he would explain he was at Tommy's house when the phone rang. It was Brad, calling from the Meadows home across the street. They made small talk until Brad mentioned Mush hung out at the party. "I told him to go home," Cody explains. "I didn't want him around Doug Sims." Brad initially argued, then agreed. He hung up to return to the party.

Regardless of the truth, Brad was with his friends at the Meadows' apartment. The party included Doug Sims. The stage was set for tragedy, but no one knew it.

Linda's mother came home, setting down her purse and keys. She did not have her own room; she let her kids have the bedrooms and she slept on the sofa. Mrs. Meadows began running around like a dramatic mama hen, clucking over the intoxicated boys. To her, Mush gave the impression of "a big kid. He didn't have the mentality of an adult." She herself spent time drinking with Mush. Brad made a show of the fact that he held a beer, and Rob

66

and Junior's journey from tipsy to drunk seemed well-underway.

Rob headed for the bathroom, tottering a bit. He had trouble standing at the toilet. His Crohn's disease made him feel a little bit off. Rob was on the prednisone as well, and mixing it with alcohol made the booze hit him harder. Rob heard the music, voices, and laughter through the bathroom door, and he heard Mrs. Meadows bellowing, something about, "He better not be pissing on the floor!" He rolled his eyes as he finished his business. "What a lady," he slurred to himself.

Linda recalled Mush inviting Mike to stay at his trailer that night. "I don't feel like it," Mike told him, lying back on his bed. "I'm sick!" Mush accepted the answer, then later tried to talk him into coming out and staying with him again.

The atmosphere felt casual, and drinks flowed as freely as the conversation. Mush, as usual, supplied the alcohol. At one point in the evening, Mushroom approached Junior with an offer.

"This Mushroom," Junior later told Brad and Rob, "has a bunch of alcohol back at his place, if we want to go." Junior nodded at the pale man who was walking around the small apartment. "He can pick us up back at my place." Rob considered. The guy looked harmless.

"My mom's closing the restaurant tonight so she'll be home late," Junior explained. "Hell, it's free booze."

Rob shrugged. They did not know of any more parties, and the night was young. Brad seemed to be cool with the plan. But first, they needed to talk to the girls about a matter.

Dollie and Linda went into the kitchen. After a quick glance around, the girls took some beers out of the refrigerator, and hid them under their sweatshirts. Then the girls headed for Linda's room. Linda set the beer down, pulled open her curtains, and lifted up the bedroom window.

Saying their goodbyes, Rob, Junior, and Brad departed the party, with a quiet promise to meet this fellow, Mush, in a few hours.

According to one account, Linda's mother wanted them to stay. "You don't have to leave!" Linda's mother nagged them. "Tell them they don't have to go!" she fussed at others.

"Nah, we gotta go," the boys told her, and they all but shoved one another away from the woman's shrill voice. They left the apartment, made their way down the stairs, and then went outside to stand under what they knew was Linda's bedroom window.

Linda and Dollie's faces appeared in Linda's window and they waved, then a few seconds later, a beer dropped down to the boys. Junior caught it. They dropped a few more down.

Dollie and Linda giggled and Linda closed her bedroom window. "Oh, I want to tape those Bobby Brown songs," Dollie reminded her, as she enjoyed the singer. She set up the VCR and began to copy two music videos to videotape.

Junior, Brad, and Rob walked back through town and tried to find something else to do, but the town, as the joke goes, rolled its sidewalks up early. Junior and Rob, with Brad in tow, headed back to the tent and settled in, listening to the night sounds in the Armstrong backyard and laughing it up, talking, and discussing the evening.

"He ain't gonna show," Rob said finally, kicking off his shoes. He began to down one of the smuggled beers.

"That Mushroom," Junior asked Brad. "He's your kin?" The *pop! Fzzz* sounded as he opened one of the beers Linda dropped down to him.

"Yeah," Brad still had the same beer he opened hours ago. "On my dad's side. My grandpa is his cousin."

A memory jiggled in the back of Rob's mind about Mushroom, or Mush, as everyone called him, and he struggled through the alcohol to remember it. Something about...

Meanwhile, Mush again tried to talk Mike into staying at his trailer that night. "I'm sick!" Mike coughed. Mush seethed, and his mouth set in a thin line.

Dollie stopped the VCR after taping the two Bobby Brown videos. Satisfied, Dollie started to comment on the music when she heard a truck's engine start up outside the window. She went to the window where Linda stood and both peered outside.

Both girls saw Mush's Ford pickup exiting the apartment

68

complex parking lot. The girls thought nothing of it and returned to their slumber party.

A truck horn blew from the street that ran alongside Junior's home, and someone looked out of the tent flap. "Let's go!"

Rob considered for a second to grab his shoes, then considered again. It just seemed like far too much effort. He crawled out of the tent behind Brad and Junior and followed them to the street. The cold pavement made his feet tingle.

Mush's brown on brown, two toned 1982 Ford F-150, with its distinct clearance lights across the top, sat curbside. Mush sat behind the wheel, looking very casual.

In a small community like Westport, drinking is a teen pastime. Perhaps the boys felt grown up, this seemed like a chance to show off, act big. They teetered on the cusp of young adulthood, manhood peeping around the corner along with soft mustaches and changing voices. Perhaps Brad saw this as a chance to be a bit of a show-off. Here was his cousin offering to give them alcohol. Brad, whose kind personality usually caused him to serve as the brunt of many a joke, now felt like the hot shot. One of the boys took a step and they fell into group formation, like a small platoon. They opened the truck door, which creaked and groaned, and piled in, the heater warming them, and slammed the door.

After the boys situated themselves and the heater churned out warmth, the truck turned into the street and started away. They hit the road and proceeded southwest to the smaller town of Sardinia, traveling the seven miles from Westport. They made small talk, laughing, as Westport disappeared behind them.

Sardinia remained an unincorporated town. The rural community rests along Southern County Road 800 West. Mush said he lived in a single-wide mobile home in Sardinia, on a road that peeled off of the main Highway 3. His parents lived in Westport, Indiana, he told the boys.

"I don't live too far from here," Rob commented.

"Where at?" Mush asked him.

Something deep in his gut made Rob lie. He pointed in an ambiguous direction opposite of where his family resided. "That way."

A stuffed toy, shaped like a dilapidated softball with a red face that grimaced through the back window, stuck to the window with suction cup hands, its legs dangling disturbingly. It moved with the truck. It was a red devil.

They turned onto a road marked by a sign, 1270 S. A large frame house sat on the corner. They passed another house. The truck pulled left into a yard where a white, single-wide mobile home sat, parallel to the street, on a plot of land between two houses. Mush parked next to the trailer.

The four of them poured out of the truck cab, tromped up two short steps leading up to a small deck surrounded by a trellis, and pushed into the home, cursing the cold. Each headed into the kitchen and living area, to the right. A hallway stood to the left, presumably leading to the other rooms.

Mush immediately began to play bartender. He handed out beers and he pulled out bottles of liquor and a few shot glasses. The place was not fancy, but Mushroom seemed to be a decent host. "Have a seat, have a seat," he insisted, pointing out the mismatched chairs. "Have another drink," he would hurry them along. "We can have shots of whiskey." He set glasses down on the kitchen counter, next to an assortment of odds and ends. On the counter was a large Bowie knife in a sheath. This was nothing strange; people who lived in the country often kept knives and guns. Something else drew Rob's attention.

"There was a digital clock on the top of the refrigerator," Rob later recalled. For some reason this one detail struck him. "When we got there it was 12:30 a.m." The cold weather sobered him up, and he noticed Junior also slowed down his drinking. Both of them took a seat in the living room and made small talk with one another and Mushroom. Brad began to play into Mush's conversations, and accepted the alcohol Mush offered.

"Have another shot," Mush told them, filling up the small glass with whiskey and handing it over.

"It wasn't anything said, or something Mush said, but it was his actions," Rob later confided. As the night went on, Mushroom's actions became stranger, until a phenomenon occurred in both Rob Nugent and Junior Armstrong; it is called "fight, flight, or freeze reaction." Also known as the "acute stress response," Walter B. Cannon introduced this physical reaction in 1915. The theory states that animals (including humans) react to threats with a discharge of the sympathetic nervous system, preparing the animal for confrontation, escape, or a state of paralysis, which in turn may save its life (think of the mouse which sits perfectly still when the predator is searching for movement).

Mush began playing with Brad, pretending to wrestle him. Brad played the game as well, and both became "champs," grabbing one another and fighting off holds and grabs. Mush would grab Brad, and then twist him around in a headlock. Brad in turn would laugh and twist out, his dark hair a mess. They would grapple, and then split apart. Brad started jumping off furniture and yelling like professional wrestlers, and Mush encouraged it.

The fight, flight, or freeze reaction began slowly coursing through Rob Nugent and Junior Armstrong that night in Mush's trailer, somewhere in between Mush and Brad's wrestling matches and the shots of whiskey Mush kept plugging. Rob and Junior felt kicked back, in a vortex of beer and whiskey haze, as Mush grabbed Brad in a headlock and stomped his foot playfully, causing the single-wide flooring to shudder at times. Rob and Junior exchanged eye rolls and shakes of the head on occasion; frankly, this wrestling was childish bullshit. They tipped their beers to sip and talk amongst themselves. Brad rarely sipped from his own beer. Brad, Rob noted, was not a drinker by any means. He appeared to be trying desperately to fit in by popping open a beer and making sure everyone saw him holding the alcoholic beverage more than doing the actual sipping. When he did sip, he tried to hide a grimace. Mush kept pouring the shots and Rob and Junior did not turn down the drinks, but Brad played the role of moral support more than partaking in the alcohol. Sometimes during the night, Mush made his way to the back of the home, his shoulders bumping along the narrow hall of the trailer.

Rob looked around at the trailer. Nothing fancy, he noted. Hand-me-down furniture, cast-off mismatched couch and chairs. A bachelor's apartment, to be sure, with no thought of decoration. Almost nothing adorned the walls. Some family pictures hung on the wall, but he did not get up to peruse the faces. A glass case showed off a collection of various knives. The apartment ranged somewhere between clean and spotless. Although the place could not be considered trashy, Rob thought of it as "red neck," the euphemism commonly used for white, low socioeconomic, laboring class folk who lived simply, not a lot of taste or class in design. Rob leaned over to tell Junior and Brad something.

A few minutes later, the boys heard the bathroom plumbing working. Junior started to say something to Rob when both boys did a double take. Mush came into the room, his belt undone and his shirt untucked. He did not expose his genitalia, but Rob could see "his big beer belly hanging out, and more than I cared to see." Mush buttoned, but did not zip up, his pants. Mush seemed to parade around the room for a moment, then he made his way back to the bedroom.

Mush interrupted Rob's thoughts when he came busting around the corner, rattling a pair of handcuffs. "Who's going to jail tonight?" he crowed.

Junior looked over at Rob and laughed, mockingly, at this bizarre display. Why couldn't they just sit around and drink? Rob pulled a drink from his beer and cut his eyes at Junior. The boys shared such a close bond, they did not even need words to communicate their thoughts.

But Brad was into the game the minute it started, jumping up at the chance. "I am!" he said, offering his wrists. "I'm going to jail!" He looked to Junior and Rob for approval.

The cuff slowly went over the beefy boy's wrist, *click-click-click*, and Brad's face showed delight.

Later, it would show a much different emotion.

"You're going to jail!" Mush led Brad down the hall and out of sight, to his bedroom, and they did not return. The boys heard them laughing and yucking it up.

Rob got up and leaned to look down the hallway. The house only had one bedroom, the last room off of the hall. Rob saw Brad handcuffed to a leg of the bed. This is when "fight, flight, or freeze" really kicked in and punched Rob in the stomach. He sat down and looked at his friend. "He's handcuffed to the bed," he whispered to Junior.

Junior became so nervous he had to go to the bathroom. He wandered down the hallway, closed the door behind him, and as he stood there relieving himself, his mind raced and he ran his tongue over his teeth. "What," he asked himself, "are we gonna do?" He watched the bathroom door nervously. "What if Mush breaks in here?" He caught a glimpse of himself in the mirror. He saw a kid, a little boy, who had no other place to go. Junior stood barely over 5'3" and did not weigh near eighty pounds. Mush was a giant compared to his stature. A grown man controlled them all, and the morning seemed far away. His very best friend, more like a brother than anything else, sat handcuffed to a heavy piece of furniture. When he exited the small bathroom, he glanced into the bedroom, where Brad was still handcuffed. Brad sat leaning back against the wall with a huge grin on his face, and Brad waved to him. Junior, feeling numb, slid back into his seat in the living room and took a long drink of his beer. He looked at Rob. "He's handcuffed him to the bed!" he whispered unnecessarily.

Meanwhile, Mush kept taking alcohol to Brad.

Rob's face was pasty, and he looked suddenly very small. "Shhhiit," he whispered.

Junior stood uneasily in the living room, glancing down the hall to ensure Mush did not overhear their conversation, and he motioned his friend over to the kitchen area, away from the hallway. Both boys, Rob later confided, "huddled up in a corner" to discuss the night's progression.

"I remember now. I've heard this guy Mush is a faggot," Junior whispered, glancing back at the hallway of the trailer. People their age often used the slang word "faggot" to mean "child molester."

His eyes bleary but cutting back toward the hall where Brad and Mush disappeared earlier, Rob agreed. "He hangs out at the ballpark," he remembered, the beer and whiskey clearing from the cerebral cortex of his brain. "Buying ice cream for little kids," he looked down at his bare toes and started to shake.

"Man," Junior shook his head slowly. "We gotta get out of here." His voice had a tremor in it, a strange sound. Junior was the tough one, the survivor, a boy who had dodged and received some hard knocks by the ripe old age of thirteen. "We gotta fuckin' get outta here," he repeated nervously.

Adrenaline is the body's natural way to prepare for an

emergency. It is both a neurotransmitter and a hormone. It increases the heart rate so the body can move faster, sharpens the vision so the eyes can see clearer, and changes the breathing pattern so as not to waste breath and save it for survival. Adrenaline increases the flow of oxygen to muscles; the nervous system sends maddening electrical impulses to the skeletal muscles to contract them, making them shorten. It also affects tissue, causing it to go into action should the body need to jump, fight, or run. It can come to the body in an instant, overriding the *thinking* process into *doing*. This is true fear at work. This is the body telling the mind, GO. If the body does not process the adrenaline, the person suffers what is called an "adrenaline dump," characterized by crying, shaking, and sweating, as the body dumps neurotransmitters and hormones needlessly into the now-useless survival mode. They have to go somewhere; useless, they float around, causing a pseudo-anxiety state.

Standing there in that single-wide trailer, surrounded by strangers smiling from framed pictures taken in safe places, adrenaline pumped as the two children formed a plot. Right there they formed an escape plan to save their lives, should it come to that drastic a measure. Later, Rob would say, "Me and Junior were trying to divide and conquer."

Junior's job involved moving to the front door, his hand on the latch. Rob stood nearby but at a planned, strategic angle. Rob pulled himself up to his full 5'3", trying to make his seventy pounds appear as tough as he could. Should Mush attempt to grab either of them, both boys needed to create a diversion. Rob would grab Brad and run, but in the opposite direction of his own home so Mush would never guess where the Nugents lived. Junior would race in the opposite direction, toward the Nugent home, but not to the house.

Adrenaline sharpens the eyesight and assists the memory. Rob Nugent can still recall, over twenty years later, the clock on Mush's refrigerator reading a bright red 2:30 a.m. As Rob ruminated over their plan, taking deep breaths, he tried to sober up. He looked down at his bare feet as he shifted his weight. Secretly he hoped his feet could withstand the run; despite being a country boy, Rob had tender feet. "If anything happens," Rob whispered hoarsely to his smaller friend, somber, "You bale."

That is when Mush came down the hallway. Junior looked down the hall and he knew Brad still sat handcuffed to the bedpost. *Brad still thinks it's a game,* Junior thought.

As Mush passed by Rob, he reached over and ran a hand casually across Rob's chest. He did it so nonchalantly; Rob did not realize what just transpired until it was over. "Have another drink," Mush told Rob.

"We gotta go home!" Rob spouted at Mush, his voice feeling a bit loud.

"Ah, come on!" Mush protested, pointing toward the alcohol. "Have another -"

Junior was pissed off. "We have to go home!"

"See? Junior's getting mad!" Rob pointed.

"My mom's gonna be home any time, and she's gonna be mad!" Junior shouted.

"She'll be home any minute!" Rob echoed, "Any minute!"

"You know how to get Junior to calm down, don't you?" Mush stepped behind the boy, placed his hands around Junior's neck and tightened his grip. "You don't choke him." He gave Junior a slight shake and then said, "You kiss him on the back of the head." He placed a kiss on Junior, quickly, on the back of his head. Then he did it again, kissing his ear, and then again. His lips pressed against Junior's skull, then retracted. "That's how you get Junior to calm down," he said, and started to amble back toward the bedroom.

Memories flooded back to Junior: from a long time ago, from a part of his past he tried his best to forget, and he felt the adrenaline mix with hate and anger and fear until it felt like bile swirling in his mouth, his brain, and his heart. He moved to the front door, trying to shake it all away, Rob's protests to Mush coming back to focus.

"Take us home, now!" Rob repeated.

Junior, his hand on the trailer's front door, said in as serious as a young voice could muster, "We have to go home now!"

Mush continued to protest and suddenly, before he knew it, Rob "was in his face," Rob recalls now; "a redheaded fourteen year old kid shaking a finger in a grown man's face, cussing him out and telling him we had to go home." Rob yelled, and he yelled some more. His face was

75

growing red, spittle flew and his shouts filled their ears. The prednisone steroid he took for his Crohn's disease, mixed with the whiskey and beer, along with the adrenaline, created a powerful effect. Rob suddenly grew fearless, mad, and ready to fight. "That steroid did it," he said later. "I never realized it then. But it could make you feel bulletproof."

Mush started backing down. He stepped back a bit, eyes downcast. Slight protests bubbled from his lips.

"Come on! Fucking take us home!" Junior chimed in now that his head cleared some and he felt, as he liked to say, "Ready to put the hurt on him."

"His mom's gonna be home at—" Rob cut his eyes to the clock "—three a.m., and she's gonna be pissed off if we're not there and we need to fucking go now!" Although a lie, the commotion seemed to work effectively. He saw the big man's shoulders droop, and Mush turned to finally zip his pants. Mush reached over to the counter to retrieve his keys.

Brad's voice arose now, from the bedroom. "What's going on?" he called out. "What's going on?"

"All right, okay," Mush said. As Mush walked back down the hall to retrieve Brad from his back bedroom, both Rob and Junior looked at one another. They did not need to speak.

Rob and Junior opened the trailer door with shaking hands and stepped outside, expecting Brad and Mush to be at their heels. They climbed into the truck, shivering from more than just the cold. They waited. The wait seemed forever. Just as the boys started to return to the trailer to see why the two did not come out with them, Mush and Brad appeared in the silhouette of the open door.

Rob and Junior breathed a sigh of relief as they started to feel optimistic; soon they would return home to safety. By daybreak, the strange night would seem like a bad dream. Junior and Rob sat in the truck, their breath heaving puffs into the night air, their hearts pounding. They turned to see Brad coming down the steps with Mush. Brad seemed none the wiser.

An awkwardly quiet group sat in the brown pickup truck at Mush's trailer that night. Brad, minus the silly handcuffs, scurried in first to sit next to his cousin. Mush climbed behind the wheel, door creaking shut. Rob sat by Brad, leaving Junior, albeit a bit smushed in, with the window seat. The night felt bitterly cold, and Rob silently cursed the fact he did not take the few minutes to grab his shoes. He wiggled his toes, hoping to keep the circulation going. It seemed like a thousand years ago when he first pulled out of the tent that evening to go drinking. He felt a bit sick, but this time it was not just the Crohn's disease making the alcohol churn in his stomach.

The fog grew impossibly thick; the glow of headlights cast shadows against the white swirls as the truck moved along North Indiana 3 toward Westport. The atmosphere grew eerie and foreboding. The fog bounced off of the truck and away as they rumbled toward home. Mush followed Junior's directions: take a left onto West Underwood Drive; pass the Westport Family Restaurant on Small Avenue, then the South Decatur Baptist Church on the left, and past West Wiley street.

"Drop us off here," Junior ordered. The truck slowed and stopped on North Kathleen Drive, just behind the Armstrong residence. Junior's feet hit the pavement as the truck door swung open and Rob scrambled behind him. Brad followed behind them; for some reason, he stopped to talk to his cousin. Rob's bare feet hit the road, the cold sending tingles through the soles of his feet, his mind on his sleeping bag in the tent. There was no sidewalk; the boys began walking down the middle of the street. Junior at his side, Rob knew Brad trailed them by some distance. They began the trek toward the Armstrong's unfenced back yard, and Rob's adrenaline disappeared and the alcohol felt like it came sloshing back into his brain and his limbs, a warm, blurry feeling taking over again. He glanced at Junior and could see his friend felt the same. Both would sleep well tonight.

The truck blew warmth as Mush passed them; his truck drove up the street, toward Kentucky Avenue and away from them, taillights disappearing in the fog and distance.

A few minutes later, both boys heard the truck's rumble behind them and saw, surprised, that Mush returned to them, parking behind them in the parking lot of the Westport Family Restaurant, on West Small Street and North Kathleen Drive, about a block away from where they stood. Mush cut the headlights on the F-150 to circle and stop the truck. The clearance lights across the top of the truck cab glowed like strange, orange eyes through the fog.

The truck sat idling, and it became the beginning of a chapter of evil for a town, a community, and a family. Rob Nugent and Ernest "Junior" Armstrong would never be the same again. Their innocence disappeared that night, in a swirl of fog and haze of anger. It disappeared so quick ... in the time it takes for a friend to slam a pickup truck door.

6 "WHERE IS BRAD?"

Junior and Rob tried to figure out why the hell that stalker freak, Mush, returned and parked in the lot across the street when Brad caught up to them and started explaining. "Hey!" Brad trotted up to them; a bit unsteady on his feet from the alcohol Mush pressured him into drinking earlier. Brad, the lightweight, felt and looked slightly intoxicated. "Mush says he's going to take me to North Vernon to get us some whiskey!" They realized Mush manipulated and convinced Brad into agreeing each time he went to the handcuffed boy, and again, when Junior and Rob waited in the truck and Brad and Mush slowly followed from the trailer home. Brad's fertile mind eagerly absorbed the seeds Mush planted in the innocent and naïve boy. Now they came to fruition.

North Vernon, a town of a little over 6,000, lies just south of Westport, a distance of about a twenty-minute drive. Although small, North Vernon still dwarfs Westport in population and size. Although little more than a speck on a map, one of many in Indiana, North Vernon provides twenty-four hour convenience stores, unlike Westport.

Junior and Rob merely stared at Brad. Junior shook his head. They all knew Brad could not tolerate much alcohol. While Junior could pour down six packs and do shots all night long, Brad merely took sips. The term the boys used to describe people like Brad is "lightweight," meaning he only needed to consume a small amount of alcohol for him to start tottering around.

Rob guffawed. From what he saw of Brad, the boy could not hold what little liquor he already consumed. Despite the Crohn's disease, Rob could drink copious amounts almost on par with Junior. Although they all drank that night, Brad seemed to only nurse his beers all evening. Brad always tried to fit in by appearing to be drinking. Small towns see social drinking as a sort of testimony of manhood, or a rite of passage, and Brad always tried to fit in by pretending to drink the beer bottle in his hand. Brad

79

wanted to use drinking alcohol as a way to prove his status as a "big man," so he would make a big scene of popping tops off of beers. He obviously wanted to fit in. But this made no sense. Rob liked Brad. Why did he try so hard to be cool, especially around someone as creepy as Mush?

"Brad," Rob said, waving it off. "Don't go anywhere with Mush. That man is a fucking faggot."

Brad's face registered shock, then anger. "He is not!"

Rob's eyebrows hiked. "Didn't you see what he did tonight?" He pointed at the idling truck, sitting in the swirling fog. "Do not go back down there! The guy's a fuckin' fruit loop!"

Brad's face was growing red in frustration and the stocky boy took a step towards Rob. "Shut up! He is not! He's my cousin!"

The booze in Rob's system hit his *challenge* button, but at the same time, Rob wanted to defend his friend. Their alcoholic breath floated and shone in the misty air as they began shouting at one another, cursing, pointing, hands curling and uncurling into half-hearted fists, unsteady feet carrying their steps forward and backward.

"He hangs around little kids at the ballpark!" Rob howled. "Buyin' 'em ice cream at the Dairy Stop!"

"Shut the fuck up!" Brad began to transform before their eyes: first, his ears grew cherry red, followed by a flush that raced to his cheeks. He began to breathe in short breaths, his huffs and puffs illuminated by the streetlight in the cold night air. His freckles, usually inconspicuous light brown marks on a pale complexion, looked like dark pockmarks on his mottled red face.

Junior put himself between them. "Come on guys, hey! Come on!" He secretly waved Rob back. "Brad, come on, man. We don't need more alcohol. And Mush is a fag. He's a fucking child molester. He had his pants—come on. Don't go. Come on back to the tent with us."

"He's not a fag!" Brad jerked away, still seething. "There's nothing wrong! He's my cousin! Quit saying that!" He made a half-hearted shove at his friend. "He's gonna go get me some Purple Passion!" Brad favored Purple Passion above all other drinks because it did not taste like alcohol, more like a fruit punch, but it still packed a kick.

By now, both Junior and Rob gripped Brad by his jean

jacket, blocking his path to the truck. They tried to get him to turn and walk in the opposite direction, heading toward the Armstrong home and the tent. Brad and Junior's sneakers made scuffling noises on the street pavement as they pushed and pulled on one another.

"He's not a fag," Brad insisted through clenched teeth, attempting to push their hands off of his jacket. "Stop it!" He shoved them off of him.

"Brad, come on, man," Junior tried his best. "Mush was kissing me on the head, he tried to feel up Rob—"

"He likes little boys," Rob kept insisting, trying to reason with Brad. "What about tonight, coming in there with us, his pants all opened up—"

"Shut up!" Brad shouted, his face so red, his freckles disappeared. He stood there, seething, with watering eyes and a deep magenta coloring adorning his entire upper body. "Shut up! He's not that way!"

Rob stepped forward again, trying to talk sense, and suddenly felt the vomit in the pit of his throat and felt the spinning start. "Brad!" He managed. "Don't—"

"Look, I'll talk to him," Junior said to Rob, and Rob finally nodded, backing off.

Rob's head spun wildly: the booze, the adrenaline rush and subsequent crash, all the fighting, his Crohn's disease, all of these factors affected his state of mind. He felt the alcohol riding his throat, and his stomach started to convulse painfully. He turned, stumbling, heading for the back yard and the tent, every step seeming impossible, until he finally climbed in, managing to settle in and (finally!) pull his cold feet into the warmth of a sleeping bag.

Back on North Kathleen Drive, Junior tried to reason with Brad. If Mush wanted to go buy more alcohol and bring it to them, fine. If Mush wanted to go get drunk alone, fine. But Brad did not need to go, too. Brad did not need to go anywhere with Mush. Junior and Rob wanted nothing more to do with Mush, and Brad, despite their familial relation, needed to stay away from the guy as well. Besides, dawn approached quickly, and they needed to get back.

"He's not a fag!" Brad insisted.

"Man, come on," Junior grabbed a handful of Brad's shoulder, shook him hard. "Let's just go home. Cool?"

81

Brad's face finally cleared, and he stared at the street. "Okay," he said finally. "But I gotta go tell him," Brad relented. He agreed with his best friend. The two boys came to an agreement, standing there on the street in the swirl of fog. Brad swore not to go anywhere with Mush. He wanted to say goodnight to his cousin and to tell him of his decision to return to the tent with his friends, as well as tell him goodnight. Brad promised to meet Junior in a few minutes if he could just tell Mush what changed.

After a while, an exhausted Junior crawled into the dome tent and crashed, drunk, next to Rob.

"Where's Brad?" Rob slurred.

"He went to tell Mush," Junior let out a whiskey-beer sigh, "To go home; Brad's not going anywhere with him."

Rob nodded, sighing in relief. He fell into a deep sleep. Junior helped Rob recreate the conversation the next day, as he did not remember it.

By then, in Sardinia, far from Rob and Junior's grasp, Douglas "Mushroom" Sims pulled up to his trailer home with Bradley Maddux as a passenger. Sims stopped the truck and they both exited the vehicle. They both walked into the trailer, and only one of them walked out.

It changed the history of Decatur County and forever changed the hearts of its residents.

On the morning of Saturday, March 10, 1990, the phone shrieked incessantly at the Meadows residence. Still visiting from last night, Dollie awoke with a start, and then burrowed into the covers. The ringing stopped and then started up again. *Why aren't they answering it?* Dollie thought grumpily, and she made herself get out of bed to pad to the phone and answer it. "Hello?"

"Hey. Where's Mike?" Dollie recognized the voice: Mush, the creep from last night.

She glanced down the hallway. "I don't think he's up," she said into the phone.

"Tell him to get up. I'll be there in a minute," Mush said.

"Okay," Dollie covered a yawn, "Goodbye." She hung up and meandered down the hallway to Mike's room to get him up. She noticed the time at 5:30 a.m.

A short time later, Mush picked up Mike at the apartment complex, drove him to work, and dropped him off. They made plans to go get a truck Mike was intended to buy. Mush agreed to cosign for the boy. "I'll pick you up after work," Mush told him, "And we'll go get the truck."

At the Armstrong residence, Rob awoke with a start and then moved slowly, as if testing his limbs inside the warmth of the sleeping bag. He looked around the tent, rolling his tongue in his mouth and tasting the nasty remnants of last night. The cold morning made him shiver violently.

Junior, as if on cue, awoke and stretched, yawning and exhaling. At the same time, he began shivering from the frigid temperature. Junior spent the night sleeping on the cold cement of the porch under the flimsy tent. He reached over to poke at a bundle of sleeping bag and blankets. They were empty.

"Where's Brad?" Rob asked him, teeth chattering.

"I guess he went home." Junior said, scratching his head. "Got too cold for him." This was Brad's usual pattern. Brad often did this; he woke up, shivering, put on his shoes, and trotted across the street to the warmth of his bed. He always caught up with the guys later in the day.

Rob waited a bit, hating to brave the temperatures, collected himself, then prepared to head home to Alert. His wristwatch read 8:00 a.m., and the incredibly long night seemed far away.

At 204 Kentucky Avenue, the Maddux family awoke early to begin the day. Daryl came home from work and he and Patti decided to go fishing. As they prepared for a day on the lake, Patti telephoned Mary to ask about her missing son at around 8:30 A.M.

Mary asked her to wait a moment, then, "Junior says he's not here," Mary told her.

Patti thanked her and hung up the phone. Brad's normal pattern led them to believe that one of his other friends invited him over to their house. They packed their gear and, with Lindsay in tow, they headed out, eager to spend some time together and ready to do some fishing. As they left the house, they noted Brad's bike, parked and ready for his four o'clock paper route. Both felt lucky to have such a dependable and responsible son.

Cody came home and then headed out to work. He wished

he could spend the Saturday at his leisure. He always found something fun to do on Saturdays: a game of ball in the street, someone having something going on inside their home, or a game in the backyard. And, as always, supervision by neighborhood parents who interfered if necessary.

Patti, Lindsay, and Daryl headed for Brush Creek, located in North Vernon. The drive was a leisurely twenty minutes, heading south and driving through the country. Brush Creek Fish and Wildlife Area, developed in 1964, boasts a 150-acre reservoir, over 2,000 acres of open farm fields, gently sloping landscapes, and public access to the Muscatatuck River. Fishermen usually leave feeling lucky with their catch at the end of the day.

Once at the water's edge, Patti, Daryl, and Lindsay settled down for one of their favorite pastimes. Clouds floated overhead, making it slightly misty. The water lapped at the shore, and wild birds called to one another. It seemed to be any other day.

It was the last day of peace the Maddux family would know for a long time. But on this day, with the birds singing and the fish jumping, Patti and Daryl had no way of knowing they should savor this feeling. Ten-year-old Lindsay laughed obliviously at the birds that skimmed over the water to hunt for meals, and she pulled hopefully on her fishing pole.

A bit later, back in Alert, a neighborhood girl named *Debbie Wells* walked down to Rob Nugent's home, calling on him. Together they met up with Kiki Weston, who caught the eye of Junior Armstrong. Kiki and Debbie spent the night together at a sleepover the night before. Junior joined them, and the four strolled down to an old cemetery, chatting and laughing while Junior flirted with Kiki. Kiki sometimes favored Junior with a shy smile, which made Junior's heart jump in his chest.

Dollie Press already returned home from the Meadows' house, and she joined the foursome as they strolled by. They headed towards one of their favorite hangouts, Mt. Olivet Cemetery.

The town initially established Mt. Olivet Cemetery in 1856. They erected the cemetery surrounded by trees off of a gravel road, called County Road 1300 South, and a small dirt road led into the cemetery for easy access. The entrance of the cemetery used gravel for the road, but once into the cemetery the road became two lanes, caused by the vehicle tires that frequently drove in and out. Rob and Debbie walked down here often, and their usual path led them to the oldest graves, located in the back of the cemetery. They enjoyed trying to read the broken and crooked headstones, wondering what history lay beneath them, speculating out loud what kind of person the grave held, what kind of personality they showed while alive, and how they ended up in this county. A low wall made of a collection of old concrete blocks the size of a brick surrounded several of the graves and separated them from the others. These incredibly old graves rested off to the side and in the back of the cemetery.

They walked through two limestone pillars and entered the cemetery. Words carved in stone decorated one of the pillars; it said:

Mt. Olivet 1856
In Memorandum
Shafer
Daniel
Whitmore
Auderiah
Shera
James
Hamlin
Kathleen
Wright

Sometimes, they walked to the huge cedar tree located near the center of the old cemetery, sat under its branches, and talked with one another in the peaceful atmosphere that inspired conversation. The branches spread up and out, like a huge, protective cover. Some of the branches dipped so low the kids needed to push them aside or duck around and under them. Rob, Debbie, Junior, and Kiki loved to sit under this ancient tree, talking, laughing, debating, and discussing anything and nothing. The quiet cemetery served as the perfect place for hanging out and engaging in typical teenaged chatter. The mist did not obstruct their view too much this morning, and a steel grey sky hung over them. They walked along the internal cemetery road, their shoes making crunching noises in the dirt and rock, and then stopped at the tree.

"What did you all do last night?" One of the girls asked. This opened the floodgates for the telling of the tale.

Rob told them about meeting Mush and drinking at his house, and the odd behavior.

"Man, we should have kicked that guy Mushroom's ass," Junior said, walking around under the cedar tree. "How about his ol' big Bowie knife?" He pulled at a tiny tree limb.

"We could've got that to scare him with," Rob agreed.

Both boys, now safe from Douglas Sims' home, began to express their regret that they did not overpower him. They talked like typical boys, each one growing tougher and stronger as they spoke. Things looked brighter and safer in daylight, away from Doug "Mushroom" Sims.

"Hey, let's see if we can find the oldest gravestone," Dollie said to the group. They often enjoyed this favored pastime. Their attention turned toward the rear of the cemetery, where the oldest gravestones were imbedded.

"I'm not even supposed to be out here," Debbie said. She looked at her friend Kiki. "My mom said," she pointed generally toward the road, CR 1300, "I'm not supposed to go past that mark."

"Oh, come on. You're already here!" Dollie started to walk to the back of the cemetery. Rob and Junior began to follow.

"I gotta go," Debbie told them. "I can't get caught out here. Let's go." Kiki nodded in agreement and both of them quickly headed for the entrance and the two large pillars.

"Scared," someone commented, and Dollie, Junior, and Rob laughed. They promptly forgot about seeking out the oldest headstone. They talked for a while longer, and then slowly left the tree. Rather than following their usual pattern and heading to the back of the cemetery, they walked toward the cemetery entrance at County Road 1300. They exited the cemetery and turned to go back down CR 1300, making a turn, to head back toward Alert. As they walked, piecing together the night's story, they decided that Brad scampered off early that morning—

probably cold, and his paper route started later that day and he would begin that soon.

They were wrong. Had they walked just a few feet further from the cedar tree, toward the rear of the cemetery as they always had, the story would be quite different. They did not follow their normal pattern and walk the additional 200 feet towards the rear of the cemetery, where, unbeknownst to them, a horrific and gruesome scene awaited discovery.

Standing under this same cedar tree with Rob, eleven years later, Junior, now an adult, looks over his shoulder. The weather outside mimics the atmosphere of that tenth day of March in 1990. "I think," he says quietly, "Brad was pulling us to him. He wanted to hang out with us, just one more time. Before it all started."

Daryl, Patti, and Lindsay came home at around 4:00 p.m. Brad's bicycle was parked in the same slot; his newspapers still laid on the porch. This was not like Brad at all—completely out of character. Brad enjoyed this paper route, especially the spending money it gave him. His customers spoke highly of him. He was punctual and efficient. Daryl instilled the value of hard work in his children. Cody, who wanted to be a farmer, already spent time at a friend's farm, learning about grain, crops, machines, and weather. Cody had goals. Brad was not too young to start learning this lesson. So where was he?

Cody trotted home from visiting with friends after work and met his father and sister at the porch. Cody immediately wondered why his brother's bicycle and newspapers were still there. "I haven't seen him all day," he told them.

"The time must have got away from him," Daryl mused. "Let's roll these papers up so he can just grab 'em and go." Daryl, Cody, and Lindsay began to roll the newspapers so that when Brad got home he would only need to grab the papers, jump on his bicycle, and pedal off on his route. Lindsay was young, but even she understood the gravity of this: Brad not here on time to deliver his papers? Strange.

Daryl, Patti, and Lindsay decided to return to Brush Creek to get a few more hours of fishing in. They drove the quick twenty minutes back and settled in, chatting and joking. Fishing was good for that.

A few hours later, as the sun sank lower and legs grew stiffer, the Maddux family decided to call it a day. They reeled in their lines and began to stow away their gear for the next day's adventure on the water. Climbing back into the truck, Lindsay, stifling a yawn, snuggled in between her daddy and momma. The return home was uneventful; they saw the same familiar fields, albeit a little darker, rolling past their windows, and they engaged in the familiar habit of waving at cars that drove past. Just another day.

The truck pulled up in front of the house on Kentucky Avenue and everyone climbed out, groaning a bit, as one does after a long day on the water. Patti's hand went to Daryl's arm. "Look," she said.

Brad's newspapers, rolled just as neatly as when they left, laid on the porch.

"That's when we started to get worried," Lindsay recalls now. "That's when they started calling around."

The phones around Westport rang tentatively at first, then with a slight case of panic, as the Maddux family began calling. After receiving word that his brother remained unaccounted for, Cody anxiously returned home. What was going on? Where was Brad?

Several miles away in Alert, Rob Nugent, Junior Armstrong, and Dollie Press spent that day together, shooting basketball hoops, talking, and just visiting. Concern for their children's safety never even crossed their parents' minds; in this tiny town, it took less than a minute to walk from one house to the next.

As the three chums talked and laughed, Cody drove up on his four-wheeler. They waved and meandered over as Cody shut off the engine. They immediately saw worry on his face. "Have you seen Brad?" he asked them.

"Not since last night," Dollie told him. "Why?"

"He's missing." Cody's eyes scanned the area as he spoke. Junior and Rob exchanged glances. "Missing?" they asked.

"He didn't come home, and he didn't do his paper route," Cody started the four-wheeler engine back up again. As he pulled away, Dollie went toward her home, and Rob and Junior "took off," she recalls.

When Rob arrived home, his mother met him.

It appeared that Patti called Mary earlier, looking for Brad. He never went on his paper route and no one reported seeing him anywhere. Did Rob know where he was, or anything about him?

"No, Mom," Rob told her. He heard the note of worry and concern for another parent and child in her voice. Part of him felt horrible for lying to her, but the other part of him knew that telling her about drinking with Mush all night could only make things worse for them.

Summer Hobbs placed a call to Rob's home and spoke with him. "Where's Brad?" she asked, wanting to chat with her buddy. "He had gone with Mush to get beer," Junior explained to her, and Summer Hobbs felt the cold rinse over her like an icy shower. "You need to go get him," she told him. "I don't trust Mushroom."

Phones were ringing all over Westport, and soon rang all over a portion of the state.

Tammy and Jack Hileman decided to spend some time together out of town before the baby arrived, knowing how precious time alone would become once the baby started consuming all of their time, and they wanted to spend quality time together. The phone rang at their hotel. Tammy answered and heard Patti's frantic voice on the other end. "Brad is missing," she told her sister-in-law, trying unsuccessfully to not sound panicked or crazy.

Tammy frowned. "Missing?"

Patti felt her stomach drop, like an elevator with a snapped suspension cable. She took a deep breath. *Something's happened*, she felt her mind say. *Something bad.*

"He's probably with friends," Tammy told her distraught sister-in-law. She felt herself sink to the bed. "He probably went to Junior's and didn't realize what time it was..." *Nothing bad happens in Westport.*

Junior Armstrong and Rob Nugent met to talk. "We have to tell," one told the other. "We have to tell everything." They thought back to the night before, which seemed a hundred years ago, and the fight in the middle of the road. "We should've made sure he was with us," one of them said in a worried voice.

Phone calls increased, buzzing across telephone wires of the Westport area. Everyone said the same thing: "I haven't seen him and he didn't deliver my paper."

89

"No, I haven't seen him."

"I haven't seen Brad at all today."

"Hold on, let me ask the boys...no, nobody's seen him. I'm sorry."

"I haven't seen him and he's not here. Have you tried—"

Meanwhile, Brad's bicycle sat unused, a silent testimony to the paper route that did not happen that evening. No one offered an explanation as to the whereabouts of the usually reliable boy. Where was Brad?

Daryl, with Lindsay as a passenger, drove their truck through Westport, his eyes squinting to look out into the shadows. Lindsay also searched, looking, watching, for any signs. They drove to the ball park in the middle of town, past all of Brad's friend's houses, back through the park, near the corner stores, along the routes he took, in people's yards. Was Brad injured? Bleeding? Was he lying somewhere on the cold ground, or shivering in a ditch? All of these horrifying thoughts and so many more raced through the worried father's mind as they looked in the alleys between businesses and behind houses. Then Daryl rolled the steering wheel so the truck would U-turn, and they began the search anew.

Back at the Nugent home, Junior and Rob still discussed the night before, but now in even more worried tones. "I'm going to go look for him," Junior said, and headed in a direction towards home.

It wasn't until 1980 that AT&T Phone Company started production of two full Enhanced 911 systems. At the time, Westport did not yet possess an Enhanced 911 system; in the event of an emergency, an automatic call went to the homes of every resident on the volunteer fire department. This included the home of Brad's classmate, Julie Ralston. Mrs. Ralston told Julie with concern, "The Maddux boy is missing." The Ralston family did not know to which of the two boys they referred. Julie thought of Brad, and of how only a few days ago they shared some Chips Ahoy chocolate chip cookies. She pictured him laughing and making jokes. Surely not...?

One of Lynn Welch's family members also set out to assist in the community-wide search. It seemed as if almost everyone in Westport assisted with the effort. Parents continuously called everyone they knew, searching for the lost boy. Everyone, in some way, knew Brad.

Rob Nugent paced in his home. Warm and cheerful before, it now appeared like the end of a death march.

At his own home, Junior Armstrong gathered up his courage. He played the scenario over and over in his head. Now it seemed like a strange, twisted play. He did not want to know the last act.

In the entirety of European and American civilization, society never learned to treat children well, or even fairly. Children always suffered the brunt of the adults' wrath, as assaulting a child proved much easier than attacking an adult in a fair fight. History, biology, a lack of law, and apathy towards the suffering of others created the world we live in today. Human greed and ambition constructed a world in which three in every ten little girls in a single classroom will fall victim to molestation in their youth; a civilization in which, in that same classroom, two in every ten little boys will at some point become prey to a sexual predator. In 95% of child abductions, the kidnapped child knows the offender in some way, while a child abducted by strangers only happens 5% of the time.

Society creates programs like "Stranger Danger," and companies sell expensive backpacks that, at the pull of a ripcord, set off an alarm and flash an unmistakable emergency light. Parents bring their children to special programs that fingerprint the children in the hope of creating some sort of protective shield. Parents dish out the age-old advice like "Don't talk to strangers" and "Don't take candy from people you don't know" and hope that their children listen. Even worse than this misguided stranger protection plan occurs when a family, neighborhood, or community ignores the danger of predators entirely. When the unexpected happens in a place unprepared for this danger, the violence of the situation does not even occur to the community for quite some time.

"Stranger danger" programs have their place. A backpack alarm, if it assists even just one child, is worth the investment. Fingerprinting identifies bodies, which can afford the victim's family a certain sense of closure. However, the greatest life-saving preparation occurs when parents engage in open communication about feelings and create a strong bond of trust with their children.

No one ever taught Brad about "Stranger Danger" or any sort of child protection skills because he lived in Westport, Indiana, where bad things did not happen to anyone, let alone children. "No one ever thought anything like this could ever happen," Tammy Hileman says later through tears. She also says,
"Now all we think about was that gruesome day..."
Brad's cousin Gretchen made plans to spend the night with her friend, *Lizzette Caldwell*, settling in for a night of preteen girl talk, staying up late, and practicing new hairstyles on each other. She just settled in when Mr. and Mrs. Caldwell called to her. When Gretchen came into their living room, her mother Judy stood there waiting for her. Gretchen's smile turned instantly into a frown. What was wrong? Perhaps she forgot something at home?
"Get your things, honey," Judy said. "We have to go."
Gretchen frowned but did as her mother asked, Lizzette trailing behind her. Was she in trouble? Something was not right ...
They made their way to the car, and Gretchen saw evidence of crying on her mother's face; even now she looked close to tears. Once they were in the car, Judy said, voice warbling, "Brad is missing."
"Missing?" Gretchen asked, as if her mother just invented the word.
"Missing," Judy repeated.
 She thought about Brad and his sweet manner, and how sometimes people took advantage of that. Gretchen thought of how Brad never knew a stranger, and how he was so willing to help everyone. After that moment, Gretchen will tell you today, "Everything was a blur; from that moment on I can't remember any details. It was like all one bad nightmare I could never wake up from."
Their car began the drive to the Maddux home and into a chapter of Gretchen and Judy's lives that, to this day, shadows both women like a shroud.
Neighbors, families, and friends began their own searches for Brad. They looked in their backyards, in one another's yards, in their own homes and alleyways and barns, trenches, and garages. Cody's friends jumped into their tractors and trucks to look in fields, swinging flashlights and lanterns. Any minute now, they told each other, Brad

would show up. They searched woods and creeks where he loved to fish and tromp, and they checked the trails on which he rode his beloved dirt bike and hiked with friends. Maybe he fell and hit his head, they pondered. Hit by a car and lying on the road. They assumed something bad, but always something fixable. If someone did not join the search effort, they showed up at the Maddux home, offering ideas, comfort, and solace, and soon the living room began to fill with people, all asking the same question: Where was Brad?

They called his name across fields, into barns, through empty houses. People shouted it into the night, into their lofts, garages, places that went unfrequented for days, months, or years on their own property. "Brad!" They shouted. "Bradley? You here?" Then they listened, ears straining. Then again: "Brad!" they yelled. "Hey, Bradley! You here!" Silence answered them. Where was Brad?

Junior Armstrong went to his mother, approaching her with caution. "Mom…?"

He told her the truth, but he amended the story: The boys camped out in their backyard, and then they went to the Meadows' apartment to play video games. While there, they met Mushroom. Mushroom agreed to take the boys back to Junior's home, but first he took them by his Sardinia home to show them his place. Mushroom dropped all three boys off at Junior's home at about 1:00 a.m. on Saturday.

Mary dove for the phone.

By then, Daryl and Lindsay already returned home from their fruitless search. In minutes, Junior bolted across the street to the Maddux home. He told his story, but in his fear, he amended it twice.

Lindsay, her eyes drooping, headed for her bed. Young and sleepy, the tiny Lindsay could not even comprehend the magnitude of it all. *Brad will be home soon*, she decided through a yawn as she climbed into bed. *And boy, was he in trouble.*

The Maddux family called the Decatur County Sheriff's office at around 8:30 p.m. and officially opened a missing child investigation.

Now his missing became official.

Patti Maddux walked away from the group of people now huddled in her home. She looked out the window again, and emptiness greeted her once more. She walked to another window, moved the curtain back, and looked out at the same empty yard that greeted her five minutes ago. A tightness twisted her gut—a feeling that said *Something is amiss.* She moved nervously through the house, wiping her hands on everything she could reach, until she finally saw Charles Whitehead, the Town Marshal, pull up into her driveway. It took him one minute to dispatch, but to a mother missing her son, it seemed like years measured in heartbeats.

Marshal Whitehead took the initial report, case # 90C003. He took down all pertinent information, such as Brad's physical description (5'0," 120 pounds, eyes blue, hair brown, white male), ID marks (freckles on face), clothing last seen (blue jean jacket & pants, Purdue shirt, gray hooded sweatshirt, "VOIT" white tennis shoes), and he began to write down a narrative of events.

Whitehead also telephoned Doug "Mushroom" Sims and asked Sims if he had seen Bradley Maddux.

Sims told Whitehead he had dropped the three boys off at Junior's house. "It was about one o'clock in the morning, this morning," Sims explained. "I dropped them off, and then I went on home."

"Is that right?"

"I had to get up early," Sims explained. "I had to give Mike Meadows a ride to work this morning."

Junior, by now, added more information to the story he told his mother, with slight amendments: Mushroom returned about an hour later after he let them out of his truck that morning. He parked at the Westport Family Restaurant. Brad left the tent to go to the truck to speak with Mushroom. Junior and Rob observed Brad speaking to Mushroom at the pickup, they then fell asleep. Yes, he knew about what time it happened; he could tell it was about two in the morning because Junior and Rob could hear Junior's older brother *Willy's* car radio playing. Yes, he recognized Willy just by the sound of the car radio. They fell asleep and awoke at 8:00 a.m. Junior and Rob figured that Brad went home early in the morning to get away from the cold, as he so often did.

Town Marshal Charles Whitehead received the information and told the family that he needed to return to

94

the Westport Police Department to complete an official Missing Persons form. He closed his notebook and headed out to the Westport Police Station.

Daryl Maddux sank back into the cushions of his chair and rubbed his eyes fiercely. He looked around the room that seemed deathly quiet without his youngest son. Then he sat up and reached for the telephone.

"Who are you calling?" Patti asked him. "We've called everyone in town."

"Jon Oldham," Daryl said gruffly. "I'm calling Jon Oldham. I'm going to ask him to start looking for our little boy."

Jon Oldham was a legend in the area. Some of the community knew him as "Jonny Uh-oh" because he was not someone to be fooled with. When spinning red and blue lights appeared in the rearview mirror and Jon Oldham stepped out of the patrol car, drivers and passengers instinctively and intelligently react with an "Uh-oh" or worse. Big and barrel-chested, he was fair, he was firm, and he was friendly, but you did not want Jonny Uh-oh to catch you doing something illegal. Intelligent people learned quickly to never smart off to him and to always mind their manners in his intimidating presence. But despite the fear and respect his appearance created, Jon Oldham cared about people. One Westport resident, years later, recalls an automobile accident from her teenage years, during which she drove her boyfriend's car into a farmer's fence. The farmer was livid about the broken fence. Jonny Uh-oh showed up and the farmer wanted Oldham to make the girl pay. "Arrest her, give her a ticket, something!" the farmer shouted. To the teen's amazement, Oldham berated the farmer. "You can fix a fence," she recalls Oldham lecturing the farmer. "You cannot replace a life. We're lucky this kid is alive, and not hurt, or worse." After promising to pay for the damages, the girl scampered home with shaking hands and a new respect for law officers.

If someone perused the majority of the personal phone books of Westport residents, they would see "Police – call Oldham" printed neatly where emergency numbers are kept. No matter the date, the time, or the situation, he answered the call personally.

Daryl knew Oldham from the time he spent working as a paramedic while Oldham worked as a detective with the Indiana State Police. Oldham responded to and investigated the break-in at Daryl's father's pharmacy, and Daryl had harbored both a personal and a professional admiration for him. Now Jon Oldham prepared to play a pivotal role in this case.

Daryl telephoned the Versailles Post. Detective Sergeant Oldham had the night off, and the assignment went to Indiana State Police Officer Terrill "Terry" Steed. Steed jotted down the Maddux address and information and hurried to their home, arriving approximately twenty minutes after receiving Daryl's call.

Steed, a local, grew up in the Westport area. His job allowed him to do the things he always dreamed of doing as a boy: catching bad guys, riding in a police car, and wearing the badge. Steed already mapped a lifetime of action in his life. He already served in Viet Nam as an Army Police Officer, running convoys in the infamous Cu Chi Tunnels northwest of Saigon, in the Cu Chi district of Ho Chi Minh City. The tunnels served as a part of the Viet Cong's operations—a literal network of underground tunnels used to run supplies and filled with booby traps. Today it merely attracts tourists. "People pay to go in there now," Terry Steed says ruefully, "And a book was written about the Tunnels of Cu Chi." Steed married a local girl. In 1971, after his time overseas, he signed up for the Indiana State Police and they accepted him into their ranks. Terry Steed worked murders, stopped fights, gave tickets, separated domestic disputes, and talked down belligerent drunks. But tonight, Officer Steed later recalls, was about to be "a momentous night for us, and for Westport."

When Steed arrived at 204 Kentucky Avenue, he noted the many vehicles parked in the yard and in front of the house. Once inside, Steed met both of Brad's parents and Brad's Grandpa Dave. Daryl told Steed the story again: about Brad spending the night with his friends, the all-day fishing trip, Brad's missed paper route, and the last time anyone saw Brad. "He was walking toward a truck belonging to 'Mushroom,'" Daryl explained.

"Mushroom?"

"Doug Sims." He told Steed how many friends and family members already joined the search for Brad. That explained all of the vehicles at the residence. Daryl explained that they already talked to Whitehead and gave him a full report, and mentioned that Whitehead already called and questioned Sims. "Doug said he had dropped the boys off at Junior's around one," Daryl said.

State Police Officer Terry Steed asked more questions, took more notes, then gave them his business card and departed the residence with a promise to be in touch. He walked back to his patrol vehicle, looking around at the neighborhood, then he drove toward the Marshall's office.

Charles Whitehead arrived at the Westport Police Station. He began completing a Missing Persons Report. He also placed a phone call.

"Doug," Whitehead said when Sims answered the phone, "I want to ask you something else. Did you come back to Westport about 2:00 a.m. Saturday morning?"

Sims did not sound aggravated, worried, or fearful. "No. I was too drunk to drive. By the time I got home, I just went on to bed."

"What can you tell me about the Westport Family Restaurant?"

Sims sounded surprised. "Why?" he asked.

"What can you tell me about being at the Westport Family Restaurant between about 2:00 a.m. to 2:30 a.m.?"

Sims did not sound moved. "Nothing," he replied, "I don't know what you're talking about."

Whitehead waited and then said, "I might call you back. Thanks, Doug."

"No problem."

Officer Steed arrived at the station and joined him. Whitehead caught Steed up on the details fairly quickly. Steed nodded, asking questions here and there.

"We better go over there to Sims' place," One of them said. "And we need to let Sergeant Oldham in on it."

Both men departed and headed for Sardinia. Perhaps, face-to-face, they could learn something else. According to the last known person who saw Brad Maddux alive, Doug Sims left with Brad. Right now they had nothing else to work with.

The officers arrived in Sardinia in minutes and turned onto

the road marked by a sign, 1270 S. They pulled left into the yard where Sims' white, single-wide mobile home trailer sat, parallel to the street, between two farmhouses. Doug "Mushroom" Sims' pickup sat parked next to the trailer. The men exited their vehicle and cast a look around, then walked up to the trailer and rapped on the thin door.

No answer.

They tried to peer inside the trailer, standing slightly off to the side of the door, but darkness engulfed the interior of the trailer. They rapped on it again and again, harder each time.

Sims answered it, and he did not look surprised, shocked, or angered. He looked tousled and sleepy.

"Hey Doug," Whitehead greeted.

"Come on in." Doug Sims stood sideways, stifling a yawn, holding open the door and motioning them inside. Both officers stepped through the doorway and took a look around. The trailer interior was neat and quiet. Sims did not look as Steed expected. He stood tall and lean, with strong shoulders, and a bit of a belly. He wore a nondescript expression on his face, and he spoke with a deep baritone voice. This marked Steed's first encounter with Douglas C. Sims, despite his service as a cop for almost twenty years in this area. He knew Doug's parents marginally because they were lifelong residents, but "I had never heard of Doug before," he recalls now.

"Doug," Steed told Sims after he completed formal introductions, "I'm here trying to locate Bradley Maddux, who is missing."

"Yeah, I know he's missing. Marshall Whitehead called me."

"I have information that says you were the last person that saw him; he was walking toward your truck about three 3:00 a.m."

"No," Doug Sims replied. "That's not true. Like I said, I was too drunk to be driving. I dropped 'em off, about one o'clock, got home, and went to bed. I was too drunk to be out driving around."

"Went right to sleep?" Marshal Whitehead asked, casually.

"Yeah."

"And what time did you say you dropped 'em off at Junior's house?"

98

"It was about one o'clock in the morning."

They asked a few more questions that netted the same answers as before. Sims showed no emotion. He seemed respectful, courteous, and soft-spoken. He appeared sleepy. Both officers thanked him and left the trailer.

As they drove back to Westport, ruminating over the conversation, Whitehead nodded. "I have to put all this into the computer in Greensburg," he said. He stared at the window into the darkness for a moment. Then, "It's time we start getting our witnesses together."

Steed agreed. "This boy's sleeping off a drunk somewhere, I bet," he said.

"I think so, too," Whitehead agreed. He laughed, "This is Westport."

Both officers considered the types of "Missing Child" cases: Runaway, Throwaway, Stranger Abduction, and Family Abduction. A study conducted by the National Incidence Studies of Missing, Abducted, Runaway, and Throwaway Children, through the Department of Justice, outlined the typical family abduction. Initially, the primary caregiver had felt no reason for alarm, as they believed the child to be in a safe and familiar place: in a custodial visit, at a family gathering, etc. Children under the age of six composed almost half of the children reported in the study; kidnappings by biological fathers comprised over half of the cases; almost half of the kidnappers kept the children less than a week; race and sex did not appear to influence the statistics. The families of only 60% of the missing children contacted the authorities for assistance, but the majority of these interactions involved recovering the child from an already known location. (Finkelhor, et. al.)

There exists a separate study by the National Incidence Studies of Missing, Abducted, Runaway, and Throwaway Children on "Non-family Abducted Children: National Estimates and Characteristics." It found that 40% of the reported incidents ended in the death of the child. 57% of the children did not get reported to the police as missing for at least one hour, and 57% of the victims, mostly teens, fell prey to sexual assault. Only 21% of the families of the missing children requested police assistance. (Finkelhor, et. al.)

This is why the Law Enforcement Department knew the first twenty-four hours were crucial when it came to locating Bradley Maddux. The officers began filling out forms and taking down information. Although it appeared a tedious task, it was a necessary and important one. "If it's not written down, it didn't happen," as the saying goes, and every officer knows forms must be filled out completely and accurately in order to do the job.

Charles Whitehead left for Greensburg to enter the information into the computer database. Officer Steed drove to Westport. He drove to Westport, hoping to speak to Ernest "Junior" Armstrong. He needed something clarified. After all, Steed spent his youth in this part of the country; he knew the tricks and the games.

By now, it appeared all of Westport knew of Brad's disappearance. Phones still rang and now police scanners buzzed with the news.

Brad's classmate, Jill Bishop, innocently sat at home, relaxing with her parents. The Bishops had their police scanner on, and it crackled in the background. "What was that?" One of the adults asked suddenly, and turned the sound up.

"What's going on?" Jill's parents provided their child with very strict rules and guidelines about where she went and whom she could leave with; tonight, to her chagrin, she remained at home.

"They said the Maddux boy has run away," came the answer.

Jill frowned for a moment. "No way it's Brad," she said, more to herself than to her parents. While other boys and girls their age complained about their parents or home life, Brad never had a bad word to say. She guessed it was Cody; she did not know Cody.

Steed arrived at Junior's residence, almost directly across the street from the Maddux home, but he could not find Junior anywhere. "He's at Robby's house in Alert," Mary told Steed. "I'll get him on the phone." Steed waited for her, listening to her side of the conversation.

A knock sounded on the door and suddenly "Grandpa Dave" Giddings stood in the room. He possessed information he hoped Steed could use. Giddings went out canvassing the area with the others, looking for any sign of Brad. A fellow named *Denny Benson,* who lived up the street from the Maddux and Armstrong houses, passed him some noteworthy information.

"Brad knocked on Denny's door about 3:00 a.m. in the morning, asking for a beer," Dave told Steed. "Denny told him no, so Brad left."

Steed nodded as he wrote his notes. "Sounds to me like the boys were pulling an all-nighter."

Mary Armstrong came into the room. "What?"

Steed nodded at Dave. "Going by what some folks are saying, it sounds like the boys were out drinking all night."

Mary's face went dark, and she turned on her heel to head back to the other room. Steed and Dave exchanged looks. Steed could not exactly hear what she said to Junior on the phone, but it was not good. "The riot act," Steed called it.

Eventually Mary returned to the room and she looked like she just finished smiting Junior with the wrath of an angry mother. "Some guy named 'Mushroom,'" she told Steed, took the three boys to his trailer at about 1:00 a.m. He supplied them with whiskey and beer. He also made unwelcome sexual advances toward the boys, like kissing Junior's ear. The boys demanded to return home. He brought them back to the tent at Junior's house, and shortly afterward, they saw Brad walking toward Mushroom's truck.

Steed got on the phone and spoke with Junior himself. He wanted to be sure the story was clear.

"Okay," Steed asked Junior, "Who is the guy that got you all the beer? Tell me his name again."

"Doug Sims."

The name never rang any bells; the name did not sound hinky. "Hinky," in cop lingo, is anything that raises an eyebrow, raises the hackles, and makes your stomach churn for no apparent reason. It is years of training coupled with thousands of years of human instinct, whispering *something is not right.*

"Can I—" Mary motioned to the receiver. She then got on the phone and said to Junior, "Tell him about the 'cuffs." Then the boy's mother handed the receiver back to Terry Steed.

"The what?" Suddenly Steed felt that jump in his stomach, that feeling that someone gave you a slight punch in the gut. On the outside, however, he showed no response.

"The handcuffs," Junior Armstrong said. "Doug handcuffed Brad to his bed. He said, 'Who's going to jail,' or something like that, and Brad said he would, and he handcuffed Brad to his bed and he wouldn't let him up, and we had to almost fight him. Finally he let him go and took us home... I mean, to the tent and..."

As his story continued, Steed nodded, listening keenly, but his thoughts raced madly. The case just took an unsettling, sudden turn, and now it did not sound like an innocent hangover.

After he hung up with Junior, Steed contacted the Versailles Post. This time, he needed to alert Jon Oldham immediately. Someone already contacted and informed Oldham about the situation. "Have him contact me," Steed requested, and he gave the dispatcher the Armstrong phone number.

Steed spoke with Oldham quietly while Mary Armstrong and Dave Giddings waited for him. It was close to 11:30 p.m. When he hung up the phone, Steed approached the two adults and asked politely, "Would you two mind having your families meet us at the Marshall's office at 11:30 p.m.?"

The Marshall's office also served as the Westport Police Department; people also referred to it as the Westport Town Hall. It only took about four minutes to drive to its location in the heart of downtown Westport from Kentucky Avenue. In happier times, Cody and Brad probably passed it when they took Grandpa Dave's truck for a spin. "That place filled up so fast with people," Jon Oldham recalled later.

The phone rang at the Westport Police Department; the Nugent household was on the opposite end with crucial information.

They told the caller to come down to the police station immediately.

The doors opened a short time later, and Mrs. Nugent walked in with her son, Rob. Patti, her eyes red-rimmed from crying, arrived earlier with Daryl. Junior accompanied his parents, and Sergeant Oldham prepared to begin the proceedings.

Rob Nugent and Junior Armstrong were separated and placed in different rooms. Because they were juveniles, their parents were allowed to be in the rooms as they were interviewed.

"The hardest thing I have ever had to do in my life," Rob confesses now, "was to tell the story from start to finish." To this day, Rob can still see the pain, fear, and sadness in Patti Maddux's eyes as he told his story. "I saw her heart break," he says now. "I can still see her eyes, to this minute." But he did it. Fourteen-year-old Rob took a deep breath and told it all: the tent and Mary's late schedule. The drinking. The party at the apartments, and how Mrs. Meadows attempted to stop them from leaving, albeit half-heartedly. Some fellow named "Mush" and his invitation to party. The drinking at Mush's trailer, and his strange behavior. Their escape and how they fought in the street, but liquor got the best of him and how he tottered back to the tent. The assumption Brad had came back to the tent late and left early. To his credit, the boy told it all.

"Mush?" Someone asked him. "You mean Doug Sims?"

"I don't know him," Rob answered truthfully. "I just know him as 'Mush.'"

Sergeant Oldham also interviewed Junior. Steed was present, along with Indiana State Police Corporal Bill Nunn and Marshal Whitehead. This is when Junior finally told the truth, after changing his story several times. It was somewhat garbled—a few missing details here and there due to the alcohol-induced memory lapses and his fear. But he told them about how Sims not only asked them to, but also encouraged them to drink, about Brad and the handcuffs and the unlacing of the belt and pants, how they practically had to start fisticuffs to get a ride home, the three kisses on his head, and—finally!—Sims drove them all home. Junior explained how he all but knocked Brad out cold to keep him away from Sims, how he thought he finally got through to him.

Investigator Oldham knew that a close family member did not abduct Brad. He did not know Brad well; his son went to the same school as Brad, but there were only two schools: the elementary-junior high and the high school. He saw Brad around town in the past and waved to him as Brad tossed newspapers. He rose from his seat to telephone Doug Sims at home, trying to appear casual. Jon Oldham kept thinking, "Brad's somewhere passed out, or waking up from a drunk; he's trying to think of what to tell his parents..."

Terry Steed listened to the somewhat garbled explanation of Junior. "This kid, Brad, has just run away," he said to himself as the boy rambled on. "He's drunk and hiding from Mama." Steed saw it happen a million times. Drinking and getting drunk was a rite of passage for country boys, a sign of machismo, talking shit—until Mama came into the picture. Although he knew of the family, he did not actually know Brad Maddux, other than the fact that his own daughter, like everyone else their age, went to school with him.

"This guy buys beer for kids..." Junior said again.

"Okay," Steed nodded. "What guy? Tell me his name again."

"Doug Sims."

Steed nodded for him to continue.

"...And we told Brad not to go with him, and we got in a fight, and I had to break it up, and Rob went to the tent, and finally he said he wouldn't."

"Wait—who said he wouldn't what?"

"Brad said he wouldn't go with Doug."

Steed nodded. "Okay. Go on."

"—And so we went to the tent, and I fell asleep, and when I woke up in the morning Brad wasn't there. We thought he went home because it was cold. He does that sometimes."

Steed nodded again. He asked the boy and his mother to wait for him in the office. When Steed met up with Jon Oldham, he exchanged looks. "This kid is laying up passed out somewhere," Steed told him. "Something weird happened, maybe he's embarrassed. He might be at this fellow's house—Doug Sims?"

Oldham nodded sagely. "That's what I'm thinking," he sighed. "Go ahead and get taped statements from the two kids, will you?" Terry Steed nodded and returned to the room where they interviewed Junior Armstrong.

With Mariah closed today, Sims should be at home. Oldham sat down in a creaking chair and dialed Sims' phone number. He asked him, casually, if he would mind coming down to the Westport Police Department to discuss Bradley Maddux's disappearance.

"I've already talked to officers about that," Sims said. "I told them what I knew. I dropped the three kids off, and then I went home and went to bed."

"Well," Oldham said casually, "I could come to your place, or you could come up here at Westport Town Hall."

Sims waited a beat. "Let me get dressed," he answered. "I'll be up there as soon as I'm dressed."

"Thank ya." Jon Oldham hung up the phone. He and Whitehead exchanged looks.

The officers waited. And they waited. The clock ticked on. The officers shifted their weight and looked at one another. Someone subdued a burp. Someone else shifted their gun belt and looked at their keys for too long.

Oldham shot a look at Whitehead.

Charles Whitehead shook his head, grabbed his patrol car keys, and in a few strides he was out the door to his vehicle and heading for Sardinia.

Whitehead made it about halfway to Sardinia when he observed Sims' customized brown Ford rumbling toward him on the two-lane highway. Whitehead waved to Sims, made a U-turn, and followed Sims to the Westport Police Station.

Later, when attorneys wrangled with each other over legal rights, Whitehead's actions created a big controversy. This is why officers must be constantly aware of their actions. For now it was just a simple, legal U-turn on a two-lane highway.

About four minutes after Oldham replaced the telephone in its cradle, Sims arrived at the Westport Police Station and parked his truck east of the Town Hall and next to a school bus, looking casual. He did not look scared or angry. Oldham could see the top lights of Sims' pickup through a window.

"I have a family reunion to go to later today," Sims said to Whitehead, who joined him just outside the doors.

Whitehead nodded. He followed Doug Sims into the building.

Officer Steed continued his interview with Junior Armstrong in the Marshall's Office as Sims drove past and pulled up into the station. Junior saw Mushroom's truck through the window. The boy broke into hysterics, sobbing and crying, asking the officer to protect him. "Don't let him see me! Don't let him in here!" The little boy howled, over and over.

In another part of the station, Sims, oblivious to the little boy's trauma, met with Jon Oldham. They shook hands, and Oldham led Sims into the Street Commissioner's Office for questioning. The tiny room contained only a few chairs and a desk. Steed completed his interview and joined them, standing behind Oldham's left shoulder. Corporal Nunn also sat in on the occasion, sitting in a chair to Oldham's left. Whitehead stood in the room as well. Sims kept his expression bland. He sat down across from Oldham.

Oldham's tone was friendly, and he talked to Doug as if conversing about life in general. That was Oldham: a cop's cop, an officer you wanted on your side, and a helluva guy.

No newcomer to this area, Oldham was born and raised to a farming family in Jackson Township, and attended Jackson Township High School. His family grew up and attended school with the Sims family. He spent two years working at Standard Packing House, now known as Mariah Foods, Doug Sims' current employer. Oldham became an Indiana State Trooper in 1965 and earned his stripes by stopping speeders up and down the Indiana highways. He smiled patiently as drivers called out expletives or made excuses for bad driving. He winced as drivers breathed alcohol-tainted breath into his face as they attempted to explain they could "drive juuust finnne, officer..." Promoted to an Investigator for Auto Theft nine years later, and then again to Detective, he worked every case imaginable, from theft to drugs, from stopping silly teens on a joyride in daddy's car to cold-blooded killers out for revenge. In the 1980s, Oldham worked White Collar Crime; he escorted corrupt state and city political officials to jail and prison many a time. "He was the most hated man in the county," his daughter would explain, years later. "He never took a bribe, and he wasn't afraid of anyone just because they were an elected official. If they broke the law they went to jail like anyone else." Jon Oldham was old school; he could talk to anyone and work with everyone, and respect equaled respect in his book. He was a living legend in this area, and whenever anyone said his name, they said it with a sort of reverence. He also had a cop's eye for detail: the way an eye shifted, how a hand moved to flick away evidence just slightly. Jon Oldham, as they say, would bleed police blue if he were cut.

And now as he sat across from Douglas Sims, working what he knew about the case over in his mind, he read Sims' body language as only an avid reader can interpret a treasured novel. They made small talk. Oldham smiled and nodded.

Doug Sims was no longer in the comfort of his own home, his environment. He was out of his element, no longer on his own territory. Although the officers did what they could to make him comfortable, they still had the advantage. "The suspect is on your turf now," explains a seasoned interviewer, "and that gives you an edge."

He asked Sims about the boys' night at his trailer, and Sims readily admitted they were indeed over at his house. Oldham asked about handcuffing Brad to his bed. Sure, Sims admitted, but he let him go. They were just playing a game. It was just a harmless, one-time-only game.

Oldham made it casual. He asked Sims if he gave the boys any alcohol to drink.

No, Doug Sims said, he never did that.

Since this was contrary to what two witnesses told the law enforcement officers, at this time Oldham read Sims his rights, or in legal terms, gave him the Miranda Warning. Rob and Junior already told the officers, on separate occasions: Sims furnished the underage boys with alcoholic beverages. Sims was the last person observed with Brad. It gave Oldham probable cause to make an arrest.

According to what is called a landmark case (meaning it changed judicial history), Miranda v. Arizona 384 U.S. 436 (1966), a person must know their legal rights when in custody and when questioned. "You have the right to remain silent. Anything you say can and will be used against you in a court of law. You have the right to speak to an attorney, and to have an attorney present during any questioning. If you cannot afford a lawyer, one will be provided for you at government expense." Everyone has these rights, no matter their offense. By law, an officer must read these rights to an individual when that person is not free to leave, or believes they are not free to leave, and when the person is questioned.

"Okay, now look here," Oldham told him. He read off of a piece of paper. "Because you are here, in custody, and I am asking you some questions, I have to advise you of your rights. You have the right to remain silent, and whatever you say here can be held against you in a court of law. Understand that?"

"Yes," Sims nodded.

"You do have the right to an attorney, and if you cannot afford an attorney, one will be provided to you at the court's expense. Do you understand that?"

"Yes."

"Are you sure? Ask me if you don't."

"No, I understand," Sims nodded.

Oldham then began the interrogation. Secretly he wondered if Brad was holed up at Sims' home or somewhere else, hung over, embarrassed, or just plain scared of momma's wrath. Interviews are conducted to gather information, while interrogations are interviews of a known guilty or suspected party. Douglas Sims fell into the latter category because two witnesses stated that he provided alcohol to minors, he was the last person seen with Brad, and Brad still remained missing. A good interrogation does not take place in a dark room with one light, a steel table, and two uncomfortable chairs, as seen in the movies. It can take place anywhere: in a musty old office, in a well-lit room. The most important thing is to establish rapport. An interrogation can take hours, and it has nothing to do with threats or physical violence—in fact, the latter will lose a case. A good interviewer is patient, charming, can establish a rapport with anyone, and does not judge. Their tactic is "Let me help you," not "Let me hurt you," because the interrogated person knows they are trapped, and now they just need a way out. A safe exit ramp, so to speak—the least painful way out of a bad situation.

Oldham finally asked, "Have you seen Brad Maddux, Doug?"

"The last time I saw him," Sims told him, "I took him, Junior, and this other boy back to Junior's house, and then I went on home."

"You went home by yourself?"

"Yeah."

"Okay then. Now, you say you dropped Brad off at Junior's place, and Junior off at Junior's, and the other boy at Junior's place, and then you went home alone?"

"I did."

"Where were you before you dropped them off?"

"My house."

Oldham nodded. "What took place there?"

"We just hung out."

"You just hung out. At any time did you touch any of the boys in any way?"

"What do you mean?" Sims asked.

"Did you kiss one of the boys?" Oldham made his voice casual.

109

"No!"

"You're lying to me," Oldham told him. It was time to bring it up a notch. "So now, tell me where Brad is."

Someone outside of the office motioned to Whitehead, who stood and stepped out of the room quietly. He had a domestic dispute to answer to. He walked quickly out of the police station.

"You're not being truthful with me, Doug." Jon Oldham said. He planned to get Sims to explain Brad's whereabouts. "Your statements aren't consistent. I need you to be honest, or it could mean trouble."

Sims looked as if he were passively watching a very slow baseball game.

Oldham needed to ask the question, but once it came out he could not turn back. This is when the clock starts ticking and the cards, as they say, are on the table. Hearts start pounding, and it is time to watch carefully: eyes, hands, breathing, changes in skin color, nervous tics however slight, all the while staying calm and collected. The question came out, and the town of Westport would never be the same.

Brad Maddux on his first birthday, 1976.
(Courtesy Daryl Maddux)

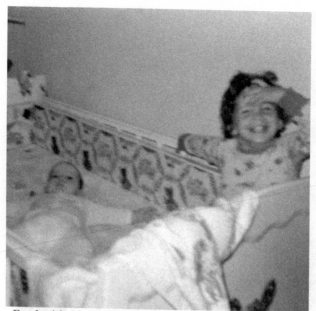
Brad with Lindsay, 1979. (Courtesy Daryl Maddux)

Brad in his first pair of overalls, 1979
(Courtesy Daryl Maddux)

1981: Brad was "always smiling" according to those who loved him. (Courtesy Daryl Maddux)

Brad, about 1988: a handsome boy.
(Photographs courtesy Daryl Maddux)

Brad in 1989. He had one year to live.

The last photo of Brad Maddux. A
school photo, it served instead for
his funeral announcement.
(Courtesy Decatur High School)

Douglas Sims, in his freshman (1977)
and sophomore (1978) high school
yearbook pictures. The devil may
have already been at work.
(Courtesy Decatur High School).

Doug Sims as a junior in high school (1979). He was always "different." (Courtesy Decatur High School).

Doug Sims' truck. Originally used to transport friends, later it would be used to transport something else. (Courtesy CSI Ed Lewis)

Aerial view of Mt. Olivet cemetery. At night it was "spooky." (Courtesy CSI Ed Lewis)

Mt. Olivet cemetery, early morning, March 11, 1990. Volunteer firefighters' lights illuminate the entrance. (Courtesy CSI Ed Lewis)

Officers found the answers in the old cemetery. They recovered the remains from where the headstone is pointing. (Author's collection)

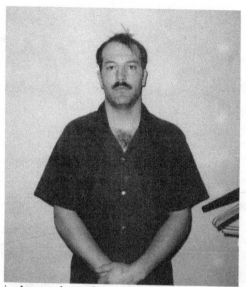

Original mug shot of Douglas Cecil Sims, 03-11-90.
(Courtesy Decatur County Sheriff's Office)

Jon Oldham in 2012. (Author's collection)

The last place Brad's friends saw him alive. They argued just beyond the telephone pole. (Author's collection)

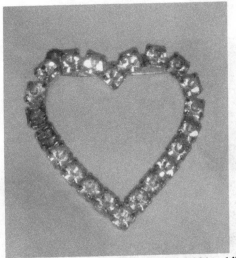

Pendent Brad gave his 3rd grade "girlfriend," Sheila Padgett. (Courtesy S. Padgett)

Dedicated to the Memory of

Bradley Daryl Maddux

1990 yearbook page dedicated to Brad. His murder impacted the community in many ways. (Courtesy Decatur High School and Sheila Padgett)

In 2011, Junior Armstrong and Rob Nugent stand as they were on the morning of March 10, 1990. Had they walked a few feet further, they could have made a horrific discovery that day. (Author's collection)

7 "THIS BOY'S DEAD, ISN'T HE?"

Jon Oldham used the interrogation tactic often. "If you know (the suspect) stole money, but you don't know how much, you ask, 'did you steal $50?' They'll say, 'oh I didn't take that much.' Then you got 'em, see, admitting to theft."

Using this old interrogation tactic, Jon Oldham asked Douglas Sims one question. He did not believe it, but he utilized it to get a reaction. "This boy's dead, isn't he?"

Douglas Sims sat there; not moving, eyes downcast. It seemed as if time stood still. After a calculated silence, he nodded his head: "Yes."

Steed was "afraid to breathe. We were afraid to break the spell." He cut his eyes at Bill Nunn, who caught his gaze and held it. Both did not dare move, and silence engulfed the room. It was almost as if you could hear the wind outside, sighing through the old trees.

"What happened, Doug?" Oldham kept his voice steady. Show no emotion; do not judge. Still, Oldham was shocked. He fully expected Brad to be passed out drunk somewhere, sleeping it off, or nursing a bad hangover and trying to decide the best way to explain it all to mom and dad. Sims' apathy toward the entire thing also floored Oldham. Sims showed absolutely no sign of remorse: no change in breathing, no sweating, no reaction whatsoever.

"I cut his throat," Douglas C. Sims said without emotion, "because he wouldn't do what I wanted him to do."

Steed could only think, "*Oh my God. This happens someplace else. Not Westport.*"

Jon Oldham nodded. "Where did it happen, Doug? Where did you cut him?"

Doug Sims said nonchalantly, "At my trailer."

No one moved. Not even a creak of gun leather or a shoe scuffle.

Oldham nodded. He let the silence work for a minute. "Doug, would you be willing to help me, here? Would you make a recorded statement?"

"Yes," Sims nodded.

Oldham stood up and left the room.

Sims looked up at Terry Steed. "Do you know," he asked, "How much time I could get for this?"

Steed did not respond.

Oldham returned with a tape recorder. He set the machine down on the desk, pressed a button, and the tape began to whirl, recording their conversation.

(Verbatim per court record)

"It's the tenth day," Oldham corrects himself. "No, it's the eleventh day of March." He tells Steed quietly, "Make sure nobody comes back here." Then he continues, "1990. This is an interview taking place at the Westport Town Hall. Present: myself, Jon Oldham, William Nunn of the State Police, Terry Steed of the State Police, and we're talking to a Doug Sims. Doug, what's your date of birth?"

"Two of June, 1961," Sims replies.

"Move up a little," Oldham suggests, so the microphone can pick Sims' voice up with clarity. "Okay Doug, last night you was in the company of a, just tell me what happened last night, just use names and the whole thing about it."

"I picked three kids up."

"What's their names?" Oldham asks.

"Junior and Brad, and I don't know who the other one was."

"Junior who?"

"Armstrong." Doug continues. "Took 'em to my place. Gave 'em a beer. I don't remember the alcohol."

Oldham waits a moment. "Okay."

"Remember having one of 'em handcuffed to the bed. I undid him. Took 'em back home and I did meet Brad. Took 'em back down home and he wouldn't do what I wanted him to do, so I cut his throat."

126

"What did you want him to do?"

Doug says, "I wanted him to go with me to North Vernon to get more alcohol, but he didn't want to do it."

"What did you cut his throat with?"

"A knife."

Oldham nods. "Where's the knife at now?"

"It's out in the woods."

"Out in the woods?" Oldham repeats.

"I don't know where I threw it," Doug's voice dips in pitch.

"Well, do you know about where it is?"

"From where I threw it?"

"Yeah," Oldham says, nodding.

"I know the direction it flew."

Oldham watches Sims as he displays boredom with the conversation and acts as if the questions are trivial. "Okay. What did you do with him?"

"I buried him."

"Where at?"

Sims answers with almost maddeningly nonchalance. "In the cemetery."

"Okay. Where's the cemetery at?"

"It's on the south side of Alert. It's on that gravel road, when you go from the highway. The first road on the blacktop."

"Okay, would you show me where he's at?" Oldham asked.

At the same time, Sims was answering him, "Yeah, yeah."

Oldham was secretly shocked. Gone was the expectation of Brad being located hung over and in big trouble. The investigation had taken a very different, and very nasty, turn. "How deep did you bury him?"

"He's not deep."

"What'd you use?"

"A shovel."

Oldham leans slightly forward. A thought occurs to him, and he knows he cannot lose this case based on a technicality. He will not allow Douglas C. Sims to walk the streets again because some legal eagle in a suit feels he violated Sims' rights. Always a thorough cop, Oldham provides insurance for himself and says, "Do you remember a while ago, all the rights I advised you?"

"Yes."

"What were they?"

Sims says, "I got the right to have an attorney present upon..." his voice fades as he explained the rest.

Oldham asks him, "Is this boy related to you?"

"Yeah. Cousin I guess. Second or third... I—" he drifts off into thought. Sims' head droops. "I think," he says softly, "I need one."

"You needin' one—what?"

Sims mumbles to himself some more, then says, "An attorney."

"Do you wanna terminate this now until you talk to one?"

"Yes."

Oldham says into the recorder, "This will terminate the conversation at this point," and snaps off the machine.

(End court record)

While Sims gave his statement, Steed slipped out of the room to move Daryl and Patti out of the kitchen area, only a few doors down from where the officers sat with Sims, to the front of the offices. Steed returned to the interview room as they completed the confession and terminated the on-tape interview. He did not want the Maddux family to overhear Doug Sims' confession, for both legal and personal reasons.

"Doug," Oldham said, "Would you do me a favor? Would you still draw that map of where we can find the body? Now I do have to tell you, this can be used against you in court of law, just like I told you. You don't have to tell us, you know."

"I know that," Sims told him. "I can take you there, or I can show you with a map." He motioned. "Get me a piece of paper."

"Well, go ahead and show me," Oldham told him, sliding a piece of paper and a pencil to him. "But remember, this can be used against you in court of law. I told you. You don't have to tell us."

"I know." Sims took the paper and pencil and began

128

drawing, explaining. It was not far from their present location. Oldham knew exactly where to find the cemetery. Sims drew and explained as if he were giving directions to a local rummage sale. It was a crude drawing, not really a map, of several lines, with an "S" for Sardinia.

Years later, Jon Oldham is still amazed at Douglas Sims' complete lack of compunction. "The entire interview took less than an hour," from introduction to confession. Of murdering a little boy in such a brutal manner, "Doug could have cared less."

Oldham knew what occurred, even if he could not, realistically, prove it: Sims had tried the boys. It had been a test. Which boy would be the easiest to manipulate, to subdue, or/and to trick? Which of the three boys who sat in the trailer that night would be the most trusting?

Sims finished his map and put down his pencil. Oldham stood up slowly, and he busied himself by doing odd jobs that needed completion. He instructed Terry Steed to transport Sims to jail. As Steed removed the handcuffs from his belt with a solid *snap* and prepared to transport Sims to the Decatur County Jail, Sims had one more comment. "I got a family reunion to go to today," he explained, as if he did not have time to go to jail.

"Doug," Steed finally spoke to him, "I don't think they'll want you there." It was the last thing he said to this child killer. He placed the handcuffs on Doug Sims' wrists.

Steed walked Sims to the patrol vehicle. He opened the back door and assisted him in, careful not to hit his head on the top of the patrol car. Steed securely locked the vehicle, then walked around to get behind the wheel. He still felt amazement and shock at what he heard. Years later, he still shakes his head each time he thinks of it. How could a grown man take the life of a child and then admit to it without at least one tear, one catch in the voice?

Trooper Steed transported Doug Sims to jail without a word, and Sims offered no conversation.

Now it was time to gather the team and move into action, to gather evidence and to start putting the puzzle together. A confession would not suffice. By the time Steed left with Sims for jail, it was already 12:20 a.m., March 11, 1990.

One of the officers involved with the case prepared to call the Decatur County Sheriff, Larry Snyder, as well as the county coroner, Mike Porter, but first called the county prosecutor, William O. Smith.

Standard practice requires the police to notify the prosecutor as soon as evidence of a homicide comes about. The prosecutor always necessitated the first phone call, before the county coroner or even the Sheriff's department. William "Bill" Smith was used to this, and he and Oldham worked well together. Smith spent four years as the Chief Deputy Prosecutor, from 1975 to 1978, then citizens elected him as Prosecuting Attorney in 1986. Indiana statutes prohibited Decatur County from having a full-time prosecuting attorney, so the elected prosecuting attorney combined their criminal law work with their private practice of law. It was a full-time, 24/7 job, but no one could be better for the job: he loved investigations; he loved history, law, learning, writing, and legal work. He was eloquent, thorough, and intelligent. William Smith headed out to join Jon Oldham and work with the other officers called to the scene.

Oldham notified Decatur County Deputy Sheriff Robert Klene (pronounced *"Klinny,"* to rhyme with "skinny"), who was working the 6:00 p.m. to 2:00 a.m. shift. It was about to get even more ugly, but Klene was a good cop who could handle it.

Klene arrived at the Westport Town Marshall's office shortly after the phone call, and Oldham briefed Klene on the situation. He did not bother using Doug Sims' map. Klene did not see the map Sims had drew until he testified in court months later. "It was pretty simple, just a couple of lines. (Sims) had written an 'S' which normally means 'south' but I guess he meant for it to mean 'Sardinia.'" Klene nodded and listened as Oldham explained. He knew exactly where the graveyard was located.

Oldham then dispatched Klene to the Mt. Olivet Cemetery just outside of Alert, with a jailer, Mike Owens, for backup. "Look for a newly opened gravesite," Oldham advised. "But be careful, and preserve it as a crime scene."

At the time, Deputy Sheriff Robert Klene was, in his own words, "fearless." His life led him to develop the kind of attitude that nothing could get to him; he controlled himself and his environment. Klene was a product of the farmland around him. Although born in Greensburg, his father purchased a farm in 1961 when Klene was a kid. Like Bradley Maddux and all the children around him, Klene grew up hunting, fishing, and swimming. He attended Sand Creek High School, a schoolmate of Daryl Maddux. He married soon after graduation ... and then the first lottery for Viet Nam came up. "I loved to hunt," he says, "And I figured, finding bad guys would be like hunting." He joined the army in 1971 as a military police officer for three years and found himself in Korea. When he returned to his hometown, he applied for and was accepted into the Decatur County Sheriff's Department and worked there from 1976 to 1997. His accolades included a Letter of Accommodation from Sheriff Snyder, quite an accomplishment.

Klene and Owens got into Klene's Deputy Sheriff's cruiser, with Owens in the passenger seat, and headed out for Mt. Olivet Cemetery. "I knew what I was looking for," he says now. He did not personally know Doug Sims, and he really did not know the victim, except that he was the son of a high school mate. Doug Sims never crossed his radar, had never got arrested, and Sims never had cause to deal with Klene, despite Klene being the sole deputy on duty for many a Sunday in the estimated 350 square miles of Decatur County.

Klene and Owens arrived at Mt. Olivet. Klene parked his Deputy Sheriff's cruiser just outside of the entryway on CR 1300, yet not in the direct entry so as not to destroy any evidence. He stepped outside of the vehicle into a light, cold breeze, careful where he stepped as he walked. Klene stayed fully cognizant and aware of his steps the entire time he searched the cemetery. The full moon did nothing to illuminate the dark cemetery. Out in farm country very little light illuminates the night sky. It can be spooky, with the rustle of animals in hay and the occasional sound of wild creatures slipping out from the woods. But even for a tough, seasoned officer like himself, the night air seemed downright menacing. The closest residence was far down the way, and its lights were off. The heavy brush and tall trees rustled, the crooked branches allowing moonlight to peep in and out. He pulled out a small, pocket-sized day planner and began to make his notes. Klene was a good officer, with an eye for details. He purposely walked as close to the outside of the

131

entrance as he could, next to the large pillar, and alongside the gravel entryway, not down the middle or on the drive, lest there be important tire tracks. He clicked on his flashlight, letting the beam scan across the dirt, grass, and gravel carefully. It almost felt like being on the moon itself, his beam crisscrossing the dark mud and gravel.

No matter how careful a criminal thinks they are, they always leave clues, or evidence of one kind or another. "We take something into every room we enter, and we leave with something from that room," explains an investigator. It is called the Locard Theory, or "'Locard's Principle.'" Edmond Locard, the director of the first forensic laboratory (in Lyons, France) theorized that everywhere a person goes, they leave something behind and take something with them. Skin follicles, hair, shoe prints, dirt—it is just a matter of finding the evidence. Forensic scientists still use this twentieth-century principle today.

Klene carefully recorded his arrival in his planner, starting on March 8, 1990, printing neatly that he arrived and observed "fresh tire tracks s. bound in to grave yard on 1300 s. ¼ m. w of 1050 w. approx. 20' into graveyard." Klene also observed a footprint and a tire track on the east side of the driveway, inside of the graveyard. The footprint was in the tire track. Klene followed the track, careful not to step near it, to the south end past a huge cedar tree. As the wind made the tree branches swish above his head, he noted in his day planner that the vehicle appeared to spin when it turned. Klene walked a bit farther, and his light caught something else. A pair of white jockey shorts hung in the thick brush on the extreme south side of the graveyard, just west of the drive. Klene carefully noted it. He continued walking past the cedar tree, trying not to let the enveloping darkness spook him, and jotted down his observation of the "low concrete foundation" that encircled a few graves. There he noted a "mound of fresh dirt 2' wide 4 to 5 ft long." This is the point where, as a cop, you have to try not to let your heart sink. To this day, it still brings out emotions in Robert Klene, for besides being a good officer, he is also a good-hearted human being.

Klene called in his findings and later the Letts Volunteer

Fire Department was notified to provide a portable lighting system with a generator. "Those firemen," Klene says today, "were so good. They came right out and helped. They did their job and were great." Klene began stringing up crime scene tape to mark off the Mt. Olivet cemetery. It was going to be a sleepless night.

As Klene worked on the outskirts of town, fellow officers went to work within city limits. They all knew it would be a long night fueled by coffee and nerves.

After he booked Sims into the county jail, Steed departed the building to drive out to the Mt. Olivet cemetery. He parked on the side of the road and, as he exited his vehicle, with the cool air hitting his face, he looked up at the moonlight sifting through the bare branches. "This is a setting for an old horror movie," he muttered to himself, shuddering. The bare limbs scratched against one another; the leaves blew, tumbling against each other. He saw Klene's flashlight play against the old headstones, creating shadows of things there—and not there. Little did he know then that he just walked into a very real horror movie.

The Westport and Decatur County law enforcement busied itself with work while most of Brad's friends were unaware of the situation. Slowly, word began to spread.

Dollie Press snuck a phone call to her friend, Tommy Stellar, the boy who lived in the house directly across the street from where the Meadows resided. They talked and laughed on the phone until 1:00 a.m., when Tommy said, "Hold on. Someone's at our front door."

Dollie noted the time and said, "That's weird."

It took some time for Tommy to return to the phone, and at first his voice was halting, muffled. Dollie could not understand a word he said, until she realized that the noises she heard were the sounds of Tommy crying, sobbing, in fact. "Doug Sims just admitted to killing Brad," he snuffled.

"Quit screwing with me!" Dollie told him. "That's not funny!" She knew the boys often teased her, and sometimes it went too far.

"I'm serious!" He almost did sound as if he were crying.

"Yeah, whatever," and Dollie slammed the phone down in its cradle. Boys, she decided, could be butt holes.

Across town, Jill Bishop's phone rang late in the night, and she answered it. It was her best friend. "Jill," her friend told her, "Brad's been murdered!"

"Oh yeah, right," Jill rolled her eyes. They talked a few more minutes, and Jill hung up. She still did not believe her friend.

It was impossible to believe, because Westport is a small community where everyone knows each other.

By this time, the Armstrong family already returned home safely, but Junior could not sleep. The phone rang in the house like a shrill warning bell, and Mary Armstrong answered, a nervous Junior pacing nearby. Mary listened, made a few comments, and then hung up the phone. She steeled herself to tell her son the horrific truth.

Junior screamed, and he began quaking and sobbing. "Let's get out of here!" he sobbed. "Let's go! We have to get out of here!" It was surreal, like a bad nightmare, and Junior bawled loudly in an attempt to wake himself up.

Meanwhile, law enforcement officers began their role in the horrific event.

At about 1:45 a.m., Indiana State Police Technician Sergeant Edward Lewis answered his home phone. Post Commander Corporal Mike Black was on the other line. Lewis knew that it was time to go to work, and off he went. Lewis' job required him to stay on call twenty-four hours a day, seven days a week. That is the way cops work: they grab their gear and go. Maybe they find time to grab a cup of coffee, kiss their family goodbye, or leave a hastily scrawled note. They become the job. A crime scene awaited him in Sardinia, and crime scenes wait for no one. Critical evidence washes away, dries up, blows away in a matter of minutes. Those minutes matter in a court of law and someone guilty could go free if no one examined the evidence in time. Lewis hustled it to the command post, Westport Town Hall.

On his way to the command post, Edward "Ed" Lewis thought over what happened in his life that brought him to this point. In the sixth grade, when most boys in his classroom wanted to be farmers or ranchers, Lewis printed carefully "State Trooper" on his career aspiration card. He still has that card. As the first law enforcement officer in his family, many more family members followed in his example. He grew up on an Indiana dairy farm. Lewis spent twenty-six years in the military, first the Navy, including a station in Virginia, and then he joined the National Guard upon his return to Indiana, and then he followed his dream when he hired on with the Indiana State Police. Lewis was an investigator's investigator; "my crime scene," he explained to others, "is my crime scene." He respected everyone but made it clear he ran the show. "I interview the dead," he says solemnly. "So the crime scene has to be controlled." Who goes in, what they carry, and what they do: this is how Lewis finds out who did what, and how. Sometimes he can even find out why and when.

Oldham met Lewis at the command post, along with Smith, Decatur County Coroner Mike Porter, and Sheriff Snyder. They briefed Lewis, who then returned to his vehicle and headed to Mount Olivet Cemetery. Smith and Porter also headed for Mt. Olivet.

The dark trees swayed above Lewis' head. CR 1300 S disappeared in a bend just a few yards away from the cemetery entrance, and the surrounding woods were pitch-black. It created an eerie effect, causing shivers down the backs of the strongest of officers.

As he pulled up on the gravel road, Lewis noted Deputy Bob Klene on the scene, securing the area. The men greeted one another and, at the same time, silently exchanged the feelings an officer exchanges when such a tragedy occurs.

"I tell you," Klene said in an aside to Lewis, half joking, half not. "I'm glad you're here. It is downright spooky out here." Lewis nodded in agreement. Illuminated by their vehicle headlights, the fog rolled and twisted in the graveyard, and the dampness gave off a chill that seemed almost foreboding.

The somberness of the crime scene also requires the policemen to put aside their emotions for later. A little boy becomes a body; a beloved family member must become an object. Without this distancing, officers cannot do their job. The tears, the anger, the frustration comes later. An emotional officer is a dangerous thing: problems enter the work and people get hurt. They miss vital evidence, and write reports incorrectly. "You have to enter the scene and start thinking, 'court room,'" explains one veteran. "Think like you are in a court room. Because if your report will not stand up in a court of law, if everything you do cannot stand up in a court of law, the guilty walk free," and all of your hard work and sincere effort is for naught.

So Lewis began processing the scene with a trained eye and steady hand. Working as a team, Klene pointed out what he found prior to Lewis' arrival and carefully marked off: the tire tracks, the footprint. The mud held them in place, so Lewis knew he could mark these off and gather them later. Sheriff Snyder arrived with a video camera in hand, assisting by videotaping the scene. The men met together in the middle of CR 1300 S.

"What do you think?" Smith asked Lewis. "I think it would be best to wait until daylight. It's dark as hell out here."

Lewis pulled the zipper up tighter on his State Trooper's jacket and considered, walking back toward his vehicle. He saw Oldham walking back to meet him.

"Ed," Oldham told him, glancing back to see Smith was talking to Sheriff Snyder, "Bill wants to wait until morning to look for the boy. I told him it was up to you. What do you want to do?" Oldham and Lewis worked well together; Oldham respected both the man's work ethic and the man himself.

"I say we do it now," Lewis nodded. "Jon, let's get the volunteer fire department out here with some lighting. But we need some boys we can trust to keep it quiet. Otherwise we'll have every person in Westport out here, onlookers, media, television, and God knows what else."

"Tearing up the crime scene and trying to help," Oldham agreed. "I'm with you." He glanced back at Smith. "I understand what Bill's trying to do," he said, "But we can always come back here in the day, too."

"Oh I will," Lewis assured him. He always returned to his crime scenes several times, searching for evidence, ensuring he missed nothing. He agreed with Oldham: Bill was a good man, a smart man, but there was no time like the present.

They notified two trusted men of the LVFD, and they quickly—and quietly—were on their way. As instructed, they did not use their emergency lights or sirens. The last

136

thing the team needed was for a bunch of people to crowd the crime scene, stomping over potential evidence, starting rumors, and for families to be bothered and harassed. Later, Smith would write a glowing letter of thanks to Rob and Byron Baltus, who were the responding volunteer firefighters that night. Once they arrived, they set up two tall floodlights powered by generators. The old cemetery lit up like some strange movie set. Under the lights, the graveyard appeared as bright as if in the midday June sun, but the surrounding area remained dark as pitch. The generators purred in the background.

Lewis removed a large trash bag from his vehicle and fanned it open. He called the team over and gave them instructions. He did not want to see someone smoking or anyone using smokeless tobacco. If someone had a cup, if someone had on disposable gloves, they must throw those things away in *this* trash bag. "If you throw anything away," his baritone voice boomed strongly, "even gum, it goes in here," and he rattled the trash bag for emphasis. As for the fire department volunteers with the lights, "please do not move until I ask you." He asked if anyone had a question. No? It was time to go to work.

Evidence photographers work from the "outside in," meaning they start taking photographs and videos starting at the largest point and then zooming in to the smallest detail. Officers take more photos and video than necessary because the rule is "more is better." The volunteer firefighters' lights cast an eerie glow in the edges of the spooky old cemetery as Lewis began to shoot frame after frame; he made sure he photographed everything.

Lewis stood for a moment, taking it all in. Then he started at the road. In a strange way, he began taking the same journey as Brad's killer, and Brad himself, only a few hours ago.

Lewis took a look around and then took a few steps. He would position his camera and take a few frames. When he asked, the firefighters would move their lights on the poles. Otherwise, they stood as still and silent as soldiers on a drill.

Slowly the evidence team made their way to back of the graveyard, where the oldest graves rested. The tombstones here sunk at a rakish angle; some toppled over or broken. Many were so old they became impossible to read.

137

Obviously no one placed new graves or tombstones in this area for years.

Lewis surveyed the immediate area, took the steps, made a photograph. "I never do a walk-through first," he later explains. "It's a process. I photograph as I go, take a step, survey." Again he would give instruction to the firefighters, who would lift their lights and move them, only speaking if they had a necessary question.

Walking toward the back of the graveyard, Lewis noted a fresh earth mound to his left. It disrupted the dirt next to several graves that sectioned off from the others by a small concrete barrier about five inches high. He saw some leaves and twigs tangled in the grey-colored earth, but it definitely appeared freshly dug. Sheriff Snyder noted this mound and carefully videotaped the disturbed earth. First, they slowly and methodically searched for evidence in the immediate area: a cigarette butt, a bottle, a piece of paper, chewing gum, anything. "It's a lover's lane out there," Lewis explains later, using an older euphemism. "There are beer bottles, trash. You have to determine if anything is relevant."

Satisfied that he recorded the area completely, Lewis set his camera kit down and knelt next to the disturbed earth. He carefully began to remove dirt from the mound handful by handful; his hands steady, his heart thumping. He prepared to set the clods of earth down and away from the immediate area.

The first clod of dirt Sergeant Edward Lewis removed solved the mystery of missing child Bradley Daryl Maddux. An Indiana State Police Supplemental Case Report summarizes the incident: "The boy was lying face down in a very shallow grave. His legs were straight, his feet and toes pointed straight down and his arms were at his side. He had a pair of socks on and was otherwise nude. There was a sock tied around his neck. The boy was discovered at 0315 Hours on 3-11-90." The body lay facing north-south, with the head facing north. The sock around his neck was blood-soaked. His face was clean. His eyes were open. The men fought back emotions as they realized that Brad's neck had a cut so deep that it almost severed his head, and they saw dark indentions on his wrists.

Years later, Terry Steed remembers those moments as if

they were happening now. "It hit home," he says of the first sign of finding Brad. "It was a kid." He still sees it in his mind's eye. "First it was the hair, then his head, and some sort of gag around his neck. We pull some more dirt away, and there's his body. His face, you know..."

Brad Maddux would never again throw a baseball, camp out on his friend's back porch, cuddle his precious dog, or say with that twinkle in his eye, "I'm your white knight in shining armor!" His parents would never get to buy him a Christmas gift, or listen to his tall tales; his friends would never again double over in guffaws at his antics. He would never tell on himself again, red face puffed up, fist doubled. His parents would feel a constant, sore, ache in their hearts forever. His brother and sister would grow up with a huge, empty gap in their lives. Junior and Rob would not have a best friend to go camping, drag their go cart to a stop, share the joys and pains of growing up, plan their futures, and watch one another grow to manhood. No graduations, no birthday parties, no joined laughter or antics with Brad. Neighbors would not wave to him as he tossed their newspaper and feel that warm sense of affection for him: Such a good little boy. Such potential. Brad was going to be somebody. Instead he ended up a cold, grey, stiff body tossed in a hole in an ancient graveyard.

Oldham departed to the command post at Westport Town Hall. They felt relief at finding Brad, but a sick, terrible sadness engulfed the team. Some of them may have felt the truth in their gut and knew all along ... But they still had to keep that sense of hope, despite their doubt.

Hope vanished when Coroner Porter pronounced Bradley Daryl Maddux deceased.

Back at the Command Center, Brad's family and friends waited in dreary anticipation. "I could not believe the amount of people that were there," Oldham said later. "It seemed like all of a sudden, that place was full of people." He found himself standing in front of Brad's family. The faces, so expecting, hurting already, knowing the truth but still hoping—that was the worst.

Silence hung in the air like a miasma. Oldham stood, and the words, "I'm sorry," seemed so hollow to him, like they

139

always did. It was, without a doubt, the worst part of the job.

Then a strange thing happened. Bradley's grandfather, Grandpa Dave Giddings, lunged at Oldham's big bulk. Oldham took a step back and deflected him, but the elderly man took another swing.

"I'm not—" Oldham deflected another blow. "I'm not going to arrest you!" he told the old man. "No matter how hard you try. So you might as well stop it now." He knew instantly what Dave wanted him to do. Arresting the old man for assaulting a police officer would place him in the same jail as Doug Sims, the man who slaughtered Brad. Sooner or later, their paths would cross, and Brad's granddaddy could take his shot at the man who took his grandson's life so callously. "Stop it!" Oldham shouted again; watching the old man collapsing into tears, Oldham turned away to save Dave Giddings his dignity.

Oldham now had a different call to make. He dialed the number and rubbed his eyes, holding the receiver tightly.

"Hello!" It was David Sims, not too happy with his phone ringing at such a ridiculous hour.

"David, it's me, Jon Oldham. Listen..." how do you explain? Oldham had the highest respect for the older Sims. Carefully, "I've got Doug locked up, David. For murder—"

"Well, what do you want me to do about it!" *Click*.

Oldham sat there in disbelief, and then replaced the telephone in its cradle.

Sometime later, Betty Sims called Oldham with a heartfelt apology. It seemed that David did not hear him correctly; David's hearing was not what it used to be. David thought Doug was in jail for something related to his drinking habit. Now, what was the problem?

Oldham made his way back to his vehicle to return to the cemetery. Tonight he would log a lot of miles in such a small town.

At Mount Olivet Cemetery, Sergeant Lewis removed clods of dirt individually and carefully, setting them away from the body. As he worked, he talked to Brad silently. "I can't do anything else for you, son. I'm sorry it's over for you. You were a child, a human being, tossing papers from your bicycle. What you could have been! I want to make sure whatever I can do now is as close to perfect as I can get. And I'll do what I can so whoever did this—whoever it was—will never do it again. I won't forget you."

Years later, Lewis says, "People forget sometimes. Officers are human beings. No policeman is tough enough to not be affected by a murdered child. We were careful with (Brad) for several reasons. I wanted to preserve the evidence because I wanted to preserve the crime scene and catch whoever killed him. Plus, he was someone's child."

After Lewis took the necessary photographs for evidentiary purposes, Klene assisted in preparing to remove the remains of Bradley Maddux from the burial site. A small amount of blood pooled under the throat area, mixing with the dirt. They placed the remains in a body bag, and they handled him gently, ever so gently, with the respect he deserved. Lewis took more photographs and videos in an effort to be as thorough as possible. Few people spoke; the noises of awkward throat-clearing the only noise to break the silence. They placed brown evidence bags over both of Brad's hands to preserve any evidence that could be under his nails or entwined in his fingers. Forensics could lift and test the dirt and residue on his fingers to help provide solid evidence for the murder. The hands do the grabbing, pushing, protecting, and holding.   Lewis zipped up the body bag without a word. Officers again forced themselves to forget that they knew the little body in the bag, but every now and then, someone needed to look away for a moment, into the inky darkness. Many blamed their watering eyes on the cold wind. Later, Robert Klene says, "This job takes a toll on you after a while."

Klene also completed a search of another cemetery just down the road, in case Doug Sims dumped more evidence there. "You never know," Klene explained. "There is a possibility of more evidence, and it was a cemetery, and he did not specifically name the cemetery we were in, so I checked the other one as it was so close. But I found nothing in there." It was after daylight when he finally arrived home, after an incredibly long shift. To this day he says of that night, "People are still trying to make sense out of a senseless crime."

By the time night turned into morning on March 11, 1990, Douglas Cecil Sims officially resided in jail after his booking. As part of the process, Patrolman Robert Herbert administered a BAC, or Blood Alcohol Test, on Sims. Testing the body for alcohol via the breath has dates as far back as the 1800s, and law enforcement officials utilized it in the 1930s. Of course, the tests advanced significantly over the years. To ensure the machine operated correctly, Herbert tested it at 1:55 a.m. Herbert carefully instructed Sims how to blow into the machine. He was tested at 1:56 a.m. The machine was then tested a second time at 1:56 a.m. to ensure the device results did not deviate.

The 6' 2", 195 pound Doug Sims blew a .00 on the Intoxiliyzer—Alcohol Analyzer Model 5000.

On local farms, the roosters and other animals began to rustle about. It was a new day.

Indiana State Trooper Greg Allen, Brad's little league coach, just finished working the 5:30 p.m. to 2:00 a.m. shift. He was off-duty when he heard the news. Up until this moment, the worst case he ever worked involved a domestic violence shooting in 1989, where an estranged husband shot their four-year-old son and 20-month-old daughter and then committed suicide. Allen remembers the horror of processing that call, as his own child was the same age as that man's son. Allen wanted to be a State Trooper since he was a small boy. However, he graduated eighth in his high school class with a scholarship, and he loved animals, and his love of animals led him to earn a Bachelor of Animal Science from Purdue. Two years in Lafayette's Animal Science Program told him this would be a long haul with many books, study hours, intricate tests, and more, so he applied for the position of Town Marshall in Westport in 1981, and in 1985 he became an Indiana State Trooper. Allen was a good cop who cared about the community, and he sat in stunned silence when he knew Brad was gone. He thought of the Brad Maddux he knew, trotting around the baseball diamond, swinging a ball bat with all of his might, and nodding in earnest to directions. He thought of the perpetrator. This all was sad and shocking news. "I always knew Doug was different," he says now, and he admits to suspecting "Doug Sims was homosexual, but I never thought he was a murderer."

After the body is removed from the crime scene, it has to be transported for the autopsy. In Westport autopsies are done at the funeral home. At the Mt. Olivet cemetery, Coroner Porter pronounced the victim's time of death at approximately 2:00 a.m. on March 10, 1990 for official documentation purposes. The body was photographed for evidentiary purposes and then transported to the Bass-Gasper Funeral Home, located in Westport, by Mike Gasper and Mike Porter.

On his way to the funeral home, Oldham studied the victim in his mind, turning it over like a puzzle. Whatever Sims used to cut the victim's throat needed to have a very sharp blade, for there were no "test" marks, meaning the perpetrator did it in one sweep. The victim's nudity indicated the possibility of a sex crime. A cut throat—the crime scene could be at Mariah's, the meat market where Sims worked, where Sims' job required him to slit animals throats, making it a sure and fast kill. The ligature marks cut deep into the wrist showed the victim struggled desperately. Oldham felt this might be evidence of a brutal struggle—possibly torture, or forced sex. The spontaneity of the crime showed in the hastily dug grave. The fact that Sims left Brad in an actual graveyard told him the killer had possessed some sort of remorse, and the hurriedly covered body and shallow digging told him his perpetrator was scared, high, or both. Obviously his first murder, the killer seemed to just want it over and done with.

Oldham had the crew stay in the cemetery for evidence gathering. Ed Lewis and the rest of the crew continued to search and photograph evidence. Tire tracks led into the cemetery and to the impromptu gravesite. If one followed them, they would see where the vehicle turned around near the grave and backed up. Lewis considered making plaster casts of these tire tracks so they could make matches later, but because of a light rain softening the earth, he realized a good cast would not be possible. A more defined set of tire tracks more suitable lay at the cemetery entrance, and they made a cast of the treads.

They found a pair of shorts and a sock just northeast of where they discovered the body. They were photographed, then retrieved and tagged as evidence. Steed's report noted that the shorts "had what appeared to be blood on them." Another sock, a shirt, and a butcher's sharpening steel, or knife sharpener, also turned up in the graveyard area. It was a "rat tail" type, meaning it was long, slender, and pointed at one end. These three items were discovered deeper in the brush surrounding the graveyard.

There are certain bags used for specific items of evidence. Wet items will "spoil," tainting the evidence, if kept in certain bag types, such as plastic. Sharp items require protective coverings over their blades, and protocol requires guns to be unloaded immediately after observation and states that they must be handled in a certain way (the movie-style "pencil in the barrel" method is incorrect). "I have actually opened a package that had a loaded gun in it," says one evidence technician. "On the inside of the package, the officer who sent it had wrote a note—'warning—loaded gun inside!'" Evidence tags should be completed and there is an evidence log for each crime scene area. A clear chain of evidence exists and requires technicians and officers to complete evidence tags and logs to fully document each crime scene as fully as possible.

Lewis ensured the scene was secured and then drove to the Bass-Gasper Funeral Home to observe the autopsy. Dr. Gene Gebele performed the autopsy with Mike Gasper, Lewis, Oldham, Smith, Snyder, and Porter witnessing.

Lewis photographed the autopsy and Sheriff Snyder videotaped. Again, it was crucial to catch every single piece of evidence.

The word "autopsy" originated from the ancient Greeks and, literally, means, "to see with one's own eyes." The first recorded autopsies include the ancient Egyptians removing the organs from the dead and mummifying them for the tombs. There are two types of autopsies: Forensic, performed for legal/medical means, and Clinical, to either determine cause of death or for research purposes. The body is brought into the Medical Examiner's room in a new, sterile body bag, which must be clean for each body so not to taint evidence. Both external and internal examinations are completed. External procedures will gather evidence such as fingernail clippings, residue, earth samples, and/or items tied on the body. Internal examinations will remove bullets or objects such as stomach contents, drug and alcohol residual, and body fluids.

Only a small section of spinal bone attached the head to the body, which was completely nude, except for one sock on each foot. Each wrist displayed red indentations carved into the skin, indicative of binds, like handcuffs, used on the victim. *Handcuffs*, Oldham thought back to the story Nugent told them, of the time in Sims' trailer, of the game he played with Brad. *"Who's going to jail?"*

Besides other pieces of evidence, Lewis noted the victim had a sock as a gag tied around his neck and through his mouth. Lewis collected this sock, holding it as evidence. Someone would make sure each piece of evidence was collected, bagged, sealed, and entered as a separate piece, evidence tags carefully and completely filled out. It was slow, meticulous work.

The goal of the autopsy is to determine cause of death. According to the results of this autopsy, the official cause of death was Exsanguination—Laceration. Due to the cutting of the series of veins in the throat, blood ceased flowing and the heart stopped pumping, rendering breathing impossible.

By the nature of the wound and the appearance, Brad did not live long after his throat was cut. His killer sliced open his carotid arteries and jugular veins, forcing the blood out quickly. Although it takes about three minutes for the brain to die after lacking oxygen, the body loses consciousness much more quickly, after about only fifteen to twenty seconds. Oldham surmised Sims probably let Brad bleed out in the bathtub, which explained the lack of blood on the floors in Sims' home. Or maybe it happened elsewhere? Oldham wondered why they found a knife sharpened in the woods at the graveyard. Dr. Gebele already declared with confidence that the cut on the victim's throat undeniably produced an "uncontrollable" blood spill and loss, a torrent of blood so swift that the cut could not even have been stopped by a doctor. The knife sharpener made no sense.

Something else bothered him: Toxicology testing showed Brad had a Blood Alcohol Content (BAC) of .04%, which indicated the murder probably took place shortly after he left his friends. Given Brad's height and body weight, he

145

undoubtedly felt the effects of the alcohol at the time of his death. Although probably not staggering drunk, the effects of the alcohol at least made him feel "tipsy." Those who loved Brad hoped this kept him from feeling any pain.

"This was a case worked that did not have DNA as a tool," one of the investigators notes later. DNA swabs can be taken from body fluids to include blood, hair, and mouth swabs and skin samples. However, it is not 100% foolproof. Although DNA testing first launched in 1985, it did not become available commercially until 1987. Although available, using it to collect and identify evidence did not occur until 1990, and not until 1992 in Indiana. The third court case to ever allow DNA evidence was in Indiana (Indiana vs. Hopkins). Deoxyribonucleic Acid, or DNA, is the genetic makeup of a cell.

Dr. Gebele returned the body to its normal appearance: he replaced the top of the skull, bagged the organs and placed them back into the body cavity, stitched up the Y-incision on the trunk, and carefully sewed the head back on. Finally, they placed the body into a bag known as a "shroud."

Someone (preferably in the family) must identify the body—a task no one should ever be forced to do. At 5:06 a.m. that morning, "Grandpa" Dave Giddings identified Bradley's body for legal purposes.

Bradley Daryl Maddux lived for 12 years, six months, and 19 days. His loved ones hoped his death had been quick, less than seconds.

Lindsay Maddux remembers her mother shaking her awake from a deep sleep. "Wake up, honey. Lindsay, wake up baby."

Lindsay took a few seconds to open her eyes. She had eyes, her mother realized, like Brad's. Lindsay would look a lot like her mother, but her eyes were Brad's. She blinked up at her mother.

"Lindsay—" How do you do this? How do you tell a child her cherished brother is gone?

Lindsay could hear the houseful of people, and she sat up, wide-eyed. She looked past her mother, mouth agape. Her dark hair was a tangled mess and she had sleep in the corner of one of her eyes. She started to give in to fear.

146

"Lindsay," Patti found the bravery from somewhere. "Brad's gone. Brad's gone away and he's not coming back."

"What?" Lindsay was not sure what this meant. Where did he go?

Patti's hands shook, and she took Lindsay's tiny hands in her own. It seemed to Patti that just yesterday they were newborn hands, tiny and wrinkled and out of the womb, perfect fingers and nails. "Doug...Doug Sims. Doug killed Brad. Brad is dead, and he's not coming home, baby. I'm so sorry."

Shock, grief, panic—it all set in on her, and Lindsay sat there, trying to comprehend it. One day Brad is there, catching frogs, playing "Army," cuddling Teddy, the dog, and the next second—? How could this be? Suddenly she found herself lying down again, her mom stroking her face and hair, soft tears dripping down, her mom's shoulders shaking hard, and Lindsay began asking herself, Dead? Where do you go when you are dead? The church said Heaven, but what was that?

Lindsay Maddux laid in bed that long night, her mother occasionally checking in on her, and she wondered what was happening, what was fair, and why Brad. Where is Brad?

Brad's schoolmate, Julie Ralston, found out as soon as her parents spoke to other volunteer firefighters. Her mother sat down with her and told her, "It was Brad Maddux." Julie felt her heart crumple. "It was very sad," Julie says today, and then hesitates. "It was...so sad."

Tasha Asher was at home, upstairs in her room listening to her radio when she heard the phone ring. She heard her mother talking quietly, and then silence. She thought nothing of it until her mother called her downstairs. Mrs. Asher sat her down and, not one to lie to her child, told her what she knew. "My friend and classmate had been murdered," Tasha explains. Slowly, crying great tears, Tasha walked leadenly back up to her room. She laid down on her bed, her mind reeling. "At that moment the song by the Eagles, 'Hotel California,' came on my radio," she recalls. "Ever since then, I associate that song with Brad."

Steve Rennekamp was the last person to go to bed at his

house that night. A news bulletin came on the local channel, announcing a "Decatur County boy was killed." Steve thought this odd; "nothing like that ever happened around here." Still, a long day full of familial activity left him tired and worn out, so he switched off the news and turned in. Probably no one he knew anyways, he decided.

The phone rang in Tammy and Jack Hileman's room at the hotel in Indianapolis. Tammy answered almost immediately. "Hello?"

"They found him." It was Patti's voice.

Tammy shifted her weight, trying to get comfortable, trying to wake up. She felt her husband awaken beside her. "What's going on?" she asked. "Is he alright?"

Suddenly a new voice came on the phone. "This is Dave, Tammy," said Dave Giddings. "Let me talk to Jack."

"What's wrong?" Tammy felt a strange twist in her throat. "What's going on? Dave, what happened?"

"I need to talk to Jack," Dave's voice sounded strange, and she could see through his attempts to protect her from something. "Let me talk to Jack."

"What is it? Is Brad alright? No, please, Dave, talk to me—" Tammy felt panic slowly loom and hang over her shoulder, and it was as if nothing existed except the phone, Dave's voice, and her knuckles, slowly turning white. At some point she stood up and found herself pacing the floor, supporting her baby with one hand, the phone in a death grip to her ear.

Jack reached for the phone and, numbly, she handed it to him. She was in a haze, and she watched Jack but did not see him. She could not hear him. He walked away from her, the phone receiver tight to his ear. He put his other hand to his face several times. Then he hung up. "We gotta go home," he told her.

Tammy managed to ask, "What's wrong?" She felt herself starting to shake, and her voice seemed to stop in her throat. Suddenly it all seemed surreal.

He started to pull bags from the closet, grab clothing and stuff them into the bags. "We gotta go home. I'll tell you later. We just...gotta go home."

"What's wrong?" Tammy asked, louder, "What's wrong? Jack, what's wrong?"

She watched in terror as he frantically stuffed toiletries into

148

their bags. "Get dressed."

She started shaking harder, and she sunk down to sit on the side of the bed.

"What's wrong? Jack, *please*..."

He stopped what he was doing and she saw tears in his eyes. He knelt down on one knee, took her hands in his and tried to look into her eyes. "Brad ..."

"No!"

"Honey, Brad was ..."

"What's wrong? No!" Tammy screamed.

"Brad was killed and..."

Car wreck, bike wreck, fell, drowned, accident, animal, motorcycle, tractor, farm...

"...And they have the man who killed him in jail. He cut his throat and buried him."

"To this day," Tammy Hileman says through tears, years later, "I can still hear myself screaming like I did that night."

Edward Lewis' day was not over. He drove to the home of Douglas Sims. Whitehead met him there to assist. Oldham and Smith arrived at the residence as well to investigate the case further. Using the same methodological care that he used at the graveyard, Lewis began photographing the outside of Sims' house. He started at the street and worked his way in, taking photographs of the white mobile home from all angles and then stepping closer to take more pictures.

The phone in Sam Sloan's home rang unusually early, and Sam tried to wake up as he reached for it. Now an adult, Sam still lived in Sardinia, and he worked nearby. He still saw Doug, of course, but their lives went in different directions. Socially, they could rarely find the time for one another. Sam had a family, and his kid was his world. Sam finally woke up enough to say, "Hello?"

"Oh my God! Holy shit, man!" It could only mean Randy Piles, his boyhood friend who also lived in Sardinia. Randy still worked for Duff's farm, on occasion. Evidently this was his day off. Sam could hear Randy's wife shouting in the background at the Pile's home. "Go look out your back door!"

"What?" Sam was rubbing sleep kernels out of his eyes.

"Go look out your back yard! Oh my God! Holy shit!"

Randy was puffing. "There's cops all over Doug's place, dude! They say he killed somebody!"

"Ahhh, bullshit." Sam started to place the receiver back on the hook when he heard Randy's wife shouting something about police taking pictures. Doug Sims? Yeah, right.

Randy apparently raced from window to window. "Something about a drug deal gone bad, and he smoked the dude and dumped him in the creek!"

Sam only wore his boxers and an undershirt, but to shut Randy up he shuffled out to his back porch, leaned on his fence, yawned audibly, and looked across to where their mutual boyhood friend resided. What he saw woke him up immediately. "What the hell?" he said into the receiver, more to himself than to his buddy.

Lewis, Oldham, and Smith located what appeared to be a fresh burn pile. This was nothing unusual for this part of the country; people burned trash often. But given the circumstances and situation of late, it did not appear to be good news for the investigators.

"I am guessing," Oldham said as he sifted through some ashes, "Some evidence just went up in smoke."

"I agree," Lewis said, using a short tree limb in an attempt to try to find something—anything—but it was a moot point. "Clothes, I bet..."

They located a shovel outside near the porch, "tagged and bagged" it after Lewis photographed it, and then they held it for evidence. Later, forensics attempted to match the dirt on the shovel to that in the graveyard.

Satisfied that Lewis carefully photographed everything outside of the home, photography moved to the inside of the residence.

Inside the residence, Lewis' careful eyes scanned the trailer. Nothing special, just a typical home for this area: used furniture, photographs on the wall; neat, but not fancy. It was obviously a bachelor's home. His eyes rested on a glass case that displayed knives.

Specially trained eyes and a closer search told them something else. "This place," an officer confides later, "was too clean, and had been cleaned just prior to our coming in. (We) touched the curtains...they had just been bleached." Someone ran his finger up over a doorframe and it came back clean. "That was suspicious for this place."

Something else troubled them, another officer confides. They found a fan set off to the side of the floor in the bedroom. Had it been used to quickly dry a floor that had to be cleaned in a hurry?

Several people involved in this case confessed that, to this date, they wonder if Doug Sims had assistance in cleaning up this crime scene. No one will ever know the answer to this, unless that person, or persons, comes forward and tells the truth.

They found suspected blood on the bathroom door and on the bathtub and collected it. Someone searching the spare bedroom located a pair of handcuffs and keys in the bottom of a dresser drawer. Technicians placed these in a sealed bag and completed an evidence tag. Lewis took pictures of all of the evidence.

Lewis noted something that both shocked and delighted him. It shocked him because of the degree of separation; it delighted him because it would make recovering evidence easier. He found a paycheck stub from the National Guard, paid to the order of Douglas Cecil Sims. Sims and Lewis were in the same National Guard unit.

When they felt they recovered enough evidence for the time being, they turned off the lights and locked the trailer. It was, again, long and meticulous work. The process remained every bit as tedious and methodical as it had been at the graveyard. Unlike crime scenes depicted on television, no one stomped around the scene, moved evidence and placed it elsewhere to photograph it, or picked up items in an attempt to taste or smell them. This is real life, and their investigation needed to be perfect.

And if anyone could do it, Sergeant Edward Lewis could. This is why he was also summoned to process Sims' truck. Also, it was all part of the same crime scene, and Lewis was in charge. He returned to the Westport Town Hall, where Indiana State Trooper Mark Strange met him. They located Sims' pickup, parked at the town hall. Lewis and Strange began processing the vehicle for evidence as it sat parked next to the school bus, where Doug Sims had last left it.

They noted a brown, 1982 Ford F-100 with 1989 Indiana state plates. They marked the VIN, or vehicle identification number, and took down the tires' make and size. They checked to see if the lights operated and if the truck had any additions, such as the top lights and a black bed liner. This was important information for witness testimony.

All of the information—the VIN number, plate number, car color, characteristics, contents of the glove compartment—gets recorded with extreme care. A VIN is the vehicle's fingerprint. Beginning in 1954, all vehicles received the number in manufacturing; in 1981, the National Highway Traffic Safety Administration required the VIN stamp on every car. The VIN number provides a history report: accidents, manufacturing, flood damage, air bags, and reports of theft. Manufacturers place their VIN numbers in varying locations: doors, dashboards, transmissions, and engine blocks, depending on the vehicle. Lewis knew the first character of the VIN represented the country where the truck was made, the second character pronounced the manufacturer, and the third designated the vehicle type. The fourth through eighth VIN characters identify body style, model, series, systems—it is the blueprint of that exact vehicle. The ninth character verifies the first through eighth characters, should someone try to amend them, and only the National Department of Transportation can establish them. Character ten identifies the model year of the vehicle, and eleven provides the assembly plant identification. Characters twelve through seventeen tell which number on the assembly line this particular vehicle came in on. Doug Sims' pickup told the officers everything they needed to know about the vehicle's history. Besides the VIN, Lewis and Strange discovered a lot more interesting information from the two-toned brown truck.

The vehicle appeared recently cleaned. Not just washed, but power-washed, like the kind used at a carwash with the wand. However, few people can truly remove everything incriminating; no one considers how residue, particularly liquids, rolls off of a vehicle to the undercarriage. They found dirt and grass samples to match to the earth and grass at the cemetery, which enabled them to provide a comparison between the soil and grass they discovered on the shovel. Evidence, but not a "gotcha," like blood evidence. Lewis and Strange went over "every nut, bolt, and screw" Lewis explains, "but found absolutely no blood

152

evidence." Both men slowly grew discouraged. The lack of sleep, the horror of the crime, and the meticulous search started to frazzle nerves.

They examined the multiple-striped brown seat cover. The truck sported a black bed liner and a custom guard, neither of which comes standard with the truck, attached to the bed and tailgate of Sims' truck. "I have an idea," Lewis said. Lewis walked over to the tailgate and began the process of removing the guard.

He turned the first screw, and blood poured down the side of the pickup truck.

Sims washed the truck with the tailgate down, and he did not consider that blood would pool under the guard. The high-pressure water forced the blood into the screw holes, literally sealing the blood into the gaps. When the officers loosened the screws, it released the pressure, revealing the blood trapped within.

Not only did blood run down in a trail along the truck, but they found blood evidence under and around the screw holes, as well as around the tailgate where the guard kept the wash from cleaning it. It rested inside of the tailgate when they opened the bed of the truck. Both officers nodded at each other, and one retrieved a kit to remove and retrieve this evidence. They later confirmed that the blood sample matched that of Bradley Maddux, and they also matched the tires on Sims' truck to the tire tracks in the old cemetery.

After they took all of the necessary steps to complete a thorough investigation of the truck, Lewis sealed the truck and kept the keys. He left no chance that a defense attorney might accuse him of allowing someone to taint evidence.

Through it all, the stuffed toy devil in the truck rear window grinned at the officers. Its white, suction cup hands against the glass, it hung there, appearing to watch them work.

While Lewis busied himself by processing the search of Sims' house and then his truck, Terry Steed returned to the Mt. Olivet Cemetery. It was about 8:30 a.m., and he knew farmers were already awake and working; the community innocently embraced the morning. By the time Steed arrived, Deputy Templeton already replaced Deputy Klene on the continuous search, but not until after Klene made another discovery: a pair of tennis shoes in the brush south of the cemetery.

"We have to find that knife, the murder weapon," Steed said grimly, as he surveyed the scene.

Strange nodded in agreement.

Steed looked around the area, his mind turning over the information. Was Sims right or left-handed? If he was into sports ... sports... how far could he throw? The two officers began combing the thick brush, slapping the bugs that buzzed up to annoy them.

Oldham and Smith arrived. Both looked road-weary, like they drank enough coffee and saw enough horrors in the night to last for years. They joined Steed and Strange at the edge of the brush.

"We need to find that knife," Steed said, and Oldham nodded. Steed looked around again. "I was trying to determine, where would he stand? How far would he throw it? But it could be anywhere."

If it is here at all, both men thought silently. Oldham and Smith began their own searches, clawing at tall weeds that slapped at them, pushing through the tangles of vines and old limbs. Their boots crunched, sounding like giants crashing about to the animals that bolted at the sound of their approaching bodies.

"Klene had found a pair of tennis shoes over there," Steed pointed to the brush south of the cemetery. He moved slowly through the woods, pushing, pulling, feeling the briars and bristles pull at his uniform and tug on his gun belt. He started to feel dejected, until he heard Oldham shout.

Everyone stopped to look up.

Jon Oldham stood about sixty feet from where the body was found, southeast from its location. He pointed at the ground. "It's here," he said, "The knife." Oldham checked his watch. It was 9:04 a.m.

On movies and television, actors pick up evidence, look at it, and return it. This taints the evidence and simply is inexcusable in real investigations. Protocol necessitates evidence must remain in place until photographed and properly documented. Oldham appointed Strange to guard this precious piece of evidence until the evidence technician, Lewis, could return and secure it properly.

"Good job," Smith sighed, happy it was located. The knife

was long, large, and had what appeared to be blood on it. Smith joined Oldham and Steed, and the three prepared to return to Doug Sims' residence.

Rob Nugent was exhausted. After he gave his story to the police and the families, reporters wanted to interview and record him, and the little boy was both emotionally and physically worn out. Mrs. Nugent received a phone call; she spoke softly, and then hung up, her hand over her mouth. She walked over to where her son slept, sank down on the couch next to him, and wondered how a person does this. Rob was just a little boy. She rubbed his thin shoulders and patted his back softly.

"Robby, honey, are you awake?" She knew he had slept fitfully. "Honey, Bradley is no longer with us. He was killed." She stroked the back of his head.

Rob did not move.

"Did you hear me? Are you okay?" She saw him nod slightly.

Rob forced his eyes to open, rolled over to look at his mother. He saw her expression and knew it was true. His heart told him the truth, but his brain refused to accept it until he heard her. "Yes," his voice sounded so small. "I already know." He turned his face back towards the couch. He heard his mother start to cry, and her voice held a treble.

"Are you okay?"

"I want to be left alone," Rob managed. He could feel her hand rub his back, shoulders, and the back of his head. He felt her stand up and move away. A tear slid down the side of his face, and another followed it. Rob squeezed his eyes tight. He could see Patti Maddux's face when he told her the truth about that night. The anger inside of him began to grow, and he did not think it was possible to hate Doug Sims any more than he already did. But most of all, Rob Nugent began to hate himself.

Jill Bishop accompanied her parents to the Westport general store, located in the heart of downtown. They met another family there and waved. "Did you hear?" someone asked.

Jill stood there while the adults told her parents when and

155

where Brad Maddux, her friend and school chum, was brutally murdered. No one really knew any details yet, but it was definitely Brad.

Jill felt "devastated. Nothing like this had ever happened in our area." She also felt heartbroken; she counted Brad as a friend.

At Sims' house, not far from the market where Jill Bishop received the sickening news, Sheriff Snyder and Technician Lewis still worked diligently inside the residence. Oldham, Steed, and Smith began a search of the exterior area, should there be any evidence outside of the home.

"The only unusual thing we found," Steed noted in his official report, "was a patch of Sims' gravel driveway which appeared to have been turned over with a rake or shovel." The men scraped some of the gravel and dirt back to search for blood evidence but located nothing. Someone noted a square-nosed shovel, caked in mud and gravel, near the porch of the trailer.

As he left at the end of his shift, Steed stretched, arching his back and pushing against the steering wheel of his vehicle, pointed the nose of his cruiser toward home, ready to get away, and hoped he fell asleep fast. To his dismay, he found it impossible to forget Sims' passive face as he calmly admitted he murdered a child. He could not stop thinking of Sims' focus on attending a family reunion instead of focusing on a confession to such a horrific deed. "Maybe," Steed mused, "He was so used to killing hogs at Mariah Packing, maybe it just didn't bother him."

By the time daylight crept into the sky, turning the shades of purple and dark blue into deep orange and pink, Sergeant Lewis' night shift was far from over. Stifling a yawn and stretching his limbs, he prepared to return to where he began: CR 1300 S, west of CR 1050 W: Mt. Olivet Cemetery. Now it was time to take photographs of the crime scene during the daylight. Sergeant Lewis began his task with the same methodical care as he had so many hours before.

In the night, CR 1300 S, CR 1050 W, and Mt. Olivet Cemetery are encased in black, as if dipped in ink. Nocturnal animals rustle through the wood, foraging for something. Lights catch their eyes in matching yellow orbs. Even with the heavy-duty fireman's floodlights, it had been difficult to see everything. A second, daytime search was demanded. Besides, Lewis returned to crime scenes several times to ensure he missed nothing.

The technicians logged the pair of tennis shoes and the knife into evidence. The officers took the shovel they confiscated from Sims' residence and compared it to marks in the earth at the burial site. Lewis took more photographs; again, far more than they felt necessary. The officers planned to take aerial photos of the area, including Sims' residence, later in the week. Lewis served in the Navy on a guided missile destroyer for several years; after becoming a State Trooper, he joined the Army National Guard as a pilot in an Air Ambulance (MEDIVAC) unit. As a certified pilot, Lewis used a helicopter to take aerial photos of all major cases and crime scenes.

Lewis made a note to return to the cemetery on March 13, 1990 for another walk around the crime scene. After one final search, and all officers and technicians agreed that nothing else could be done on that day, they "released" the scene, meaning the officers departed the area. Upon his return to the Decatur County Jail, Sergeant Lewis seized Douglas Sims' clothing and bagged it as evidence.

Lewis' long night and even longer morning left him tired and weary, but he still had work to do, and he diligently filed his reports. Popular television shows such as "Cops" and "CSI" do not often show this boring and tedious side of police work. Officers spend more time writing reports than doing the actual investigative work. If it is not written down, as the saying goes, it did not happen.

When officers completed the evidence list for case #42-8321, it read:

Plaster casts of footprints from cemetery
Plaster cast of tire tracks from cemetery
Beer can from cemetery
Pepsi can from cemetery
Wash cloth with possibly blood from cemetery
Under shorts with possibly blood from cemetery
Beer bottle from cemetery
Yellow Purdue shirt with possible blood
Knife sharpner steel from cemetery

Tennis shoes from cemetery
White socks with possibly blood from cemetery
Shovel from residence of accused
Army type tee shirt from accused residence
Handcuffs and key from bedroom
Pants and shirt from bedroom
Suspected blood from bedroom door
Suspected blood from bathroom
Knife from cemetery
Suspected blood from truck
Chrome tail gate protector from truck
Sock from victim used as gag
Victims socks
Victims blood
Victims stomach contents
Victims hair
Rectal and oral swabs
Suspect clothing
Suspect shoes
Knife from National Guard
Map and cash register receipts
Grass from pickup wheel well
Accused blood
(*Sic*)

Lewis transferred the items to the GHQ laboratory with a request for tests. It was not enough for Sims to confess to the murder of Bradley Maddux. Evidence needed to prove, beyond a shadow of a doubt, that Sims did in fact knowingly and intentionally take the life of a twelve-year-old boy. Absolute proof assured that Sims could have no appeals, no innocent pleas, no backtracking on what he told Oldham. Officers needed Sims' fingerprint, so to speak, on the crime. Witnesses, confessions, and audiotape all helped build the case, but evidence—blood, prints, hairs and fibers—was nearly impossible to argue. Still, the defense could argue anything, seeking loopholes in the investigation.

The situation demanded that officers be constantly ready; they soon were glad that they took the appropriate precautions while investigating the case.

Junior Armstrong and Rob Nugent could recall that morning stroll with the girls, where they stopped to rest under the huge cedar tree.

Normally, they always walked around that cedar tree to the back of the old cemetery, passing under its branches. For some reason, that morning they did not go around the tree. They walked as far as the gravel, stopped to chat for a while longer and escape the falling mist, then turned to go back to CR 1300 S.

Had they followed their normal route and unleashed their natural curiosity, the scene unearthed would have haunted them for the rest of their lives.

8 MITIGATING & AGGRAVATING CIRCUMSTANCES

At 6:00 p.m. that Sunday, March 11, 1990, the Indiana State Police handed out an official press release on the murder of Bradley Maddux and subsequent arrest of Douglas Sims. The neatly typed, one page piece meant to answer the who, what, where, and when of the murder. The press release did not reveal half of the horror. It did not give an iota of the terror. It read, in part:

Bradley Maddux's body was recovered from a shallow grave south of Alert (a small unincorporated community in SW Decatur County) at approximately 0315 HRS. Sun. 03-11-90. His cause of death is still under investigation   pending further medical investigation (sic).

It listed the officers involved in the investigation and their badge numbers, the agencies involved in the investigation, and reduced the victim and perpetrator to a name, date of birth, and series of informational bits on a sheet of paper. Already "the story," as newsrooms referred to this crime, grew into a local legend; Decatur County never experienced anything like this murder since its founding. To this day, when someone mentions the name "Bradley Maddux;" the eyes of the community grow sad and their expression grim.

Prosecutor William O. Smith held a press conference in front of the Decatur County Jail. Sergeant Jon Oldham stood behind him in a somber dark suit and a white shirt and tie. Westport Town Marshall Charles Whitehead attended, along with Trooper Terry Steed and Sheriff Larry Snyder, all in uniform. The men's faces were grave, their appearance professional.

The hype of the case started. "It was the shock of the century," recalls one long-time resident of Sardinia, who taught Doug Sims in high school. The chorus began by so many residents saying, "It could never happen here."

"It was a complete shock," echoes a friend of both the

160

Maddux family and Doug's family. "A huge shock a young boy was killed, and that Doug Sims did it." Trying to make sense of what had happened, the friend considered that Doug Sims was "a closet homosexual and panicked... but I never suspected him of being gay or a pedophile."

"I'll be honest," said a Sardinia resident, a man who lived alone, "I never locked my door until that (murder) happened."

Another resident referred to the news of the murder as, "Horror. Just horror."

Brad's third-grade romance, Sheila Padgett, rode in the car with her parents on their way to church. The route took them from Westport to Alert. As they drove the usual, leisurely route, the elder Padgetts noted a vehicle whose driver was waving them down. When they stopped, they realized it was Judy, Brad's maternal aunt and good friend of Mrs. Padgett. They noted with alarm that Judy was sobbing.

"Judy, whatever is the matter?" Mrs. Padgett asked. Sheila, still in elementary school, just sat and listened to the adults. "He's gone!" Judy managed to say through the nonstop tears. "Brad's gone! Brad's gone!"

"What do you mean?" Mr. Padgett chimed in now. "Missing?"

As the adults talked frantically back and forth, Sheila tried to make sense of it all. Her family finally drove to church and Sheila did still not comprehend. "Gone?" she asked. From then on, "I can only remember bits and pieces," Sheila Padgett says today.

Summer Hobbs awoke that morning and received the news. "I woke up to the tragic news Mush killed Brad." Years later, Summer Hobbs cried unstoppable tears at the mention of that morning. "I didn't like the idea Brad was around Mush anyway," she sobs. "And he never came back." She thought of Brad's smile, his laugh, and his freckles. She thought of that eerie feeling she always got around Mush. Where did he come from, anyway? "It had just seemed like, plop, and he was there," she recalls. The ache hurt so badly, she found it difficult to breath.

By now, Rob Nugent fled his house and sought refuge outside, trying to get his mind to function, trying to make sense of it all. He did what he did best, what he knew he

161

could control: he worked on an engine. He saw one of his friends, a girl from the neighborhood, walking across their lawn. Rob glanced about and noticed the girl walking toward Mrs. Nugent as she tried to keep her mind occupied by hanging up the day's laundry on the clothesline. He returned to his work until his mother's scream pierced the air. Rob ran over to where his mother held onto the clothesline, a hand covering her mouth, tears gushing forth. His mother had lost control, and now, in the little boy's presence, she had to walk away. "What's going on?" Rob demanded of their visitor, who looked back at him with red-rimmed eyes. He could only think of Junior. Junior was Brad's best friend, and he had such anger already. Did Junior do something bad or horrid?

"I can't," the girl shook her head, her face contorted with pain.

"What is it?" Rob demanded. "Is it Junior?"

The girl's eyes rimmed with tears. "They found Brad's clothes in the bushes," she finally admitted. "They found Brad in the cemetery. I...they say his head was almost cut off."

Rob stared at her stoically, nodded, then returned to his project in the shed. Each step he took, words rang out: why...not...me? When he went to lean over the engine project, the tears gushed forth and his small frame shook. "Why, God?" he asked aloud, "Why didn't you take me, not Brad?" He looked at his hands. He was sickly, always something going wrong. "I'm a burden anyway," the little boy told God that day in the shed. "I'm always sick. I always cost money." He punched the engine, and came close to falling into a heap. His anger for Doug Sims rolled in his stomach like a hot, putrid lump; it hurt so much his body ached, and at the same time, he felt even angrier with himself. "I could have stopped it," he said to the ground, to the machine, to himself. "I should have stopped it." He doubled over, holding his stomach. "It should have been me," the boy sobbed. "It should have been me." And this became Rob Nugent's personal anthem for a long, long time.

Kenny Nugent, now living away from Westport, received a phone call from a relative. He could not believe the son of

162

his friends died such a brutal death, at the hands of someone he knew. Kenny graduated with one of Sims' siblings. What could he say to them? "We're still friends," he says now. "I have never mentioned it."

One farmer, who lived down the road from Sims, just shook his head as he perused the daily headlines. Doug Sims? The farmer lived in Sardinia his whole life and grew up near Sims, who was a year ahead of him in school. "We rode the bus together for three or four years," he recalls. They passed one another in the hallways of school, or saw each other in public and spoke socially. The farmer recalls no one really disliking Doug Sims, but he was one of those fellows who "wasn't overly outgoing, nor was he overly reclusive. He was just an average guy." The farmer does remember one detail, but at the time he had no idea it related to his acquaintance. The night Sims buried Brad in the graveyard, this gentleman happened to drive past Mt. Olivet Cemetery. "I noticed (tire) tracks," he said, which was unusual, which one did not often find "coming out of the graveyard."

The rumors blossomed like tall stalks of corn during a fertile season. To preserve case integrity, those who knew the details of the case needed to remain silent until the right time. Mt. Olivet Cemetery became akin to a tourist trap. A line of cars wound through Alert, Indiana and down the gravel road both day and night. People came to pay respects, to gawk, or to show out-of-towners the spot of the worst tragedy Westport knew. The cemetery drew particularly heavy traffic at night.

Another dynamic took place: people began locking their doors. Parents no longer allowed their children to play out of their line of sight, if they allowed them out at all. An awareness of evil, of meeting the devil, was born.

One of Lindsay Maddux's best friends was Shona Erwin, who attended the same school but lived out in a rural area. "We lived in a very, very small town," she explains now. "Things got strict, after Brad was killed." Shona's mother, once so trusting, began insisting she meet the parents of her child's friends, and she required the presence of adults with children at all times. The days of riding a bicycle around with friends, or lazing together at the swimming hole unsupervised, vanished. Shona's family lived "'way

163

out in the country," but she says they "started to lock our doors at night."

Cody Shane Maddux was angry. It emanated from him, as if every pore in his body sweated hate and anger. His hurt and pain scared people. "He was so angry," says a mutual friend, "I was afraid, wondering how he'll grow up."

A family member said of Cody, "He scared me. He just walked around pissed off. God, he was mad." It shone in his eyes, in his body, in the way he sat and walked and stood. He yearned to go tear the jailhouse apart, brick by brick, to get to Douglas Sims. Then he was wanting to slowly, literally, tear Sims apart.

"You have to understand Westport, and because of its size," explains a resident. As a preteen, "You could only choose who you hung out with so much. That group of kids (Brad, Rob, and Junior) could have been anybody that night. It's scary... As a mother, you can do everything right and this still happens. In Westport, you always knew where your kids were. It could have been anybody. And it didn't have to be anybody at all."

Secretly whispering to one another, parents and young adults began discussing the factor of alcohol in the crime. Alcoholic beverages were a part of everyone's history. Restaurants and bars in Indiana serve alcohol Monday through Saturday from 7:00 a.m. to 3:00 a.m. They served alcohol on Sundays from 10:30 a.m. to 12:30 a.m.

There was still so much to do for the investigative team. Oldham conducted a background search on Sims. He carefully typed in the information: Douglas Cecil Sims, DOB 06/02/1961, white male, height six foot, one inch, weight 195 lbs., brown hair, brown eyes, and other information. The NCIC (National Crime Information Center) received the information for processing. NCIC is a computerized index of information, including information on missing persons, weapons, criminal history, and stolen property. It is an FBI maintained database, available to limited law enforcement agencies 24/7 and provides information, agency to agency, on criminal behavior and crime scenes. Oldham checked to see if Sims had a warrant, prior arrests, or any illegal activity that had been reported prior to this date.

Nothing major came back. Oldham's eyes scanned the

flimsy Teletype. The only record found of wrongdoing by Sims was the January 14, 1982 traffic ticket received in Kentucky for driving the wrong direction on a one-way road. Of course, the system was not foolproof. If an agency did not report an incident to NCIC, if Sims gave a false name or DOB, false social security number, he still existed in the system somewhere. Nothing is foolproof, and all computers are just machines run by humans. A wrong keystroke, a missing letter, or a missed piece of paper could keep someone from showing in the system. To be sure, Oldham would submit a fingerprint card to match with the billions of other fingerprints. Unlike data, fingerprints cannot be faked or manipulated.

He prepared a list on a sheet of yellow legal paper of "Witnesses to contact" in painfully scripted cursive:

David Mangrin — saw Sims working gravel in driveway on Saturday morning. Works at Mariah.

Jeff and Ann — brought Bradley to Jr's from downtown? Time? Where picked up?

The Meadows — what time did Jr. Armstrong and Robbie Nugent leave apartment? At (address).

D.J. Braddick — Was walking in tent area with Bradley in early a.m. — possibly at Bensons?

Denny Benson — Said Bradley knocked on door for beer.

Chan Vandecall — Sold liquor to Sims, including 'Purple Passion.'

Irma Cottage — Sims' neighbor. A former teacher. Said Sims was "SLOW" in school! Saw nothing.

Kevin Mangrin (David's father) said Sims' "elevator did not go to top floor."

Check bank records of Sims — rumor is he paid boys with checks for-?

Check military for Sims' bases. Ed Lewis said unit at Shelbyville had given him several "boning" knives (He was a cook).

Rodney Casey — lives across from Sims. Did not get a chance to interview. I get the impression he was avoiding me.

Ed Lewis followed up on the pay stub from the National Guard by old-fashioned police work; people used to call detectives "flat foots" because people joked that detectives wore out their shoes and feet from so much walking. Lewis paid a visit to his own company and asked someone, "This guy is in our unit?" He received an affirmative response and found out then that, yes, Sims was a cook in the unit.

"The military will assign you property for your job," he explains carefully, "And when they do, you sign a form, a receipt, stating you have that property. It is a way of both keeping inventory of an item and maintaining accountability." Sure enough, Sims the cook signed out for a large boning knife.

This receipt went into the evidence file.

On Monday, March 12, 1990, the state of Indiana, represented by William O. Smith, the prosecuting attorney, formally filed charges of Count I, Murder, a Felony I.C. 35-42-1-1 (1); and Count II: Child Molesting, a Class D Felony I.C. 35-42-4-3. In a criminal court, only probable cause must be proven. The court felt, thanks to the excellent job of the law enforcement officials involved, such probable cause existed. Douglas remained imprisoned without bail. Case number 16500-9101-CR-00042 began.

The child molestation charge was "alleged and filed to make it possible and relevant to admit a greater range and variety of evidence in a jury trial," explained one of the legal professionals involved in the case. This trial tactic allows for the possibility of the death penalty at sentencing. It would be the State's position to prove molestation occurred "Beyond a Reasonable Doubt." Law enforcement and judgment cannot automatically throw someone into a death row cell just because they committed a horrific crime; "to secure a conviction in which the death penalty is involved almost always requires a jury trial." Under Indiana law, even if the team could prove child molestation in this case, it would dovetail with the murder charge and become part of the sixty-year sentence. Indiana could not increase Sims' time to seventy, ninety, or one hundred years.

William O. Smith was in his fifth year as prosecuting attorney for Decatur County. He was not one to say, "It can't happen here" because he knew it could, and it would. He knew all kinds of crimes happened in this little county, just like in "the big city." The things people did to one another never amazed him, and this local attorney saw, and heard, just about everything. Smith originally started working as an attorney in Greensburg. He was also active in his community doing philanthropy work. He was also interested in the history of Indiana, and he loved research.

The case would be tried in the Circuit Court of Judge John Andrew Westhafer. Some people in the legal community saw this as good news; others raised an eyebrow.

Judge Westhafer first ascended the bench in 1976 upon election, and he began serving in January 1977. Born a "local boy," he attended Greensburg High School until he graduated in 1958. He attended Purdue University and graduated in 1962 with a Bachelor's Degree in History and English. Westhafer continued his studies at Washington University, earning his law degree in 1965. After practicing in Lafayette, he returned to his roots in 1969. He practiced law before becoming the Greensburg City Attorney in 1971, and he held this position until 1975. When not serving on the Bench, Judge Westhafer was "grandpa" to his grandkids; he enjoyed traveling, particularly to the ancient, romantic city of Paris, France. He looked more like a "grandpa" than a judge, with his easy smile, short, neat hair parted on the side, trim moustache, and eyeglasses. But when the black Judge's robe came on, he was all business.

Westhafer served as the Judge in the 1989 capital murder case of Stuart Kennedy, a month-long trial that left nerves jangling. In October of 1986, Kennedy, a twenty-six-year-old white male, abducted twenty-two-year-old Michelle Seagraves as she got into her Ford Grenada at her apartment complex in Columbus, Ohio. Kennedy and an accomplice then robbed The Peoples National Bank in Moores Hill, Indiana and used the Granada as a getaway car. His accomplice later led the police to Seagraves' body. They shot her execution style to the back of the head and strangled her with a leather strap, cruelly left around her throat. The horrific case landed in Westhafer's courtroom due to a change in venue. Judge Westhafer sentenced Stuart Kennedy to the death chambers. In 1992 Westhafer again sentenced Kennedy to death, overriding a jury recommendation and without a hearing in compliance with the state's Supreme Court. In 1995 Kennedy came before the judge again, and he received a sentence of 118 years in prison. The technicality saved Stuart Kennedy from the gallows, but he would no longer walk the streets a free man. Judges do not like their sentences overturned, but they acknowledge that it is part of the process. Later, Judge Westhafer remembers the Kennedy case as the most memorable in his career.

This time, in 1990, Circuit Court Judge John Andrew Westhafer was facing another high profile murderer when Douglas C. Sims stood before him.

The state appointed Attorney Brent Lee Westerfield to represent Sims, who was declared indigent. Sims had less than $200.00 in a checking account. The bank financed both his truck and his home; he still owed payments. Westerfield was from the Public Defender's office. This irked some people—how can this killer receive free legal advice? How fair was that, when Brad still lay unburied? Brad Maddux, with his easy smile and sweet ways, never received justice.

It angered many, to the point of shouting over tabletops in restaurants and angry arguments in family homes. "Some people were trying to get arrested, hoping they'd be locked up with Sims," recalls Greg Allen, "So they could get a hold of him." But this is how the United States legal system operates. Everyone charged with a crime receives a guarantee of Due Process—the right to an attorney, the right to have their case heard by a jury, and protection from self-incrimination. They have the right to fair and equal treatment; no one has the right to automatically condemn someone because of their race, nationality, or by the crime they are charged. Despite the fact Douglas Sims admitted guilt and told where he buried Brad, he still legally received Due Process: law enforcement could not beat or torture him, the courts could not skip the trial, and prisons could not make up new rules for him to live by because he murdered a child. Some people argue this is unfair.

Observations about legal proceedings throughout history led to the creation of due process. The U.S. based its laws and rules on those of England, while also incorporating the changes the founding forefathers wished to make. If accused of a crime in England, the suspect received no opportunity to defend him or herself, regardless of guilt, innocence, or lack of proof. Douglas Sims received these "unfair" rights as a result of hundreds of years of effort towards creating equality in the court system so that a person could have a chance for a fair and equal trial. And a fair and equal trial was what he was to have.

They set the trial for July 9, 1990 at 9:00 o'clock a.m. sharp. The attorneys prepared themselves; Douglas Sims entered a plea of "not guilty." They had four months to prepare for the biggest thing to hit this part of their world since the fire of 1872.

Murder is the unlawful killing of a human being with malice aforethought. Every murder perpetrated by poison, lying in wait, or any other kind of willful, deliberate, malicious, and premeditated killing; or committed in the perpetration of, or attempt to perpetrate, any arson, escape, murder, kidnapping, treason, espionage, sabotage, aggravated sexual abuse or sexual abuse, child abuse, burglary, or robbery; or perpetrated as part of a pattern or practice of assault or torture against a child or children; or perpetrated from a premeditated design unlawfully and maliciously to effect the death of any human being other than him who is killed, is murder in the first degree.

The unlawful killing appeared obvious, but the prosecutor's job included proving Douglas Sims did take the life of Bradley Maddux beyond the shadow of a doubt. Along with the confession, officers must provide physical evidence to prove the crime. A confession simply was not enough. Officers knew the defense; Sims' attorneys could and would try to throw any confession out of court. The prosecution needed to prove beyond a reasonable doubt that Sims did take the life of Bradley Maddux, both willfully and premeditatedly.

"Willful" might prove difficult. The prosecution had to prove the murder was not accidental. Bradley did not slip and fall, he did not commit suicide, and he did not die as a result of a struggle for the knife. Again, the investigation team needed to gather evidence, including photographs, lab reports, and coroner's testimony. This was not like a popular television drama where everything magically fell into place in fifty minutes, including airtime for commercials. Officers wanted to close the case on Douglas Sims and ensure this man paid for his crime, and they wanted it done professionally and legally. Each time they looked at the photograph of the smiling little boy, their hearts melted. No one deserved this, and Bradley was a gentle soul. Anyone who knew him immediately described him as such. "He was a sweet boy," his first cousin, Gretchen, would say over and over. "Sometimes people took advantage of it." Not anymore, investigators vowed.

"Premeditated" would be, possibly, the most difficult to prove. The State would have to explain Douglas Sims' mindset and show, by testimony, evidence, and confession, how he lured Bradley Maddux back to the trailer for the purpose of attacking him.

The crime of murder is specific in the United States; states can also define what they consider "murder." There is no "murder of a child." The law usually defines first-degree murder as "an unlawful killing that is both willful and premeditated" meaning the killer planned the murder "lying in wait."

The legal system usually views second-degree murder as a non-premeditated murder resulting from an assault in which death was a well-defined possibility.

After first-degree and second-degree murder, the next possible charge is manslaughter. Manslaughter is usually defined as the unlawful killing of a person without malice or premeditation to do injury.

Little of this mattered for Sims, as Indiana only employs one criminal charge for murder; there is no second- or third-degree. "Once a person is convicted of murder, the nature of the murder is considered at sentencing," explains an Indiana attorney who practiced in the state for the entirety of his legal career. "Once a person is convicted of murder, the death penalty could be imposed; certain statutory factors can be proved beyond a shadow of a doubt, in a separate trial, on that issue alone."

In Indiana, there are aggravating factors for capitol capital punishment:

(1) The murder was especially heinous, atrocious, cruel or depraved (or involved torture).

(2) The capital offense was committed during the commission of, attempt of, or escape from a specified felony (such as robbery, kidnapping, rape, sodomy, arson,

oral copulation, train wrecking, carjacking, criminal gang activity, drug dealing, or aircraft piracy).

(3) The murder was committed from a motor vehicle or near a motor vehicle that transported the defendant.

(4) The murder was committed by intentionally discharging a firearm into an inhabited dwelling.

(5) The defendant killed the victim while lying in wait.

(6) The murder was committed by means of a bomb, destructive device, explosive, or similar device.

(7) The defendant caused or directed another to commit murder, or the defendant procured the commission of the offense by payment, promise of payment, or anything of pecuniary value.

(8) The victim of the murder was less than 12 years of age.

(9) The victim was a pregnant woman, and the murder resulted in the intentional killing of a fetus that has attained viability.

Had Brad been only one year younger, Doug Sims would immediately be on his way to the Death House. If the incident happened only seven months earlier, before Brad turned twelve, Sims would have no chance to escape death.
Indiana's method of execution has changed over the years. Until 1913, those sentenced to death walked the slow, long walk to the gallows "to be hung by the neck until dead." The electric chair came into use in 1994, sending volts, at one minute each, through the condemned person's body until the doctor pronounced them dead. Lethal injection began in 1995; Code 35-38-6 requires executions take place inside Indiana State Prison at Michigan City Institution prior to sunrise. In 1990, the Indian courts sentenced three people to death row. Currently, ninety-four murderers reside on Indiana's death row, the majority of them white males in their twenties who had shot and killed a stranger. Sims would not claim a cell with these inmates, carrying a

neatly folded bundle of sheets, blanket, and inmate clothing to set up his new home. Cody Maddux ruminates over this, years later. "You know, in Indiana you can get the death penalty for killing a cow," he refers to an ancient law that remains on the records. "You can be hung in the public square."

Three main factors make the prosecution of criminals in crimes against children difficult to achieve successfully: law, time, and people.

Prosecution of molestation relies heavily on the victim's testimony. Some victims are as young as newborn, which makes their testimony impossible to receive. Many well-practiced molesters know how to leave no traceable physical evidence, which makes proof difficult at best, impossible at worst. To add to the difficulty of gathering evidence, some parents refuse to allow their child to testify or be questioned for a variety of reasons: shame, guilt, religious reasons, trauma, or simply wanting to leave well enough alone. "The past is the past," one victim's parent explained to an investigator. "We'll let God take care of it." Because cases are often time-sensitive, evidence trails fade quickly and investigators must act quickly and efficiently.

The average criminal spends about one year waiting—from the time of their arrest to the moment of their trial—while the police investigate the crime thoroughly.

Some people who are charged with a crime are innocent; many are not. The system is not perfect. Like everything else run by people, it has some flaws. Consider that out of about every one hundred crimes committed, fifty of those people get arrested; and out of those fifty, twenty will go to trial, yet cases still overload every court in the state. If every case went to trial, courts would back up for years and years. Thus the reason for plea-bargaining and probation: there would be no possible way to hear every case that resulted in arrest: listening to and judging every case that resulted from an arrest is impossible. If cases overloaded the courtrooms, the system would soon be bankrupt.

Through it all, Brad's friends heard the adults talking amongst themselves, over and around the little ones' heads. Some wanted to go burn Doug's trailer to the

172

ground, as if that would solve something. Others discussed lynch mobs—old-fashioned justice. This was scary; no one said things like that in Westport... Until that day.

As Doug Sims was being arraigned in court, the staff at Brad's school, South Decatur Elementary, prepared for their own drama. The Decatur County Community School Corporation implemented their crisis program in full force for their students and staff, bringing in social workers, guidance counselors, an additional nurse, and substitute teachers to offer solace and help answer questions. One of their tasks involved providing instructors with a packet of materials on the grieving process, as well as which signs of behavior to look out for per each grade level. Teachers willingly sat down with several of Brad's closest friends, catching their tears and, sometimes, crying with the children. One of Brad's acquaintances recalls that first Monday was "weird and painful."

Teacher Jean Hickey prepared for that morning still shocked herself. "I think everybody was affected," she says now. "No one expected something like this to happen in a small community."

Despite the fact that spring break was lingered just around the corner, the students of South Decatur Elementary came in on Monday, March 12, very quietly. Even the school bus ride was silent. One of Brad's friends recalled waiting for the bus, then hopping on and finding a seat next to a friend.

The students made no noise, looking down at their shoes instead of playfully calling out to one another. "What's going on?" The boy punched his friend.

"You don't know?"

"My family was busy all weekend," he explained.

The other boy proceeded to explain. "Brad Maddux was murdered. He's—he's gone."

"What!"

"Brad Maddux was murdered," whispered the boy. A few others glanced up and quickly away.

Silence enveloped them for the rest of the ride to school.

They did no schoolwork that day. "It was as if a black veil hung over South Decatur Elementary," recalls a school chum of Brad's. Guidance counselors went room to room to make announcements and answer questions, when possible, trying to do their best to quell fears and catch tears. Brad's seat sat obviously empty in his sixth grade classes. Students walked the halls and went to class, but the conspicuously silent hallways lacked the boisterous chatter and whispered giggles that usually filled the air. The school "was a somber atmosphere," Lindsay's best friend, Shona Erwin, recalls.

Tasha Asher felt what she called a "solemn" atmosphere and "stayed crying" all day. Where was her "Top Gum?" They were all children, trying to understand the enormity of what had just shaken the community. They also had a friend to grieve.

Dollie Press could not shake the image of Doug Sims holding her arm; she could still see his eyes, hear his voice. Every time she thought of it, she got a tight feeling in her belly, numbness in her limbs. Then she thought of Brad: "Brad's whole face," she says, "would light up when he laughed."

As Jill Bishop walked into the school building, she thought of the last time she saw Brad. She saw him on Friday when they played a game together on the blacktop. Now, Brad would never play another game. Jill was eleven years old, and she comprehended most of what had happened, but it did not mean her heart hurt any less. She met up with her best friend, and they sat outside with a teacher, talking softly. The teacher took them to a guidance counselor. Jill Bishop ended up getting so upset, the school needed to call Mrs. Bishop to come get her.

Sheila Padgett ended up talking to a guidance counselor. She talked of how Brad had been her little boyfriend. She still had the love note and the heart shaped pendent. Sheila's father was a preacher, and he brought her up under strict rules, and he never allowed her to go out and "party" like the other kids. She wondered just how and why Brad would end up at this man's house, this Doug Sims character. Who was he, anyway? Some people in the community started saying Doug was "slow" and had mental problems. It still made no sense. Brad was her age, twelve years old.

The school planned what they called a "Parent Information Meeting" for Thursday, March 15. The school principal, John Secor, said of Brad, "He was a very fine young man...good to have among our student body" in the March 12, 1990 edition of the *Greensburg Daily News*.

The following Wednesday, *Greensburg Daily News* reporter Jean Reed followed up with a special piece on the grieving process for children. Reed discussed the emotions of fear, stress, being overwhelmed, and feelings of survivor's guilt. There is a marked difference between the death of an adult and the death of a peer. Children, Reed wrote, are ill-equipped to handle such serious emotions, much less have the skills to deal with the turmoil following. The newspaper offered free publications on how to work with children as they cope with fears and stressors.

As part of assisting their student body to understand and cope with the incident, the school officials had Junior Armstrong and Rob Nugent go to each of Brad's classes to explain what had happened that night. The boys kept out details but explained as honestly as possible: the boys went to Doug Sims' house to drink; after Sims dropped them off, Brad left to go back out with Doug. He disappeared after that, but few knew it until the next day, late Saturday. Julie Ralston recalls the two friends explaining to her class, and how the words "underage drinking" rang through the presentation.

"It was so sad," recalls one student who knew of Brad, ruminating over the horror. "I mean I didn't really know him as a friend. It was just sad the *way* he died."

Another man, who was a student at the time, made an observation as an adult. "Kids who didn't really know him were all saying they were his best friend, suddenly. After he was gone, kids who didn't even like him were saying what a great kid he was. I didn't understand it at the time."

Rob Nugent went home to his family, his church, and a strong support system. His mother and father ensured he was cared for, hovering over him and being there through the bad dreams, the tears; they held him close and told him how much they loved him and that he was safe.

Junior Armstrong did not receive a phone call from his biological father, checking in on him, until several days after the murder. His older brothers did not seem to understand that Junior was traumatized. Junior slept between his parents for a long time; eventually he moved to a pallet on the floor beside their bed. Finally he moved to his little brother's room and slept in his own bed. Brad's house was still right across the street, but no Brad to come bounding out of the front door to greet him. No parent to hold him after a particularly nasty nightmare, which never seemed to end, and no one to tell him he was safe now.

Junior recalls the rumors that flew about the case, and his child's mind struggled to process everything from survivor's guilt to the stages of grief. Over and over, he saw in his mind Doug Sims handcuffing Brad, then kissing him on the head, and then fighting with him to stay in the tent.

The older Lynn Welch, although she was not Brad's age, "never felt so unsafe in my life." She knew Patti as "kindhearted" and Daryl as "kind—they were good people." Lynn Welch saw "the (Maddux) family stop dead in their tracks." She says, "It is so scary to me that you can do everything right for your kids and this can still happen." She is emotional still to this day, ruminating over the situation. "It was scary and sad," she will repeat. "Scary and sad."

On her next visit to her friend's house, Tasha Asher took the same route and began the trek across the field, alone. Suddenly, she stopped and fear overwhelmed her. She thought to herself, "I'm being silly," but she could still not bring herself to walk across that field. She took the long way around and never cut through the field again. That night, safe in her own home, Tasha insisted all the doors and windows to be locked tight or she could not sleep; her heart started pounding, her eyes clamping on shadows in the room. Although she was one of five children, and she knew Doug Sims to be locked away, Tasha insisted her parents lock up once dusk fell. Tasha Asher remained afraid into adulthood: "His death set something off in me. Fear. After that, I stopped walking to friend's houses. I am still this way."

Tasha was not Brad's only pal who began to fear for her safety. Jill Bishop grew fearful of the world as well; "I was afraid to go anywhere," she explains now, "It was always in the back of my mind." Despite Jill's parents' strict parenting, Jill still felt she should stay close to home.

176

In an attempt to return to normalcy, Sheila Padgett accompanied her mother to a store. They perused the various goods, from groceries to clothing. Turning a corner, Mrs. Padgett saw Patti Maddux. She greeted her with sympathy.

"I'm picking out Brad's clothes for the funeral," Patti told them bravely. "Will you give me an opinion?"

"Of course, anything," Mrs. Padgett nodded. Patti showed them a few pieces she had selected. Meanwhile, shoppers walked past and around them, heedless of a woman shopping for burial clothes for her youngest son's funeral.

"I love this," Sheila told Patti, pointing out a baby blue turtleneck sweater. "It would match his eyes." She tried to smile.

"Yes, and the turtleneck would cover... would cover it." Patti laid the sweater out across her arm to show them.

"This would look good over it," Mrs. Padgett held up a matching blue sweater. "Will he be in trousers or jeans—?"

"Dress slacks," Patti nodded. Her eyes were swollen and red-rimmed.

"Then that would look good," Sheila agreed. The three spoke a bit longer, then the Padgetts bade Brad's mom a farewell. As they walked away, Mrs. Padgett reached over and pulled Sheila close to her, holding her a bit tighter and longer than usual.

The crime hit the front page of local newspapers and was precedent and remained there for several days. The Tuesday, March 13, 1990 front page of the Columbus, Indiana daily newspaper, *The Republic*, featured a full color photograph of Doug Sims being escorted to the Decatur County Courthouse. He wore a brown jumpsuit and the plastic sandals issued to inmates. He wore handcuffs and leg shackles. Reporter Danny Lee interviewed Mariah Packing Company President John Stadler, who described employee Doug Sims as "a decent worker... very well-liked (with) a decent work record." Lee also noted the number of vehicles parked at the Maddux residence as well as the lack of activity at Sims' trailer. The headline utilized the adjective that went up and down Westport streets: "Slaying shocks Westport."

In the same edition of *The Republic*, Prosecutor William O.

Smith issued a statement explaining the county appeared to be "experiencing a high level of personal violence" with "the fifth victim in the last seven months" involving a person under sixteen. Smith urged parents to keep an eye on their children and those who are around their children, reminding the community the perpetrators knew all of the victims in these crimes. A black and white photograph of Mush's trailer accompanied the article.

On that Tuesday, March 13, State Police Sergeant Ed Lewis arrived at the Mt. Olivet Cemetery again, this time during the day. He conducted a search for any overlooked or lost evidence and took some final measurements.

Despite the shining sun, the cemetery still had a strange air about it. The weather-beaten headstones sitting at various angles, the dark woods looming just a few feet away, and the crime scene tape fluttering in the breeze gave it all a sad, heavy feeling. Lewis spent some time searching, but did not find anything else.

Tuesday, March 13 also marked another event in the saga: It was the day of visitation for Bradley Maddux. The service would be held at the Bass & Gasper Funeral Home in Westport at 2:00 p.m.

The Bass & Gasper Funeral Home, by Westport standards, is a giant building. It sits at the corner of North East and East Bennett streets. It takes up half a city block. A sturdy, clapboard, white building with bright blue awnings, it has a history in Westport and, like most businesses, is locally owned and operated. The first undertaking business in Westport was opened in 1872; from there it grew to include two businesses, a furniture store, and an undertaking department. In 1945, the funeral home was moved to its current location and changed to meet the needs of a growing and changing community. In 1985, the Gasper and Bass families united in business and the funeral home added more parking, more visitation rooms, and better accommodations. That Tuesday night, they needed it, as visitors for Bradley Maddux overflowed the parking lot and building.

Visitation was scheduled from 4:00 p.m. until 9:00 p.m. that Tuesday, but one look at the cars in the parking lot across the street from N. East and the traffic along the way told a different story. The undertakers told Brad's immediate family, per tradition, to stand up front near his casket to receive guests. Patti received so many "I'm sorry" statements it all became a blur. Daryl was numb. One family member wondered—did people come to look at Brad one last time to pay their respects and say goodbye, or did they come to try to see the damage to his neck, as if in some sort of macabre show?

Several school buses arrived. Students filed out, solemn, dressed in what they usually would wear to church. They were the students of South Decatur Elementary School. They came to pay their respects to their lost comrade, and some of them wept openly. This was a first funeral for most of them.

"Westport is a poor farming community," explains one teacher. "Those little boys and girls were dressed in what they considered their best clothes," which meant department store specials. "It broke your heart to watch them."

Julie Ralston arrived on a bus. She filed past the casket with the others, and when it came time to say her goodbyes, she tried to shield the vision of Bradley lying there. She managed to see his blue turtleneck sweater and this horrified her. Julie heard the rumors and stories; she believed she knew what happened to Brad. "It's so hard, seeing that turtleneck," she told friends later. "Thinking of what happened to him."

Brad wore dress slacks and the blue turtleneck with the blue sweater Sheila and the Padgetts helped chose; Sheila was glad to see this and felt special that she chose an appropriate outfit for her friend to wear for eternity.

Sheila Padgett saw her little boyfriend in her mind's eye, but when she saw Brad in his casket, she was taken back. Because of the damage to his throat, his head rested at an awkward angle, his chin forced to rest on his chest in an effort to cover it all. Sheila vowed she would never let go of that note or the pendent Brad had gave her. In her heart, she would always check YES.

Jean Hickey had arrived, and thus began, "The hardest experience I even went through as a teacher." She reminded herself to be compassionate but professional. Her duty was to provide comfort and leadership for the children. She led students up to the casket and held them as they cried, and she allowed them to say prayers or

179

whatever they wanted to say to Brad. It was still "unbelievable shock." She could not think of any other words. "Unbelievable shock."

In the group sat two boys, brothers, dressed in their Sunday clothes. Jean Hickey wondered how they would act. In class these boys were horrid; they tried a teacher's patience and exhausted them by the end of the class just from trying to control them. Mrs. Hickey noted they each carried a red rose. She thought she needed to watch them more than anyone. She escorted the boys up to the casket and forced herself not to give them a behavior warning. Each boy lifted his rose... and set it on Brad's chest. "That's when I lost it," she says, years later. "Those two mean little boys, doing something like that."

Teachers clutched moist tissues and shared thoughts with the family, friends, and one another. Brad, they consoled one another, was fearless. If there was something new, he was not afraid to try it. He was a cut-up, but he never disrupted class with pranks or silliness. He still said, "yes ma'am" and "no sir," said "please" and "thank you" and always volunteered to help. Sometimes he could be hardheaded and want to do things his way. Some felt that Brad did not have enough self-esteem in his schoolwork. He never acted like a mean or bad child, just one who did not trust he was smart enough to do the work. But most teachers recall Brad as a student who made them laugh and made it a pleasure to have them in class. Instructors pulled students close to them to talk if they seemed to be taking it worse than others. Brad was a popular boy; they did not cry or act out in an attempt to show off—they were genuinely mournful.

One boy that could not bear the pain sat with tears rolling down his cheeks, head bowed, sobbing. Danny Kennedy lost control of his emotions in that room. He could not attend the funeral later.

Patti Maddux, tears streaming down her cheeks, hugged each of the sixty to seventy-five children who came to pay their respects and say goodbye. Some of them were close to her son and were still trying to understand the how and why of death. Others only knew Brad marginally, due to the nature of the small school. The murder hurt them as well; how could this happen? Especially in the safe cocoon of Westport?

Jill Bishop says she can still see, hear, and feel what this day felt like for her. It was Jill's first time to a viewing; she never had cause to go inside of a funeral parlor, much less a funeral. She saw Brad lying there, saw his turtleneck sweater, and felt "horrible." Because she was innocent of how he died, she later asked her parents why Brad had to be buried wearing a turtleneck sweater.

Lynn Welch attended the visitation also. She filed past the casket, tears in her eyes. At high school, none of her friends talked about Brad's death to one another. Not openly, at least. She found it difficult to believe this was the same smiling boy who loved life and laughed so much. As she made her way into the various clusters of people, Lynn Welch heard whisperings: Betty Sims was going to show up tonight. "How could she do that?" certain people scoffed. Others asked, "How can she not?" The rumor spread like a hot commodity tip. Lynn Welch was old enough to understand this, but young enough that she did not recall seeing Betty that night. Besides, Doug Sims' mother was a good person, "a proper lady," Welch recalls. It wasn't her fault Doug committed this crime.

Tasha Asher also rode on that bus, and she was overcome with sadness. Brad was a good boy; he always did what he was asked to do in class. He never even complained or harped about his parents, like so many other kids their age often did. He made her feel special, he had a sweet personality, and he was so funny. So why did she see him lying there, so still and cold, in a casket? Tasha could see his freckles, which she loved, but it was not the same Brad. She made up her mind then; she would not attend the funeral. "I don't want to see him again, like that," she told herself.

Steve Rennekamp did not attend the viewing or the funeral. He did not know Brad as others did, and he had so much strife in his own family. He was a little boy trying to get through life one day at a time. Guilt gnawed at him for years for not attending. "I always wanted to know where he was buried," an adult Steve says now, "So I can pay my respects." In a strange way, Steve admits, Brad's short life and sudden death taught him much about his own life.

The doors did not close at 9:00 o'clock p.m. Too many

181

people continued to file in. The tears flowed, the sobs quickly muffled, but not hidden from sight. There was Brad, in his casket, so still. How could it be? Someone mentioned that just a few days ago Brad was pedaling his bicycle and throwing their newspaper. Another person told a story of about the time Brad made a whole group of folks crack up laughing, a twinkle in his eye; God, that kid was funny! And the teller of the story laughed until they had tears in their own eyes. One teacher reminisced on Brad's politeness. Yes, sometimes Brad played the jokester, and no, he never took gruff from another kid, but Brad unfailingly acted politely and courteously towards his elders. It grew later and still people filed in, squeezed family hands and gave hugs that lasted longer than usual, tousled Cody's hair and patted Lindsay's little shoulders. The doors to Bass & Gasper Funeral Home closed several hours after 12:00 a.m.

On Wednesday, March 14, 1990, at 2:00 p.m., Bass & Gasper Funeral Home was again filled with grief. The sadness was palatable. Brad lay in his casket as the Reverend David Scaggs of Westport Baptist Church officiated. He spoke highly of Brad, for he knew him; Brad and his family attended Westport Baptist.

Sheila Padgett's heart broke each time Patti Maddux let out a sob, and it felt shattered for most of the service. "You can't completely guard your children constantly," Sheila, a parent, says today. "But I just remember his poor mom, sitting on the first pew, crying and crying." Sheila felt useless, not knowing what to do.

Junior walked past the casket to say one last goodbye to his friend. He noted something and smiled. Brad, in perpetual boyishness, always seemed to have a bit of a dirt ring around his beefy neck from playing so hard. With the funeral home's repairs to the vicious slash to his throat, that ring still appeared to be there. Tears in his eyes and flowing down his cheeks, Junior smiled down at his pal. How could he go on without Brad? He was the best friend Junior ever had. Sometimes it seemed he was the only friend he had. Besides loving his friend, Junior's guilt plagued him: if only—if only. If only he would have dragged Brad back to the tent and held him there that night. If only they had not gone to Mushroom's house. If only...

Junior heard something that will stay with him forever, and to this day he cannot face the Maddux family. His memory is unclear about when, but sometime during the services, he heard Patti Maddux's voice. "If he wouldn't have been with Junior," she said in her grief, "Brad would still be alive."

"I know it's not true," Junior says now. "I know she was only hurting. But then, I was just a kid." A lonely kid full of self-blame, of pain, and nowhere to put it.

That evening, Brad's loved ones laid him to rest at Westport Cemetery. Good, trusting, loving Brad. The white knight in shining armor, the best friend who always had your back as a faithful sidekick, who loved his puppy and his family. He tried to be tough, but it just did not fit him; he trusted too much and believed the best in everyone. He loved laughing and making people laugh. They inscribed "Precious Memories" on his headstone.

This time, it was a proper burial. If there is such a thing for a murdered child.

The legal process continued throughout March in 1990. Brent Westerfield, Sims' court-appointed attorney, tried everything legally possible to block evidence against his client. It was his job, and he took the responsibility seriously, as any good attorney would have.

Decatur County Deputy Sheriff Robert Klene testified at a Suppression Hearing. It was the sole time he was called to testify. Sims' attorney's tactic involved getting as much evidence thrown out as possible, and if he could get Sims' confession to Oldham thrown out, the rest would follow. This included the map Doug Sims drew of where Brad's body was buried in Mt. Olivet Cemetery. Klene remembers turning the map around in his hands while sitting on the stand, as the lawyers wrangled over the slip of paper.

A copy of a loan application for a Chevrolet S-10 Blazer was recovered. The amount requested was $4750.00. The person requesting the loan was Mrs. Meadows. On the lower half of the application someone had written "Doug" and a telephone number.

Sims' bank records did not yield much information. He penned several checks to Ben Frost totaling less than $50.00. He wrote a check to Mrs. Meadows for $50.00. He had written several checks to Mike Meadows in amounts of $20.00 and $40.00, but they did not total over $100.00. Later, someone told officials Doug Sims would pay the boys for "odd jobs" and the check to Mrs. Meadows was for vacation money. She planned to repay Sims when her child support check arrived.

Law enforcement officers interviewed Dollie Press, but they told her, "Your time frame is off. Are you sure of the right times? Are you positive?" Dollie insisted her stories were true, to the point of growing angry. "I was scared," she told law enforcement officials about her encounter with Doug Sims. Dollie did not disobey adults; for the first time in her life she had lied to an adult, and later he ended up killing one of her schoolmates. "It has haunted me," Dollie Press says today.

On the 16th, Brent Westerfield filed an objection to the court's discovery order and requested a protective order for his client. On the same date, the State filed to seize blood samples from Sims. On the 23rd, the court set the hearing to seize the blood samples and a psychiatric interview Sims for the 26th.

On March 26, the court granted the State the right to obtain a sample of Sims' blood. The court also allowed the defense attorney to permit psychiatric testing and, at the same time, the defense requested a change of venue. Westerfield did not feel his client would receive a fair trial in this county, let alone this immediate area. "This (murder) was the worst thing that had happened here," Jon Oldham explains later. "Everyone was talking about it."

Not only were they talking about it, but Brad's death also affected people's lives in other ways. His family still struggled to get over the shock and grief. It was not easy being the center of various kinds of attention.

South Decatur Elementary officials brought the students together in a ceremony behind the school. The students planted trees in memory of Bradley Maddux. To this day, a grove of trees stands just behind the school, swaying in the wind as if to catch the children's innocent laughter and hold it in place. Julie Ralston was there, placing her tree in the earth just so. As she scooped the fertile soil around the tree, she thought of how she had shared cookies with Brad just a few days before he went missing. It seemed so trivial then. This memory stayed with Julie far into adulthood.

Lindsay Maddux tried to get back into the routine of things; she returned to class. Lindsay had a select group of girls she liked being with; they were not the most popular clique, nor were they the least popular group. They were just a few little girls who came together because they enjoyed each other's company.

"Lindsay was a sweet girl," says one of the friends, Shona Erwin. "She was so funny! And so much fun to be around." But upon her return to class, her pals noted a marked difference in her demeanor. Nevertheless they were little girls, and many in Westport believed it was best to not tell their children the truth, so some did not even have an idea of what took place. "I knew because my mom explained it," Shona Erwin confides now. So the day Lindsay broke out of class to run to the girl's restroom and sob in grief, it was Shona who ran to her to console her friend. The tears seemed nonstop, and Shona's heart ached, wishing there was something she could do for her friend. Shona only knew Brad marginally; he was Lindsay's big brother who playfully teased them if they came over for a sleepover, or else a boy whom she saw in the hallways at school and recognized as her best friend's kin. She had difficulty thinking of something to say; Lindsay appeared to not want to talk about her loss, and her friends were too young to truly understand it all.

Cody tried to get back to normal. He scooped up his schoolbooks and his football gear and returned to class. Cody played for his high school football team, the South Decatur Cougars, and he desperately hoped a return to normalcy would help him. Cody did not share his feelings easily. His family started attending a special group his Aunt Judy had located, called Angels of Mercy, in Indianapolis. There was also a group, called Parents of Murdered Children, in Greenwood, Indiana. Cody refused to attend, rejected any type of help. He buried it deep inside of himself, where no one else went, and it stayed there.

So it was with excitement and anticipation as Cody Maddux headed to the locker room, ready to struggle into his pads, stamp into his cleats, and hit the field to work off anger, frustration, and hurt. Then the coach stopped him.

"Maddux," he told the boy, "You're off the team."

"What?" Cody asked in disbelief.

"You've missed too many practices." The coach shook his head. "You know the rules. Can't let you play."

Cody stood there, feeling very small, then very angry as he swallowed hard. "Sir, I had my brother's funeral, and—"

"Sorry, son. Rules are rules." The coach shook his head and walked away.

The Cougars had an amazing year in 1990. People in the community said they were on their way to state. Two weeks after Brad's murder, the boys gathered in the locker room, suiting up for the game.

Chase Mullery finished applying the wrap around one of his arms, as he thought about his friend, Cody. He completed the taping and sat back, stewing. He thought of Cody, then Brad, and the times he had spent at the Maddux house. Mr. Maddux was a great guy, and he always took the time to show him how to grip a football or to ask him how he fared, and he meant it. Brad was a great guy, a funny kid, sincere, not like those asswipes that pretended to be your friend and then stabbed you in the back. He thought about how Brad probably would have been in this locker room next year. Chase tried not to let anyone else see the water in his eyes and he put his face in his hands, acting like he was rubbing his face. When he looked up he saw a big, black marker on the board where Coach gave instructions. Chase nudged the friend sitting next to him, flexing his newly-taped arm. When the other boy turned to look, Chase said, "I got an idea."

As the group of South Decatur Cougars came trotting out of the locker room, their coach did a double-take. Printed neatly on the wraps of some of his players' right arms, vertically, were the words IN MEMORY. Printed neatly on the wraps of their left arms, vertically, were the words OF BRAD.

"Take that off of there!" Coach bellowed as he herded them together, clipboard clenched in hand. "Knock it off."

The boys looked at one another, communicated as a team, and someone said, "Okay." They turned and loped back into the locker room, the coach at their heels. He watched

186

as they began peeling off their jerseys.

"What are you doing?" the older man demanded.

"We're not playing," someone answered for them.

"Brad was my friend," someone else said.

Coach stared at them in disbelief, and then respect crossed his features. "For tonight," he said finally.

He allowed the boys to wear the wraps for another game after that evening. The South Decatur Cougars went on to win the State Championship that year, in 1990. They got to play in the Indianapolis Colts stadium, just like the pros. All of the players got a State Championship ring—all except for Cody Maddux, who had to cheer his pals on from the sideline and pretend it did not hurt.

The football field was not the only scene where drama, affected by Brad Maddux's murder, played out in the schools. Students had returned to their school desks that following Monday in a strange stunned silence. Once Lindsay, Cody, Junior, and Rob returned to class, they all clammed up again. No one knew what to say to her or the boys, or how to say it. "It was the biggest elephant in the room," recalls a fellow student. "It was also horror. Just horror." It was difficult not to unintentionally ostracize Junior, and Rob and make them part of the group, as if nothing occurred, to help them feel normal again. And the whisperings went on, usually gossip they brought from home: The boys should not have been out drinking. Where were the parents in all this? What really happened in that trailer?

Officers also attempted to determine the answer to that last question. Doug Sims still refused to discuss it, and on the advice of his attorney, he kept his mouth shut tight. On March 28, 1990 they took a blood sample from Sims. An A-EMT, or Advanced Emergency Medical Technician, took the sample at 10:14 a.m. Indiana State Trooper Lewis took the sample from the A-EMT and filed it as evidence. They would use the blood sample to match to the blood located at the scene and on the body of Bradley Maddux.

Sims' attorney, Westerfield, also filed against the police department and cited the time Whitehead was driving to Sardinia to locate Doug Sims for questioning. Whitehead had observed Sims' Ford coming toward him on the highway, made a U-turn, and followed Sims to the

Westport Police Station. Westerfield argued this was when Sims actually became under the custody of law enforcement, and not later, when they read his Miranda Rights to him; therefore, his rights should have been read to him immediately upon arriving at the station. Because they were not, everything Doug Sims told Jon Oldham was inadmissible.

The court disagreed with Westerfield, arguing the Westport Police read Sims his Miranda Rights lawfully. Whitehead's simple U-turn was just that, and Sims did not become a person in custody until he lied to Jon Oldham. Oldham did the right thing under the law.

On April 20, 1990, Jon Oldham received a "Report of Laboratory Examination" from the Indianapolis Regional Laboratory. The analysis had discovered hairs "of possible evidentiary value" on the following items:

"Under shorts with possible blood removed from the cemetery'
"Yellow Purdue shirt"
"Army type tee-shirt removed from the accused residence"
"Shirt removed from the accused bedroom"

Legal maneuvers continued through April and May. Lawyers filed for orders approving funds for psychologists and investigators. They also filed notices of delivery for both audio and video taped evidence. The courts ordered both parties to file their briefs by May 30, 1990. May was a busy month for those involved in The State of Indiana vs. Douglas C. Sims. On the 14th, the State filed a petition for an order to seize hair samples from Sims. Sims' attorney filed an objection barring the sample on the 29th. The hearing was slated for June 5. Still, Sims' attorney fought to prevent evidence, any evidence, which would weigh against his client.

"I don't think Doug did this crime alone," says one close friend of Sims. They do not suspect the Meadows family, nor do they see Ben Frost as a potential accomplice. "Doug was jealous of Ben, because Ben was Mike's best friend, like a brother," the friend explains. "So Doug would never have confided in Ben." Then who? "I don't know," admits the friend.

Mike Meadows believes Doug Sims was not the culprit—that Doug took the blame for someone else. He reminds a researcher that Doug was upset over Brad's well-being, and perhaps the murder had something to do with that. Another friend echoed this sentiment: "They need to get Brad out of that house," Sims reportedly said quite often. There was also the rumor that Brad was going to be adopted, or at least the elder Sims planned to adopt Brad. A lead investigator in this case calls these allegations untrue, and Daryl Maddux responds with a stalwart, "No." In May and June, Doug Sims penned a few letters to friends in looping cursive on jail-issued, lined paper. He awaited trial in the Greensburg County Jail in Greensburg, Indiana, and he used this address as a reply address, 119 E. Railroad Street:

*It is alright to take awhile to write to me, I am glad
to have your new address and telephone number.
I hope you really enjoy your house the family moved
into last weekend. Is your dad going to live there also?
If so I hope he will not mind me calling on Sunday
morning's sometimes. You will not miss Westport if
Whitehead leaves to be a deputy or, he is running
for County Sheriff. That will make (name withheld)
town marshall of Westport. That would be trouble for Linda and
Mike.
I hope you enjoy your own phone. Tell the family hello for me. I will
enclosed a letter for you to give to Mike. Is he working a lot and tried
or what? How are you doing in school? Will you be going to South
Decatur next year or what? I hope enjoy going with (name withheld).
But remimder about drinking and driving right now. This is election
year and the police are real thick right now.
They just brought in 4 drunks thru the door. Our little door is open,
and we can look down the hall. One of the drunks just hit a police
officer in the   mouth, and he is wild right now. I hope you enjoy
softball this summer.
Have to go now.
Friends forever,
Doug
PLEASE WRITE BACK*
(Sic)

189

Sims mailed the above letter in early May 1990. On his next letter, he drew a smiling face with the words "Be Happy" on the outside envelope flap. Again he appears obsessed over Mike Meadows; he gives sage advice, and writes as if he is away on vacation rather than behind bars for the murder of a child (edited by the author for privacy as indicated by parentheses):

*It's nice to hear all of the voices in your house. I
know Mike hasn't forgotten me, but ask him to write
once in a while. It would be nice to hear from him.
I am glad he is going to night school. Tell him thanks for going back
to school. Please ask Mike to write.
I hope you stay with (your significant other) has long has you can. I
am glad and happy for you. How's school for you anyway? I hope
you passed this year.
You should ask (your significant other) to tell (your ex) that it is
over, between you and (the ex). But   don't let two friend fight about
it. That would be real bad for both sides. I will try to call, bit
sometimes we get the phone to early or not at all. Are you helping
mom clean house or what. I hope you enjoy your trip this summer.
I guess you are the only one going by your letter. But if you do not get
to go, do not get mad. Find you a summer job somewhere.
I hope you have fun playing (sports) this summer. Do you or the
family go to Westport anymore? Who is Mike seeing now? Tell
everyone hello for me. Ask Mike to write. Love all of you and hang
in there.
Some day we will all have a beer. You, Mike, Mrs.
Meadows, Doug, and Dollie
Doug
"Mush"
P.S. Have a nice summer. I will be 29 years old on
June 2. Please tell me when Mikes birthday is.*
(Sic)

A close friend wrote to Doug Sims. "Please stop writing me," the friend asked, "and let me go on with my life." The friend did have a question: "For the sake of putting it all to rest, for peace of mind, did you commit this crime?" Doug Sims never answered.

On June 2, 1990, Doug Sims turned twenty-nine years old behind bars. There was no party, no alcohol, no one to sing the traditional song or bake him a cake. Instead of a specially prepared meal and his beloved iced tea, it was a meal on a plastic tray, served just like the other inmates around him, within the confines of the Decatur County Jail.

On June 5, the court granted the State the right to take the hair sample. The judge signed Cause Number 16C01-9003-CF14 with a flourish and it was stamped "FILED" in red ink. The court also listened to the argument regarding change of venue.

Law enforcement received a call that could, potentially, change the course of the case. A neighbor of Doug Sims was home after one of their regularly scheduled vacations and found some strange items partially buried on their property. The items were seized, all legal paperwork completed, and appeared to be tainted with "an unknown stain" believed to be blood. The items were: a brown/beige rug, green size 35L work pants, one pair of Nike shoes, one brown tee shirt, and a cloth hand towel. The investigators completed a request for a laboratory examination on June 6, 1990 and sent it to the Indiana State Laboratory Division; Jon Oldham personally delivered it, along with the evidence and samples of Sims' head and pubic hair, for testing. Someone printed "TRIAL 7/21*" on the top of the request, as if in a plea to prioritize the test.

On a letter postmarked June 21, 1990, Sims wrote to a young female friend who also knew Mike Meadows:

Hello, how is everything going around home? Do you have a boy friend yet? How's the family doing? I hope you are enjoying the summer so far. It has been a wet one so far. But it should start getting better. How's Mike doing, he has not written in a long long time. I wished he would write me a letter.

Are you going to Missouri for the summer or what. How's your mom doing? Will have to go, please write, and ask Mike to write. Take care of yourself.
Doug Sims
P.S. Have a nice summer.
(Sic)

On July 7, the court overruled the motion for the change of venue; Sims would receive his trial in Decatur County, where the "alleged crime" occurred. Until the person is legally convicted, it is an "alleged" crime, no matter what evidence is seized or who admits guilt. Thus, Brad's murder was referred to as "alleged crime." Doug Sims would appear in the courthouse in Greensburg, Indiana.

On July 16, 1990, a letter from William O. Smith's office was typed out and sent to the office of Brent Westerfield. It would be marked a turning point for Douglas Sims. "I have," the letter stated, "decided to request the death penalty if this case is going to trial." It continued to read: "In the event the defendant is prepared to plead guilty, I will not request the death penalty." The prosecuting attorney went on to offer a fifty-year sentence with a dismissal of the child molestation charge in exchange for a plea. Would the Sims team take the plea or take a chance and go to trial?

Legally, the prosecution must allow the defense to review any and all evidence the prosecution has against the defendant. Again, some may feel this is unfair, but it is a part of the due process, a part of the trial. Prosecuting Attorney William O. Smith sent another formal letter to Sims' attorney, Brent Westerfield, on July 17, which read: "I am tentatively arranging to have the physical evidence in this case available for inspection ... sometime after 5:00 p.m. Wednesday August 1, 1990," Smith invited. He also explained that the laboratory "has been slow" in completing the evidence requests sent by law enforcement. The officers did an amazing job in gathering evidence and logging their work. They had logged their findings, and they also worked on gathering more information after the fact. The noose, so to speak, was tightening on Sims.

Finally, on August 10, 1990, Jon Oldham received the much-anticipated eight pages of Indiana State Police laboratory report results. He leafed through them carefully; some of the results surprising him, some of them not:

"No latent prints were found on the beer can, the Pepsi can, the beer bottle, or the knife with the camouflage handle, all recovered from the cemetery."

"Bradley Maddux's blood was identified in the under shorts from the cemetery, Brad's yellow Purdue shirt, the knife with the camouflage handle, and from the pair of Nike shoes."

"Blood was either inconclusive or could not be found on certain items. For example, no blood could be found on the knife sharpener, or the handcuffs and key seized from the trailer bedroom." This is perhaps because both were washed thoroughly, or because neither came in contact with blood.

"Semen was found on the Army type tee-shirt from the accused residence, and listed the genetic profile. "This genetic profile is consistent with Douglas Sims but not consistent with Bradley Maddux," noted the report. Also found on this shirt: "pubic hair 'sufficiently similar'" to Douglas Sims. No semen was found on any other items submitted.

"A head hair 'sufficiently similar' to Douglas Sims was found in the under shorts of Bradley. A head hair and a head hair fragment 'sufficiently similar' to Douglas Sims were found in Bradley's Purdue shirt."

"A pubic hair and head hairs 'sufficiently similar' to Douglas Sims were found in the brown T-shirt removed from his home."

There was no real "gotcha" here. It placed them together, which witnesses already established. It placed Bradley's blood on the knife. It identified semen, but not on Bradley, indicative of a sex crime. Both the prosecution and the defense could use this information at their desk in court. What it all came down to was Sims' confession: The confession, the legality of his confession, and whether or not his attorney could get it thrown out of the case. Then anything associated with it would follow: evidence, reports, and witnesses. Doug Sims might walk. Doug Sims might plea to a lesser charge and just be a probationer, passing Brad's friends and family on the streets of Westport tomorrow. Buying more alcohol or ice cream for the next little boy and asking him, "Want to go to my house?"

Meanwhile, there were meetings, discussions, and many late nights spent pouring over documents, files, and photographs. The defense team met with the prosecution, who met with the officers, who spoke with one another. Days turned into weeks. And then the involved parties made a decision that angered some, confused others, caused a lot of tears, but in the end seemed the right thing to do, based on legalities and evidence.

On September 12, 1990, an Agreement to Disposition was signed. It carried the signatures of William O. Smith, Brent Westerfield, and Doug Sims; most importantly, it also held the signatures of Patti Maddux and Daryl Maddux. The two parties compromised that the Attempted Child Molestation charge would be dropped if Sims pled guilty for Brad's death, in exchange for the State not seeking the death penalty. The Agreement to Disposition also recommended the state consider "Aggravating factors" and the court "may impose whatever sentence that complies with the law and evidence." Both the state and defendant could present "any admissible evidence." Sims retained the option of appealing his sentence.

On September 14, 1990, the prosecution requested the maximum possible sentence or the maximum sentence with the least amount of time suspended. The prosecution cited Brad's age, the nature and circumstances of the crime (evidence of confinement, body buried and hidden to avoid discovery), the condition of the body (neck cut, hands bound, undressed, mouth gagged), and the fact "that until sentencing in this cause, the defendant has shown no remorse." The prosecution cited "an aggravating factor" of the evidence to be the fact that "the age of the victim and the brutality of the killings are heinous..."

They knew that if they utilized the death penalty and Sims received the death sentence, he could spend ten or more years utilizing the appeals process while postponing the sentence. And what if it were appealed? An appeal would mean even more years of hell for a family trying to get through it all.

194

Throughout all of the legal proceedings, after all of his court appearances, one thing did remain consistent. According to David and Betty Sims, Doug's legal team had advised their son to tell them nothing. "At one point, we were asked what we knew (about the murder details)," David shakes his head. "We kept explaining, we knew nothing. Nothing. They told us not to talk to Doug."

"Doug wouldn't talk to us," Betty says, years later, the pain evident on her face. "We kept asking him, 'what happened?' We would ask his attorney, we would ask what was going to happen to him." No one answered them, she says now. They had to get their news from the local papers. According to Betty, it was 2012 before she heard the details of Brad Maddux's last night.

According to one witness, during a courtroom appearance, Betty did tell officers at one point, to "take these (handcuffs) off of my boy! It makes him look like a criminal!" Shock, grief, anger, and misery worked together to create a personal hell for the innocent loved ones of the accused.

Greensburg lies in a straight shot north of Westport, about an hour's drive up I65 North. Today it is a pretty little town, with approximately 11,000 inhabitants. It has an old-fashioned feeling, with plenty of historical buildings downtown, but with a modern edge around the borders. It served as the county seat for Decatur County since 1822. The months of April and May in 1822 were filled with setting up a court and a government, in that order. Thomas Hendricks' wife named the town Greensburg in fond memory of her home back in Pennsylvania. The first building, the jail, as if in anticipation of problems, went up in 1823, southeast of the courtyard.

The courthouse tower in Greensburg, Indiana is famous for an oddity. Sometime in the 1870s, trees started growing from the roof house tower without soil, after taking root in the crevices. It is now a national and international tourist spot. Experts from the Smithsonian Institution have even paid the trees a visit. The trees have made their way into multiple newspapers, magazines, books, and television shows. The trees made international news. The trees, in and of themselves, are celebrities. It is normal to see tourists of all nationalities stop in the middle of the sidewalk to snap pictures of the tower and the trees. Locals, particularly courthouse employees, are quite proud. Only a select few may enter the actual tower for a close look at the trees, causing the trees' type to be hotly debated. Employees at the courthouse will tell tourists about berries that land on the lawns, sidewalks, and their vehicles during a certain season, debunking a few hypotheses as to tree origins. The courthouse has a flyer full of information on the trees for anyone who requests it. It was in this courthouse that the case took a serious turn that would affect lives forever.

On September 17, 1990, Douglas C. Sims, along with his court-ordered attorney Brent Westerfield, appeared before Circuit Court Judge John Andrew Westhafer to enter a plea.

The Maddux family was in attendance. They alone almost filled all of the galley seats in the courtroom. The months of wretchedness showed in their faces. Grandpa Dave sat, seething, the rage and pain visible on his face. Officers in the courtroom had passed the word on to keep an eye on him, and trained eyes searched him for anything concealed. It seemed as if the old man shrank in stature from the toil of heartbreak, but he also seemed to be able to crush Doug Sims with one hand.

Tammy Hileman did not attend. She did not make it to any of the legal hearings. "I couldn't," she explains later, tears welling in her eyes. "I couldn't bear to go there."

Junior Armstrong sat in the galley, flanked by his mother, stepfather, and his biological father. They had attended every one of Sims' hearings, watching him closely. Junior watched Mushroom from a safe distance, but his heart still palpitated and he needed to feel his family physically next to him. Junior still did not sleep in his own room or even away from his parents, and nightmares often caused him to awake screaming.

Rob Nugent attended with his family. He noticed Mush never looked up, never looked around, but kept his eyes averted. Rob recognized the unease in Sims' behavior as a result of undergoing his own personal trials and dilemmas with survivor guilt.

Doug Sims' parents attended, along with his siblings. The months of misery and embarrassment, the pain and shock they had to endure showed in their faces as well. They

196

were, after all, relatives of the Maddux family. Many in the community blamed them for Doug's crime.

Then it came time for Douglas Cecil Sims to stand and face Judge Westhafer, his back would be turned towards the people who loved Brad.

Judge Westhafer asked, "How do you plead??"

The officers who stood guard in the courtroom saw movement in the gallery. Junior's biological father leaned forward slowly in his seat. The officers stood at ready, their hands crossed over their belt buckles. One officer nudged another and nodded to his partner, then to Junior's father. Both watched the man as he slowly leaned forward, reached for his pants leg and pulled it up, his eyes on Douglas C. Sims. The pants leg came up, came up, and both officers' hands started to separate. The man then reached into his boot... and pulled up his sock. He let his pants leg down and sat up straight. The officers relaxed.

Sims answered Judge Westhafer, "Guilty." Guilty of Count I, Murder, a Felony I.C. 35-42-1-1 (1). The second charge, Count II: Child Molesting, was dismissed.

"Do you understand the nature of the charge?" Westhafer asked.

Sims stated he did.

When asked if he understood the possible penalties, Sims acknowledged he understood. When asked if he waived his rights and if this was indeed his plea, Sims stated in the affirmative. And it was over. In less time than it took to bring Brad Maddux into his home and then murder him, Sims had turned over his life to the State of Indiana.

Westhafer set a sentencing hearing for September 28, 1990 at 9:00 a.m. The judge's face was unsmiling.

Through it all, Douglas Sims remained emotionless. His expression was bland. Officers led him away from the courtroom.

Eleven days later, Douglas C. Sims stood in front of Circuit Court Judge John Westhafer again. Next to Sims stood his attorney, Brent Westerfield. Also present was William O. Smith, representing the state of Indiana. The state and the defense could present evidence that, if considered relevant to the case, would affect sentencing. Each side was well-prepared for this.

Westerfield argued people in the community liked Doug

Sims, he brought up Sims' military record, and he was employed in a good job. Westerfield also declared Sims was remorseful.

Representing the state, William O. Smith argued for the statutory maximum under Indiana statutes at the time, without probation, of sixty years.

It is the trial court's job to weight mitigating and aggravating circumstances, explain in their sentencing statement the mitigating to aggravating circumstances, and give reason, specifically, why each circumstance was mitigating or aggravating. Judge Westhafer considered this, citing, "the particularly brutal nature of the wound inflicted." Westhafer ruled circumstances outweighed the fact a remorseful Sims had no prior criminal history.

The trial court was not bound to agreeing to all of the mitigating circumstances. Just because Sims was well liked or had been in the military did not sway a decision. Just because he had a good job and worked for a living did not change the fact Brad Maddux had been only twelve years old and enticed by an adult with alcohol. Emotions aside, legal expertise and knowledge in the forefront, the law determined Sims' sentence.

Judge Westhafer explained that he knew Sims hoped to receive the standard punishment of forty years. However, Judge Westhafer explained, "In balancing the mitigating circumstances with the nature of this crime, the court finds this offense so brutal and outrageous," he added "an additional twenty years." He continued to explain the case did not meet the criteria for a death penalty case, and he knew some people did not understand this. In reviewing the case files, the judge agreed Sims had shown remorse, but disagreed with Brent Westerfield that "This crime will not happen again."

"The court cannot predict that," Judge Westhafer explained. He added, "I don't think anyone fully understands what happened when Bradley Maddux was killed. Bradley was no physical match for the defendant." Although no one could prove confinement, there was evidence that Brad had been bound and gagged—the ligature marks on the wrists, the gag around his mouth—"this is aggravating circumstance." The court could not prove "improper sexual activity," although "the court does

198

find (Sims) had contributed to the delinquency of Bradley Maddux by giving him alcoholic beverages to drink" and ruled that these crimes and the "wound to the victim" (the throat slash) were both aggravating circumstances. "This attack on this victim was so brutal and was almost decapitation," the judge said, calling it "A very strong aggravating circumstance."

Doug Sims looked on placidly as the judge sentenced Sims to the maximum sentence: sixty years in the Indiana Department of Corrections for the murder of Bradley Daryl Maddux. Westhafer also explained Sims received 202 days credit for the days he had served in the county jail during his arrest and trial. This made Sims' projected release date March 9, 2020.

In the year 2020, Brad would have been forty-three years old. Old enough to have his own family, a farm, and a college degree; old enough to race motorcycles, work at a business, or fulfill any dream he fancied. Instead, his body lay buried in the cold ground in a Westport cemetery for the six months it took for Sims' legal wrangling to proceed.

According to witnesses at the sentencing hearing, not once did Douglas "Mushroom" Sims show one iota of compassion, regret, or remorse. He may as well have been watching it all on television, a story about someone he never met.

He let the officers lead him away from the courtroom without incident. He never shed a tear, never looked back.

"Do you know the worse part of this whole case?" Indiana State Trooper Terry Steed asks today. "The worst part of this whole thing? We went to trial, and Sims didn't have to stand up in court and tell what he did. He didn't have to tell because he struck a plea bargain. His attorney spoke for him, the district attorney spoke, and he didn't have to say a thing," Steed sputters. "He said absolutely nothing. Not one thing. He never had to tell what he did." Doug Sims' silence and lack of emotion left a line of law enforcement officers grinding their teeth and showing white-knuckled fists, exasperated and furious, boiling in anger at the fact he did not have to own up to his actions. Every law enforcement officer who had worked this case, and even some that did not, had shed tears for Bradley

Maddux. The Maddux family, Brad's school friends and teachers, the community—so many people had ached over the loss. Doug Sims, who butchered the little boy like a Mariah Packing Plant animal, never even had to tell the court he played a part in the death.

The defendant has a constitutional right against self-incrimination. Although the defendant, Doug Sims, pled guilty, he did not speak at the hearing so he could appeal the sentence. It also protected him during post-conviction remedies. This is standard legal practice.

The guilty plea was the same as a jury trial conviction without using the time and money, and it provided long-term certainties. Sims could appeal his sentence; he could not claim the evidence, found during the investigation, was obtained illegally; Sims could not claim his confession was obtained illegally. This was of utmost importance, for if he could prove his confession was retrieved illegally, anything located because of it, including Brad's body, would not be admissible as evidence; this is called "fruit of the poisonous tree."

For example, one rumor had Jon Oldham driving to Doug Sims' trailer and demanding to know where Brad Maddux was located. In this tale, Oldham slammed Sims against the truck, held him in a vise-like grip by the throat, and choked him until Sims spilled the truth. There is no truth to this story. Harming Sims in any way rendered the confession obtained under duress: Doug Sims could have admitted to killing Brad Maddux, Jimmy Hoffa, kidnapping the Lindbergh Baby, and crashing Amelia Earhart. Despite his confession, all of the evidence—the bodies of Maddux and Hoffa, the baby, Earhart's plane—would be thrown out of court, allowing Sims the possibility to walk because the confession was illegally obtained. The bodies and the plane served as the "fruit" and the confession the "poisonous tree."

"I don't let my kids go one block away to the park by our house," Jill Bishop says firmly. It does not matter they live in a small town. "Brad was nice to everybody," she recalls, "Everybody."

Junior Armstrong began to have brushes with the law, and his life appeared to be spiraling out of control. He pushed away anyone he believed was getting too close to him for fear of losing them. He became drug and alcohol addicted, racking up DWI's. At the same time, he feared what would happen if he found himself imprisoned in the same institution as Douglas Sims. "I know," he says now, "I'd kill him. Then I'd be locked up forever and never see my kids." His mother had divorced his "Dad" and "ran off with a convicted child molester." Junior keeps an overprotective eye on his own children. He educated them about safety and ensured there was an open communication with them. He describes himself as "paranoid, skittish, leery" when it comes to anyone being near his own kids. "I sleep best when they're in the house with me," he confides. He also holds contempt for Ben Frost and Mike Meadows; "I heard they had something to do with Brad's murder."

When things finally returned to normal at South Decatur Elementary, Dollie Press noticed something. She has remained friends with the Meadows, but now it seemed that the taboo subject created unspoken rules in their friendship, such as, "Don't talk about Brad's murder." Gone was their innocence, their feeling of invincibility, and their beliefs that youth guaranteed a long, happy life. And Dollie Press noticed something else.

She sat next to Ben Frost in typing class. She watched Ben furiously type away, page after page. One day, Dollie saw Ben's papers, at what he so feverishly worked on. On the pages of typewriter paper, Ben Frost had typed three words repeatedly:

Doug killed Brad
Doug killed Brad
Doug killed Brad
Doug killed Brad
Doug killed Brad
Doug killed Brad
Doug killed Brad
Doug killed Brad
Doug killed Brad

"Ben never recovered from all of it," adds a close friend, and Summer Hobbs agrees. "There was a sadness over

201

Ben," she explains.

Gates are now placed in front of the cement pillars to keep the curious out of the Mt. Olivet cemetery after Brad's remains were located. It became, for a time, a spot of curiosity for people. "Cars were driving up and down the road at all hours," confides a resident of Alert. For some time, at night it was particularly crowded; on Halloween it was an area attraction. The quiet little hamlet suddenly became akin to a drive-through. "I don't know why," says another resident. "I guess people just needed to see."

Douglas Sims settled into the Indiana Department of Corrections' Correctional Industrial Facility (CIF), becoming inmate # 910253. To get to CIF one drives past the maximum-security institution, Pendleton Correctional Facility. CIF is in the Fall Creek Township, in Pendleton. Inmates are housed in mostly two-man rooms, not cells, in housing units which surround a grassy yard. Sims was given khaki pants, khaki shirts, sweatshirts, white socks, and underwear. He could wear state-issued black shoes or white sneakers. There are strict policies on visitation, jewelry, food, and movement, but not as strict as Pendleton Correctional Facility. Sims became one of the 24,000 inmates incarcerated in Indiana's state prison population.

All inmates, unless they have a legitimate medical excuse, are given a job in the prison. Douglas Sims fell into the prison routine. His parents visited him when they could. His siblings refused.

Visitation with inmates by family and friends is held Monday through Friday, from 4:30 p.m. to 9:00 p.m. and from 7:30 a.m. to 1:00 p.m. on weekends and holidays. Visitors are not allowed into the institution after 8:30 p.m. on weekdays, and their entry is stopped from 5:15 - 6:15 p.m. to allow for shift change processing. Sims' parents could visit him for a limit of two hours.

An inmate must present his visiting list request to their counselor for approval before visiting may occur. A background check is completed on the listed persons; family members must be confirmed as legal or blood relatives. Clothing regulations for visitors is strict: shorts cannot be fringed; no revealing clothing, and shirts must have sleeves. If a visitor is wearing a blazer or jacket they cannot remove that jacket. The visitor is limited to what

202

they can bring into the institution; no paper money is allowed. Each visitor is limited to eight dollars. The institution has lockers in the lobby for visitors to place valuables and items not deemed legal in the visitation area. Visitors place a quarter into the locker to utilize it and retrieve their items, and their quarter, upon departure.

Visitation takes place in a room with tables and vending machines. Prison officers carefully search the area prior to visitation and afterward. There are many ways a visitor could secret contraband into the room. There are large spaces inside the backs of soft drink machines, perfect for large items. The visitor's restroom must be carefully searched. "The strangest thing I have seen visitors smuggle in," says one prison correctional officer "was three pounds of cooked shrimp. It was bagged and stuffed inside the toilet tank" waiting for the inmate to pick it up and smuggle it into the prison compound.

Anyone visiting Doug Sims could pay for a photograph together. Inmates will create backdrops to hang for this purpose, so the inmate and those in the photo will have a nice background in their picture. At $2.00 apiece, visitors could have up to three pictures taken. If an inmate or his visitors do something inappropriate, such as a gang sign or gesture, the visit is terminated immediately and the photo destroyed.

Visitors are monitored for where they sit and how they sit. An inmate may enjoy something from the visiting room vending machine, but only if the visitor makes the purchase. Inmates and their visitors are not allowed to wander about. Sims is allowed one kiss and one hug per person when they came into the room, and one kiss and one hug per person when the visitor leaves the visit. He may hold a female's hand, but only if it is on the tabletop. The institution is tobacco-free, which irks many visitors.

Despite the strict rules and regulations, visitors are able to smuggle in anything from food to drugs, and they will do so. Visitors are not strip-searched and are adept at hiding the items on their person, in their baby's blankets or bottles, and on visiting children. "Visiting is the worst," confides an officer. "There are many of them and only so many officers to watch them. I wonder how many children were conceived behind vending machines?" The officer recounts how, at one institution, one inmate encouraged his wife to "flash" his friends; she wore a skirt but no panties. She would sit, legs uncrossed, and open her legs wide any time another inmate looked. Another visitor smuggled in a tattoo gun and ink, hiding it inside the cavity of a soft drink machine.

Official visitors must have their photograph taken for identification purposes. Jon Oldham visited Sims some time after his incarceration. Oldham attempted to get Doug Sims to tell him more about the case. Sims remained nonchalant about what he did. He refused to discuss the case further. And there was one more thing.

Doug Sims had the job of photographing people who entered the institution so they could be properly identified upon departure. "You can't leave this place without my help," Sims smugly told Oldham as he snapped the photo. "I take the pictures." It was as if he had some sort of power over who must stay and who was allowed to leave. Doug Sims, Oldham confirmed to himself, was a strange bird.

Meanwhile, outside of the Correctional Industrial Facility, Brad's family and friends struggled on to survive without him. At the same time, Doug Sims' parents stayed away from the public; some people blamed the elder Sims for Doug's behavior. They saw one another in church, but sat on opposite sides of the room and averted their eyes. Both families continued to grieve, sharing many of the same dynamics. Later, the Maddux family and Brad's friends explained they held no grudges against Doug's parents. They understood it was Doug, not his parents, who took Brad's life. And each felt bad about what the Sims family had to endure, knowing their son was a convicted child killer. At the same time, the Sims and the Maddux families would cross paths in public, catching each other's eyes at the local store or standing behind the other in line at the grocery store. It was not easy, living just minutes away from one another.

Inmates spend a lot of time attempting to shave off one day, a week, or a year from their sentences. The minute they are sentenced, incarcerated individuals plan to appeal the sentence. Doug Sims was no exception. Attorney Brent Westerfeld filed an appeal on behalf of his client, Indiana Supreme Court no. 16S0C – 9101-CR-42.

204

Justice Jon D. Krahulik wrote the response to the Appeal. Like most of those involved in the case, Krahulik was a local; he was born December 31, 1944, in Indianapolis. He had attended Indiana University, where he received his A.B. in 1965 and a J.D. cum laude four years later. Justice Krahulik had been admitted to the Indiana Bar in 1969, as well as the U.S. Court of Appeals, Seventh Circuit, the U.S. District Court, Southern District of Indiana, and the U.S. Tax Court. Justice Krahulik was one of those people who lived the law: he served on the Indiana Legal Forum from 1967 to 1969, he was the predecessor to the Indiana Law Review, and served as director of the Indiana Lawyers Commission in 1973. Besides his work on the bench Justice Krahulik shared his knowledge and love of the practice as an adjunct professor at the Indiana University School of Law in Indianapolis in 1992, teaching State Constitutional Law. He was square of jaw and his short hair was swept neatly over the top of his head. He was definitely a family man, and known for having a keen sense of humor. He was well thought of by his students. He was a fair and just man who took his work seriously. Justice Krahulik was the Justice who had reversed Judge John Westhafer's sentence of murderer/kidnapper Stuart Kennedy in 1995. Now he was responding to the Appeal by Doug Sims.

"The only issue Sims raises," Justice Krahulik wrote, "Is whether the trial court properly considered certain mitigating circumstances in imposing the maximum sentence."

Westerfeld argued the court did not consider Sims' "character and condition" and the offense. The court should have considered the lack of criminal records, Sims' community involvement, how popular he had been in school, and the fact he held a good job and was a soldier in the Army as well as a member of the National Guard. Attorney Westerfeld also reminded the Supreme Court that Doug had admitted guilt and pled guilty, saving the state money by not dragging out his case by trial.

Justice Krahulik explained, "Sentencing is conducted within the discretion of the trial court and will be reversed only upon a showing of a manifest abuse of that discretion." The trial court had discretion to increase or decrease a sentence, based upon "aggravating or mitigating circumstances." Justice Krahulik cited Leticia v. State 1991, which determined a sentence was not unreasonable "unless no reasonable person could find such sentence appropriate" to the offender and their offense. For example, if Circuit Court Judge John Westhafer had sentenced Sims to the maximum-security prison for 100 years, based solely on the fact Westhafer did not like Sims' offense, the Supreme Court could certainly reverse the sentence. Westhafer had taken into consideration that Sims did appear remorse for his actions and had no prior criminal history.

It was the trial court's job to weight mitigating to aggravating circumstances, explain in their sentencing statement the mitigating to aggravating circumstances, and give reason, specifically, why each circumstance was mitigating or aggravating. Judge John Westhafer had done just that, listing the aggravating circumstances to be the fact Sims had supplied alcohol to a child, that Brad was a child, "and the particularly brutal nature of the wound inflicted." Judge John Westhafer ruled these circumstances outweighed the fact a remorseful Sims had no prior criminal history.

The trial court was not bound to agreeing to all of the mitigating circumstances. Just because Sims was well liked or had been in the military did not sway a decision. Just because he had a good job and worked for a living did not change the fact Brad Maddux had been only 12 years old and enticed by an adult with alcohol. Emotions aside, legal expertise and knowledge in the forefront, and the law had determined Sims' sentence.

The Supreme Court affirmed Judge Westhafer's decision. The file was stamped January 23, 1992. Douglas Cecil Sims would remain in prison to serve his original sentence.

In 1996 the senior class that should have included Brad Maddux was preparing for graduation ceremonies. "Brad should be with us," his buddy Tasha Asher thought as she tried on her cap and gown. "Something doesn't feel right," she said out loud as they practiced the walk across the stage, had friends sign their yearbooks, and the students planned their futures. "I wonder what Brad would be, who he would have been?" She contacted Daryl and Patti

Maddux, and then contacted the officials at South Decatur High. With their permission, at graduation, a huge wreath with the last photograph ever taken of Brad in its center was on display. Tasha placed a teddy bear in it, and it wore a cap and gown made by Tasha's mother. The class flower is a daisy, so the wreath was adorned with the sunshiny flower. The class president paid homage to Brad in the class speech, and the school gave a memento in Brad's name to the Maddux family. Brad may not walk across the stage to receive his diploma as he should have, but he was in the hearts and minds of the young people as they crossed the threshold from high school to adulthood. Tasha still could not hear the song "Hotel California" without crying; sometimes she would play the song when she missed her friend the most.

Most of Brad's friend's have stayed in the area of Westport. Many have children of their own. Because of what happened to their friend and schoolmate, these adults are "overprotective" of their own children. "Once it happens in your home," Tasha Asher explains, "You never forget." She has told her own children about her wonderful friend, but she also keeps "a strict, sometimes too strict eye on them." The Asher's doors and windows remain locked, "even during the day." Lynn Welch and others agree with her sentiment and practice the same precautions.

In 2010, Sims filed state government form 1213, a Request for a Clemency Hearing. He included his inmate number, the charge, the county where his trial was held, and length of sentence. He completed a block for "Circumstance of Offense" and one for "Reason clemency is requested." There was paperwork for the Trial Judge and the prosecuting attorney to complete. Because he had served one third of his sentence and had no disciplinary actions the last year he was incarcerated, the Request was accepted.
The Clemency Hearing was scheduled for April 1.
Again, the Maddux family and Brad's friends felt the sting of being victimized all over again. Some become confused – clemency? How could he get out sooner? Was this like

parole?

Clemency is not parole; parole is the release of an inmate from prison under certain conditions, for a given amount of time, as stipulated by the court. Clemency is the shortening of a sentence, the pardoning of an act, or a reprieve. The governor of the state or the United States President can only grant it, based on the recommendations of the Parole Board.

A "pardon" is the official act of forgiving a crime. If a person receives a pardon they cannot be retried for the crime, the crime is cleared from their criminal record, and the person cannot be punished or penalized for the crime.

A pardon is not the same as a "not guilty." Patty Hearst received a presidential pardon in 2001 for her role in the SLA activities during the 1970's, because numerous professionals proved she was brainwashed and forced to take part in the SLA's illegal activities.

A "reprieve" is a temporary delay in imposing the death penalty. Inmates request a reprieve because new evidence may have been found, errors in legal records, new testing such as DNA is available, etc. Reprieves are only delays. Doug Sims was requesting the shortening of his sentence because, as he wrote in his request, "I got drunk and killed a man."

This time, family went into action and put together a petition on the World Wide Web, using the personal computer as a weapon. They found a website called ipetition.com and signed on, creating a petition to fight Sims' early release and a plea to the Parole Board to deny him clemency. The petition included the last school picture taken of Brad and read:

On March 10th 1990 a 12 year old child was taken from us due to the evil, malicious, and downright sick acts of a murder. Bradley Maddux was a son, brother, grandson, nephew, friend, and so much more to the Westport Indiana community. Douglas Sims took Brad from this community. Took a son away from two loving parents Daryl and Patti Maddux. Took a brother away from Cody and Lindsay Maddux. Douglas Sims left this small town absolutely terrified and heartbroken. It has been only twenty years since the evil acts of this man took place and now he is asking for clemency. He wants to come back to our community and live his life. What about the life he took? What about the family and community this man destroyed? This man murdered a child. On March 10th the Maddux family lost a part of their life because of this man. Please help us make sure he does not get out of prison and be able to live his life. I am asking everyone who does not want this murder in our community to please support us and sign this petition to keep him in prison (sic).

The petition link gained exposure through the web via emails, Facebook, Myspace, and more; friends and family of Brad and complete strangers signed the petition. An online news article by this writer featured the story and more signed up, furious the state would even consider releasing Sims earlier than 2020.

Lynn Welch, the Maddux family neighbor, signed the petition immediately. Although she left Westport for a big city, she kept up with news via her family. "It was shocking to me how light (Sims') sentence was in the first place," she says. "And he did it so fearlessly, really. I wonder; can he trust himself to be in society?" She signed the computer-generated petition and hit "save." Lynn wonders how many boys Doug Sims had taken advantage of, and why they were not murdered.

Dollie Press demands more answers. "How is it this (case) is not talked about? We can talk about a horrible murder, but not about sexual molestation. If we don't talk about (sex crimes), it will creep into us." She talks to her own children about safety, and educates herself on crimes against children. She will never forget her encounter with Mush: "I would know his eyes, I would know his face, from a mile away."

Sheila Padgett cannot comprehend a system that would allow Doug Sims to "walk." She still has the love note and the pendent Brad had given her all those years ago, when they were innocent and no harm could be done to them. "Brad would have done something good with his life," she vows, and not just because he was murdered. "He was that type of person. He would have made a difference." She looks at her own children today, and remembers Brad. "He was the way I want my kids to be."

The family brought the petition with its signatures, the online news article, and their stories of Brad to the Board, and subsequently to the Governor of Indiana. All they could do was prepare for the response.

The response appeared to shock even those on the Parole Board.

9 HOW?

Sexual predators woo their victims over time; very few attack a stranger on the street. They begin with a child they know—a family member, a neighbor, or a student. The perpetrator will carefully select a child who is lonely or needy in some way, who has self-esteem issues. Perhaps they are a child who needs an ego boost or who lacks in certain areas of life: perhaps an absent parent, socioeconomic issues in the family, or poor sports skills in a society that takes these talents to heart. Initially, the perpetrator, like Sims, becomes the "big buddy" in an effort to create a connection with their victims. They relate to the child at the child's level. They may play video games, sports, or enjoy the same recreational activities, movies, theme parks, or music the child enjoys. Their social world may consist of only or mostly children. They may give themselves a moniker, such as "uncle," when there is no blood relation. They allow the child to call them by a first name, where the child normally calls adults by last names. The perpetrator may set themself up to be the child's confidant, or helpful friend, best friend, or the absent parent that the child "needs." They give gifts for no reason, and they also give gifts to the family. These are not gifts of love but "hush money." The perpetrator attempts to buy silence, for silence is the molester's secret weapon.

The web is spun and, eventually, the molestation begins. Now the child finds that he or she fell prey to fear or manipulation, and the offender snared them in a web of deceit and a hunger for power. Like a fly on a spider web, the child flails helplessly in its silky prison, and the culprit leaves them no escape. The transgressor worked diligently to fool all of the adults. Uncaught malefactors have long lists of victims, and as few people notify the police immediately, they have the benefit of time on their side. Before starting any abduction, the criminal usually guarantees that the family will remain silent.

211

Multiple studies prove that inmates age seven to ten years faster than non-inmates, appearing older than their chronological age due to substance abuse, their poor health, and the stress from living behind bars. They are also "older" medically, suffering illnesses and symptoms of people seven to ten years older than their actual age, usually due to substance abuse. A sixty-year-old Doug Sims will have the medical issues of a seventy-year-old man. Sims released at fifty-nine years old would be equivalent to a Sims at sixty-nine years old, both medically and physically—if he lived that long. Still, he lived, and Brad died. The Westport community argues: Would that be too old to prey on children? Away from children for so long, would he have "grown out of it"? According to extensive studies, child molesters rarely have only one or two victims.

"Mush was the cool one," says one of his friends. "He provided the alcohol. He was big in the young community, because he did allow drinking and we'd all go to his house."

Douglas Sims did not have time to cultivate Bradley Maddux, Junior Armstrong, or Rob Nugent that night. Instead, he stalked and tested his prey in an attempt to find the weakest link in the quickest way possible. Any one of the boys could have been his victim, or all of the boys could have fallen for his ruse. It is possible that Brad got out alive at first, but he probably broke the one rule of child molestation and said the two words that caused Sims to panic, perhaps two words Sims never heard before: "I'll tell."

Sims selected a victim that night. Mike could have been his original target. Then he tried Dollie. Then, at his home, he tried each boy, testing them, seeing which one would be easiest to trick and then molest. At some point he saw Rob and Junior were not malleable, nor were they easily manipulated, despite his many and various attempts. He approached all three, plying them with alcohol to lower their inhibitions and then pulling out the handcuffs to see which boy he could dominate.

He did this in steps, in steps that usually took a while, but perhaps Sims was in a hurry—perhaps his need for power and control had overtaken his need to be careful. Or perhaps he had too much to drink.

Step 1: Ply the boys with alcohol to lower their
inhibitions.

Step 2: Start a "wrestling match" to see who lets
him physically touch them.

Step 3: Test boundaries by not buttoning his
pants after using the bathroom.

Step 4: Further push a boundary by kissing and
touching.

Step 5: Pull out a "harmless / fun" way to
dominate yet capture with the handcuff
game.

Step four and five took place at different times with
different boys. He probably sensed, like most molesters
can, who had been a previous victim. He knew who to kiss
and who to avoid.

Step by step, Sims carefully made his way, testing. He
pushed the boundaries. When he saw which boy would
"work," he zoned in on Brad. He quickly figured out how
to play Brad, who Brad was, and how his mind operated:
Brad is innocent.

Brad is eager to please.

Brad trusts me because I am a relative.

Brad wants to show off and be macho.

Brad may suffer bullying because he is so sweet and good.

Brad's tolerance to alcohol is low.

Sims formed a quick plan and, as child predators do, took
advantage of all that Brad was. In hindsight, as adults,
Junior and Rob believe he worked on Brad's mind as he
unlocked him from the handcuffs that night. They can
almost hear Douglas Sims coaxing Brad into a plan: "Hey
buddy, let's you and me go get you all some more booze."

"Hey buddy—"removes the boundaries completely,
diminishing the fact more than fifteen years separate this
child and this man. An adult and a child cannot be
"buddies."

"Let's you and me—" security specialist Gavin de Becker
refers to this as "Forced Team Planning"—creating an
unwanted/nonexistent teaming between two individuals, a
kinship that does not exist. It's a "we're-in-this-together"
gamble where the stakes are usually dangerous. It is a sure

sign of manipulation.

"Go get us some more booze—" as if a twelve-year-old boy could purchase or procure alcohol in the middle of the night, or could even have a reason to accompany an adult on such an excursion.

An adult would be suspicious; a streetwise child may not have taken the bait. But Bradley Daryl Maddux was a trusting, nice kid who loved his family, and Douglas Sims was family. Sims was also a predator who lived on the innocence and silence of victims.

Sexual orientation has nothing to do with sexual molestation of a child—no more than rape has to do with making love. Like all crimes, a sexual offense is about power and control: asserting power over someone helpless. Child sex offenders who attack the same sex are not homosexual or bisexual. Offenders who attack opposite-sex victims are not heterosexual. They are all predators. In a 2001 study conducted on over 4,000 admitted sexual predators in forty-seven states, more than seventy percent of the male predators who molested male victims were heterosexual. The majority of the perpetrators who molested male victims were married, divorced, or widowed from a female (Abel & Harlow).

Studies show that nothing cures or stops molesters despite psychotherapy or even castration. Behaviors may change, but mindsets cannot. It is akin to trying to force a lion to stop acting like a lion. You can declaw the lion, remove the teeth, cage it and teach it to do funny circus tricks, but one day the predator instinct will come to the forefront of the lion's brain, and it will attack someone. The predator strikes at a hapless victim and tragedy ensues. This is why a wild animal can be a pet for years and then, one day "out of nowhere," attack its trainer/owner, the one who raised it, fed it, loved it—because a predator remains a predator, no matter how many times it is treated with love and care. The same law applies to a human predator. No matter who loves them, or how many times they go through psychotherapy, jail, or counseling, they will be stay quiet or subdued and obey the rules for a while. But one day...

10 "I DON'T KNOW"

On April 1, 2010, Douglas Cecil Sims took a seat before the Indiana State Parole Board for his clemency hearing. His hair now grey, he wears it neat and short. He now sported a full beard and mustache. He wore the prison-issued pullover tan shirt and tan slacks with a white T-shirt underneath. His expression was bland.

The board consisted of three members this morning: two white males and an African-American female. They sat at an impressive-looking desk, shaped like a half moon, with an austere wooden emblem of the state of Indiana nestled in its center. Files and papers lay stacked about the desk. Each person leafed through the files during the hearing.

Indiana performs its hearings via live satellite, so Sims appeared on a television screen before the board. In turn, he watched the board from a camera.

Vice Chairman Randall P. Gentry led the hearing. He served as a board member since 2003. Gentry introduced Board Member Valerie Parker, who served as a member since 1998, and Board Member William Harris. Mr. Harris began his tenure on the board in 2006. Gentry explained for the record that this was a five-member board, but the three members present would legally constitute for the hearing. Gentry listed the sentencing date as September 28, 1990 and Sims' release date as March 2020. Gentry identified himself and introduced each of the board members, who both issued a cheery "Good morning."

Doug Sims sat in a straight-backed chair looking into the monitor. They asked him to state his name and his prison number. His voice was a deep baritone, and he held up a piece of paper to show his name and prison-issued identification number. "Douglas Sims, 910253."

Vice Chairman Gentry asked if Sims needed any information or wanted an overview of how the hearing would proceed. "You can give me an overview," Doug said to him, "'Cause I don't even know what to expect."

Vice Chairman Gentry carefully outlined and explained the hearing procedures. The Indiana Parole Board acts as a Clemency Commission for all capital cases and makes recommendations to the governor concerning clemency or commutation requests. The purpose, Gentry said, "was for fact finding." They planned to interview Sims about the crime and, based on information and records, make a recommendation to the governor. He explained it would take six to eight months for Sims to receive a response. Clemency grants by the governor are rare. "Clemency," said Gentry, "Is a long shot." Doug Sims stated he understood.

Then it began. Vice Chairman Randall P. Gentry asked the first question, requesting Sims to elaborate on the crime that led him to prison.

Sims' expression was nondescript. "I was totally drunk," he said slowly. "Alcohol had my life and I killed a young boy." He sat, unmoving, emotionless.

Gentry granted Sims time to say more, and then asked, "Do you care to elaborate?"

"No, not really." Sims added, "It's something I'd like to put in my past."

Gentry reviewed pages in a file and did not accept this answer. He continued to ask Sims to elaborate and explain. "What else was going on in your life?"

"Ah, it was alcohol. Alcohol controlled my life back then." Sims stared into the camera, emotionless.

Gentry became frustrated, but remaining the quintessential professional, he gave Sims other opportunities to detail his past. "Did you go to sleep with a bottle in your hand and wake up with the bottle in your hand?" he asked. "Did you work? I mean, what was going on in your life?"

Doug Sims elaborated, "Well, when I got frostbite in the army I could not reenlist no more. They let me join the (National) Guard. But it just—alcohol took over. I wanted to stay in the military but they wouldn't let me reenlist. I started drinkin' too much."

Gentry quizzed him on his employment at the time of the crime.

"I was working at a pork processing plant." He did not explain what the job entailed.

Board Member Valerie Parker leafed through the files as

the two men spoke. She spoke up and asked Sims how he knew his victim.

"Relation," Sims said shortly.

The board members waited for elaboration, emotion, anything that could assist in their decision. It was akin to pulling extremely rotted teeth.

"I got drunk and that's it; I killed him. I don't know. I killed him," Sims appeared to struggle with his thoughts. When asked how Brad was related to him, he also vacillated. "On my mother's side of the family. It's like a cousin, or something like that," his tone sounded as if it did not matter. He reduced Brad to "It."

Board Member Parker's response was not positive; she obviously felt frustrated. She reminded Doug Sims of the circumstances of the crime, to include Brad being found "in his underwear...buried."

Sims listened and then, after a pause, said, "I couldn't tell you. I blacked out."

"Well, what can you tell us?" Parker asked him, incredulous.

"I blacked out. I couldn't tell you." Again, the vacillating.

Parker heard enough. "You were at the trial. Did you black out then or were you drinking there, too?"

Sims stumbled in his answer, and then said, "Well, it was long ago..."

Parker blasted him. She told Sims the crime was something he should be able to recall every day of his life, every moment, for the rest of his life. She spoke of the body's condition, the appall she felt due to Sims' responses and noncommittal behavior. "This is a crime you should never forget," her voice rose. "You sit here and say you don't remember. How can you have any remorse? You sit here like somebody made it all up." She moved papers in frustration. "I'm just one vote on the board," she said, the anger palatable, "But I can tell you, I'm not happy with your presentation."

The camera caught Sims glaring at her. He pursed his lips. "They told me he was found in his underwear," he deadpanned.

There were other kids, two other kids. What happened with them?

217

Sims corrected the board: "He was the only one. The other two were out walkin' around." When asked, he could not recall Brad's age. "Thirteen, maybe?" A board member corrected him.

"Twelve," Harris said loudly.

The Board wanted, again, for Sims to elaborate, but it was almost impossible. How did Sims come into contact with Bradley?

"I picked him up." Silence.

How? Where?

"From Westport."

And where did you go?

Sims said, "We went to my place."

Board Member Parker asked Sims if he felt sexually attracted to Bradley. Did he engage in previous sexual encounters with the boys? With any boys? What was the nature of their relationship?

"Strictly friends." Sims' voice had an edge to it.

Parker told him it made no sense and was incredibly suspicious. "You're an adult with a twelve-year-old 'friend,'" her voice was strong. She asked him to explain this.

"I don't know. Loneliness." The board waited, but he said no more. Did he have friends his own age? "No," Sims answered. They inquired, who was Ernest Armstrong?

"I don't remember that name." The board reminded him of Ernest "Junior" Armstrong's testimony regarding the kisses on the head.

Parker read from her notes about Junior and Rob's presence and how Junior told of Sims' kissing him.

"They might have been there. I don't remember," Sims said it as if he were bored.

Board Member William Harris appeared just as exasperated as Board Member Parker. "How in the frickin' world," he asked Doug Sims, could Sims be trusted in public? How could the board make any decisions based on the answers given today? Alcohol intake cannot be regulated. Behavior cannot be watched all the time. What makes him think he is trustworthy?

"'Cause I don't drink no more," Sims answered simply.

The course of questioning took a turn, and they asked Sims about his activities and work in prison. Sims

218

explained he attended AA (Alcoholics Anonymous) every Wednesday; he was a member of a prayer circle and a union. He had a job.

Where did he work now?

"In maintenance."

The board noted that his conduct history, during incarceration, was clear at the time. No infractions, no write-ups, no negative reports.

"Given the opportunity to be released sooner than 2020," Vice Chairman Randall P. Gentry asked Sims, what did he plan to do? Where would he live?

"I'm hoping to find a job in a restaurant 'cause I know how to cook," Sims explained. He "had an aunt and an uncle . . . a father and mother" who would welcome him home.

Vice Chairman Gentry explained he did not intend to trick Sims, but he sought only to obtain honest answers in an effort to make an informed decision. He discussed the size of the community and how it would be inevitable that Sims encountered the victim's family in public. What would Sims say to the victim's family?

A pause, then, "I'm sorry that it ever happened." Another pause.

Gentry asked him how he planned to explain to the victim's family and friends that he was allowed to walk free early?

"That my conduct in prison showed I was good enough to be given a chance back out in civilian life," Sims replied.

The board noted he possessed a high school diploma upon entering prison. They asked him if he took part in any education programs in prison, perhaps a college degree?

"I tried to get a grant when I was in Michigan City," Sims explained, but he was denied because "I had used my grant when I was in the Army." Because of his sentence length, he did not qualify for grant monies with another program. "I had too many years to qualify."

Parker continued to attempt to obtain information on the crime itself. She reminded Sims, by his own self-admission, he had been arrested a day after the crime. "By then, you should have been sober." She gave some details about the aftermath of the murder; he was questioned by law enforcement; he was a part of the puzzle.

219

"I didn't really know at the time. I was not sober," he repeated.

"But you were sober enough to lie (to police)" Parker shot back. Again, she asked him about what occurred, how he felt, and why he blamed alcohol on his crime.

Sims had no answer.

Parker asked him, "Do you believe you killed this little boy?"

"After I got all the way off of alcohol," Doug Sims sighed, "Sitting in the county jail for three days, yes."

"Do you know why," her voice softened, "You killed him?"

"No. I completely lost it with alcohol and—and everything."

Board Member Parker remained unsatisfied. "Do you have any concept of what transpired between you and that young man?" She explained, that any parent would want answers. It was the responsibility of the board to release those who seemed eligible for clemency. Also, part of the board's responsibility involved explaining to victims' families why a person was released early.

She gave him a chance to respond. He did not.

Harris noted that the crime occurred in 1990, and asked Sims when he had left the Army.

"1987," Sims replied.

And did he have any criminal history before the murder? Any misdemeanors, criminal acts, other crimes on his record? Anything at all?

Sims said, "Nothin'." He seemed to forget the charge he received in the Army and the traffic ticket in Kentucky.

Harris repeated, no criminal history at all? Not even a misdemeanor, or anything?

Sims did not respond.

Vice Chairman Gentry then began the conclusion of the hearing. He asked the board members if they had any more questions or comments. Neither Board Member Parker nor Board Member Harris had more questions or comments. Gentry asked Doug Sims if he had any final thoughts.

"Just hope you release me," Sims said.

The meeting came to an end. Sims returned to his residence at the state prison to await the governor's

220

decision.

Throughout the hearing, Douglas Sims acknowledged the murder of Brad Maddux only when pushed. He blamed alcohol addiction for his crime and the Army on his addiction. The sole time he apologized for the act was when he was pushed for an answer. Perhaps it was because Doug Sims could not articulate clearly. Perhaps it was because he felt nervous and did not prepare for the hearing. Perhaps he did feel guilt overwhelming him, but he feared a show of emotion.

Or perhaps it was because he felt absolutely nothing at all for the heinous murder of twelve-year-old Brad.

The wait became brutal. Brad's friends and family members asked the fearful question: *What if Sims got out?* They comforted each other with the information passed on from various officials: There is no way Douglas Sims is going to be released early. And if they do let him go—well, plenty of people in town would gladly take care of him. The last few words sent chills down everyone's backs, particularly some of Cody Maddux's relatives. They all feared Cody might take the law into his own hands. Cody's life was going well; what if he threw it all away in the name of some perceived justice? Their worry teetered back and forth: Sims might get released. Sims might not get released. Brad's siblings had children now—what if Sims took revenge? What if he targeted Junior and Rob? The authorities provided Daryl with a phone number to the parole board for victims' family members to call, but each time he telephoned, he received the same reply: no information yet.

The word "victim" conjures up a horrible world thrust upon the helpless, from which they will never fully recover. What they thought they knew is gone. Their lives split into two time periods: before the crime and after the crime. People fundamentally change after becoming a victim, and no one wants to be a victim. Law enforcement saw the need for creating specialized departments for victims; they provided people who are specially trained in everything from suicide models to molestation, and they also supply community resources to assist the crime victims. Some victims have never set foot inside of a courthouse before the crime. To some, it seems as if the justice system protects the perpetrator and ignores the victim. Court procedures and legal issues such as arrest powers, child visitation, and protective orders can seem confusing; the proceedings grow even more confusing if one is injured or mentally shaken from being victimized. Add to this the stress of funeral arrangements, of the loss of someone dear, of making arrangements for the lost person's belongings, and of little plans—like how to tell friends and family while also balancing their feelings of guilt, anger, and frustration. Losing someone to murder is particularly heinous—some judge the parent (*"Where were they?"*), others blame the victim for his actions (*"Why did he go there?"*), still more apply a grisly label to the community (*"That's the place that kid was killed"*), and everyone gets tainted at some point.

"Sims is out and he is living in Sardinia."
Maddux family members telephoned one another asking, "Is it true? Have you heard?" In a small town, rumors catch like brush fire, die down, and start up at another flash point. Someone confirmed they saw Doug Sims in Sardinia. Someone else said they heard another person report that Sims was in Westport. Others claimed Sims was in North Vernon, talking to some kids.
Daryl Maddux attempted to call officials, but the number did not work. He waited and tried it again; still inoperable. After a few more tries, Daryl gave up. He had no idea what to do next. He did not know who to call or how to get through the system.
On October 17, 2011, a friend called the Indiana State Parole Board to discover the truth. Douglas Sims' plea for clemency had been denied on March 11, 2011, and they assured the friend that Sims would not be able to apply for another clemency hearing for another five years, in 2016. The Indiana Department of Corrections would be his home until 2020. No one had notified Brad's family. After some research, the Maddux family signed up for notifications of any changes to Sims' record, movement, or anything effecting his imprisonment, such as parole hearings.
But as prepared as they feel, they know it is never over.

11 PUTTING THE PIECES TOGETHER

Afterwards, there were so many unanswered questions. How could a grown man prey on a child in the open? How could he get away with it for so long? How is it that the laws do not stop these predators?

Because being homosexual or the label of "homosexual" is often considered the worst thing to be in our society, males will often refuse to admit to being sexually abused by other males. They fear being labeled: "fag," "queer," "gay." They hear it in the media, in churches, in schools, and in some homes. Even with friends, the words, "That is so gay!" serves to indicate something is negative or bad. The Boy Scouts and United States military openly refused to allow homosexuals to serve, as if gays are pariahs or gay males are not masculine or a sexual threat (since the induction of Don't Ask / Don't Tell / Don't Pursue, more officers have been discharged for either being gay or being suspected as being gay than before it was introduced).

All of these negative stereotypes are not lost on children. In small towns, where there is not much diversity, this rings true the most. Small towns demand males to show a certain amount of machismo, act a certain way, talk a certain way, and create a role model for young men and boys to follow. Boys who have more interest in the arts than, say, hunting and fishing, suffer suspicious attention in the town's eyes. "After Brad's murder, it came out there were more boys molested by Doug Sims," says one person who resided in Westport but asked to remain anonymous. "But they did not want to tell anyone because this is a little town and (the victims) were afraid people would call them names (of a homosexual nature)." Often the molester uses this homophobia to wield power over his victims: "If you tell, people will call you a fag."

Also, people deny these things happen, claim that the

223

father would never harm the child or the grandfather would not "do that." We want to believe people can change, get better, find Jesus, or heal by reading a good book. Chemical castration, finding a nice spouse, going to church, moving to another parish, settle down—whatever cure they need to implement to get people to "stop bothering kids." Most of all, people do not want to think poorly of others, and if we are suspicious we immediately stuff the feeling. If people suspect something, people tell them that they are just paranoid, over-excited, jaded, or just "crazy."

Bud Allen and Diana Bosta's "Games Criminals Play" is the Bible for those who work in corrections, but everyone concerned with safety should read this timeless and important book. The authors write of that "gut level" feeling, that sense in the pit of the stomach that says something is wrong:

> ...most often the suspicion that something
> being wrong has no initial foundation in fact,
> but is simply something one feels. There is an
> innate desire in human beings to want good to
> come from their relationships with others, so
> when this inner feeling of uneasiness occurs . . .
> people chide themselves and cast the matter
> aside as foolish . . . they rarely analyze the
> feeling . . . most people tend to back away from
> situations or feelings they find difficult... (208)

People rarely deny suspicious feelings in regards to any other crime. Let us say you are en-route to enter a bank in July, when you observe four grown men at the bank entrance. All four wear heavy trench coats and gloves. Prior to walking in, they stop to don ski masks. Then two stuff their hands in their pockets and two have heavy sacks. All of them take quick looks around. They run into the bank. Would you still enter the bank or would you call for help? It is highly unlikely you would say to yourself, "Stop being silly! You're being too suspicious!"

You are out for a walk when you see a young man carrying a large, empty trash bag sneaking around the side of a house. No cars line the driveway; no lights shine in the windows; no sounds of a television or radio come from the home. The man looks around then eases open a side window, waits, and then carefully slips into the house. Would you feel slightly suspicious? Or would you think, "He's probably locked out and that's his house." It is highly unlikely you would think, "Stop thinking the worst! You're so suspicious!"

An average person would instantly suspect the men in the above scenarios plan to rob the bank and burgle the house. Their body language, their clothing, and their actions tell the observer that something is amiss. It would be rare to brush off feelings of, "I'm being paranoid" or "I'm just overreacting." The brain takes in all of the information (body language, clothing, actions) in a millisecond and processes it, then it sets off the little warning bell called Instinct (millions of years of survival) that says, "Something wrong here" without making the rest of the brain even consciously aware of it. If it works with a robbery or burglary, why would it not work with a child predator? Because polite society force-feeds the world phrases such as "don't talk about such evil things." Shut up. The predator's greatest tool: silence.

People also do not want to believe that certain people would harm children because of who they are or how they make their livelihood. Suppose a single man lives on a ranch that is tailor-made for children. He provides them with video games, movies, music, even animals and carnival rides. He takes the kids with him to Disneyland and has fantastic parties for children only. He buys them lavish gifts and admits the children sleep with him in his bed. He has few adult friends. Would you be suspicious of his intentions? Everyone should be. Would you allow your child to visit him? No one should allow the child to even speak to the person.

Society elects to believe someone else's word over the child's. People hear on television, "four hundred people missing in earthquake" on the news and do not question it. Yet they refuse to believe a person would sexually abuse a child, simply because that person seems nice, or is married, or is good-looking, or successful. Often we adults assume the child must be lying because they have an active

225

imagination, watch too much television and bad movies, or play video games. Overall, society accepts the words of a stranger (the newscaster selling the news) over their own children on any given day. Those who work with children on any given day can tell stories upon stories of children left to the system because a caregiver refused to believe the child's story and instead believed the molester's tale.

Some women will take the word of an abuser over their children because society tells women they must have a man to be worthy. Women grow up hearing how Snow White, Cinderella, and all those other pretty, strong women needed a man to save them. A handsome prince will save them from despair; all they have to do is wait. If the prince shows up, hang onto him. If he does not, grab the next best thing. A woman, we are often told, is nothing without a man. Even "women's magazines" carry this subtle message. At the risk of losing her man, the female will take his word over the abused child, because she fears losing him.

Child abuse laws appear toothless. In Indiana, to "Knowingly and intentionally cause bodily injury to a person under age 14" § 35-42-2-1(a)(2)(B) and (a)(4) is punishable by a minimum of six years if the injury is "serious" and one year if it is not. With good time (time served in prison without a negative incident gives inmates credit toward their sentence length) and time served (the time spent in jail awaiting trial or going before the judge for sentencing), the perpetrator could serve less than five years for, say, a scalding, beating, cutting, or burning. In less time than it takes for a person to earn a college degree, a child abuser walks free. The legal system believes that the term "child abuse" can be loosely defined, just as "bodily harm" and "neglect." In a southern state, one caller to Child Protective Services related how a family member's children had to forage for dog food behind the furniture while their parents slept off drug and alcohol binges. CPS told them a "home check" could not be performed on a family simply for "being messy."

In the years following Brad's death, his best friend, Junior, grew well-acquainted with the penal system while he battled a devil within himself. He now speaks openly

226

and honestly about his journey. He admits to being suicidal and trying to kill himself because of the guilt Brad's demise has caused. Junior only found refuge in drugs. "Something is wrong with the (legal) system," he says. "Why is it, someone with an addiction, with a problem, can be put away for life? But Sims killed an innocent child and gets sixty years! Sixty?" Junior has tried various programs in his attempts at sobriety. "When Brad was murdered, I didn't have anyone help me get through it, so I turned to drugs and drinking to escape," he admits. "Now that I'm sober and facing it, I have to learn new coping skills. And I don't know how."

Lynn Welch still visited Junior Armstrong when she could possible. She saw pain and loss etched in Junior, as clear as black ink letters on a white board. Lynn Welch could plainly see the "guilt and loneliness" that Junior carried. She also saw Junior as flotsam, moving from here to there, married then divorced, in and out of jail and slipping in sobriety—just floating from one incident to another. "Between his family and Brad's murder," she says today, "I am not surprised."

Potential victim Rob Nugent, as a father, now looks at the United States laws made to protect children with disdain. "We (the United States) look down on and put down certain countries," he sputters in anger. "We shouldn't even refer to them as 'third world.' Look at their system of punishment. If you're convicted of hurting a child, you're put to death. Their prison systems are made to punish." When he is reminded of the problems with these systems, he considers the subject carefully. "But," he says slowly, "We have to make a change, somewhere. These are our kids."

One of Rob's best friends confides, "Rob was suicidal. It was like he didn't care about death. He didn't care about living." It was only when Rob became a parent he gained a true will to live, says his friend.

On Monday, March 12, 1990, the *Greensburg Daily News'* headline read, "Sardinia Man Jailed for Murder." A byline read "Grieving." A story beneath it ran, "Alleged murder sparks crisis program implementation." Brad's obituary also appeared in this issue.

Brad was the youngest person listed in the obituaries on this date. Most of the others were in their eighties. He was also the only one with a posted picture. As a side note, the column mentioned he delivered newspapers for the *Greensburg Daily News*. Underneath the obituary, the front-page story continued under one simple headline: "Murder."

The Maddux family had asked that in lieu of flowers, donations be made to Decatur County Youth Baseball Program in order to fund the teams and care for the baseball park where Brad loved to smack the ball into the field and to trot around the bases. It was difficult to imagine the next season already, not to be clapping and whistling and yelling "Goooo Braaaad!" The thought of the team without Brad next season troubled many people, both on and off the team. His legacy, though brief, would live on through other little boys able to learn sportsmanship, and coordination, and friendship through teamwork, in the same way that he met his best friends, Junior and Rob. Today, both Junior and Rob drive past the field where they once played sports with Brad. Their chatter becomes silent. "It was supposed to be named after him," one of them says quietly. "The Bradley Daryl Maddux Sports Center. I don't know what happened to that."

Tasha Asher finds it difficult, years later, to discuss the boy who would share her childhood so briefly—such an engaging young man. "I will never forget," she says, "His smile, his freckles, even his voice."

12 AFTERWARDS

Eight months after Brad's murder, on November 29, 1990, the United States President signed the National Child Search Assistance Act of 1990. This required each federal, state, and local law enforcement agency to report every case of a missing child (under the age of eighteen) to the National Crime Information Center (NCIC) of the Department of Justice. It also directed the attorney general to publish an annual summary of such reports, so that law enforcement and the public obtained a clear summary of just how many children went missing, from where they happened, and if whether they were stranger abductions or family custody kidnappings. The act "Requires States reporting under this Act to: (1) ensure that no State law enforcement agency establishes a policy which requires a waiting period before accepting a missing child or unidentified person report; (2) provide that each such report and all necessary and available information is entered into the State law enforcement system and the NCIC computer networks and made available to the Missing Children Information Clearinghouse of other designated agency within the State; and (3) require the law enforcement agency that entered the report into the NCIC to verify and update such record with any additional information (including, where available, medical and dental records), institute or assist with appropriate search and investigative procedures, and maintain close liaison with the National Center for Missing and Exploited Children for the exchange of information and technical assistance in the missing children cases." (Public Law No: 101-647 Title XXXVII) The government planned to assimilate information as quickly as possible, share information with other agencies, maintain records and keep them updated, and, if necessary, be able to identify remains. Everyone knows time is of the essence when searching for a missing child. The initial twenty-four hours are crucial. Strangers who take children do not keep them alive for long, and relatives who kidnap children do not stick around. Both types of kidnappers plan out their abduction in advance and prepare for all situations, leaving them hyper-alert. Like the sports player who has practiced for the Olympics or the musician about to step onto the stage at Rockefeller, they have usually prepared.

Shortly after the murder, Patti Maddux received a diagnosis of, and then lost her life to, cancer. Some of the family feels she was initially misdiagnosed. Some say losing her little boy brought on the cancer. Others swear she died of a broken heart.

Daryl Maddux married a second time and lost his second wife to cancer. During the writing of this book, Daryl remarried a final time. He and his new wife live near Westport, Indiana. Daryl is now retired. As a paramedic, he instigated the painting of one of the company's vehicles a bright pink, the color of the breast cancer awareness ribbon. The purpose is to remind people of the horrors of cancer. He hopes women will see it and be reminded to have regularly scheduled examinations.

Cody Maddux lives near Westport and works as a successful farmer. In 2011, his home was struck by a tornado. Cody watched as three 35,000 pound silos flew over his head; one landed on his roof, one landed on his garage. Cody was uninjured but said, "The sounds alone felt like my eardrums would burst." Once again, Cody found himself picking up the pieces of his life and placing them back together. As a result of Brad's murder, Cody still brews with anger and sinks himself into work. It is still difficult for him to discuss Brad, and Cody still refuses to attend therapy or counseling. He has recently wed.

Lindsay Maddux lives in the Westport area with her family. She has a steady job and is a hard worker, well-liked by her peers. Lindsay has lived through some ups and downs, but she "keeps her chin up," according to a friend. Lindsay is kind-hearted and funny. She hopes this book can assist at least one family in their grief, or prevent at least one child from being murdered. Lindsay closely resembles both her

230

mother and Brad.

The murder of Brad Maddux has followed Ernest "Junior" Armstrong for life, and life did not go easily on Junior. After Brad's murder Junior became heavily involved in drug use and later attempted to lose himself in addiction. Admitting suicidal thoughts, Junior found himself traveling cross-country, marrying and divorcing, fearing the closeness of relationships, and admitting he feared losing people if he became close to them. He has children he loves dearly and finds he is overprotective of them. He still cannot bring himself to visit the Maddux family in person. He is currently engaged to a woman who was friends with Daryl when Brad was murdered. He admits that he developed a lifelong fear of the dark and other phobias. Ernest "Junior" Armstrong wants to act as a motivational speaker for youths, teaching against drug abuse, and sexual abuse, and telling the story of that night in the hopes of saving at least one life. Small towns, however, offer little outlets for such dreams, and Junior does not know how to start. "How do you do something like that?" he asks. "Brad was an angel," Junior says now, "and still is."

Rob Nugent, for a long time, blamed himself for the slaying of his friend. He dabbled in drinking and smoking marijuana. In high school he became interested in racing motorcycles. The sport demanded sobriety: "It is what saved my life." During one motocross accident, Rob looked up into the face of the emergency responder to see Daryl Maddux was the EMT transporting Rob to the emergency room. Rob eventually met and married a woman who helped him overcome adversity and they now have a child. Rob no longer drinks or does drugs. In time, he began to understand the dynamics of what occurred that evening with Doug Sims. He controls his Crohn's disease correctly and says it has made him a better person, showing him what is important in life. "I wish I could go back in time," he says now. "We would have tied Brad up, pinned him down, anything" to keep him from leaving with Doug "Mushroom" Sims. At the same time, he knows Brad was determined to leave with Sims. Thinking of the last thing he saw of Douglas Sims that night, Rob

231

Nugent says, "I refuse to buy a truck with top lights, to this day."

When Tammy Hileman's child was born, it was a boy, just as Brad had predicted. She named him Brandon William Bradley Compton (William was Tammy's grandfather's name). Brandon plays semi-pro football and loves music, both of which he attributes to Brad's influence while Brandon was in the womb. Brandon is now married and

is a proud father. He talks about Bradley often.

The Maddux home where Brad grew up burned to the ground in 2007. The site of the home remains an empty lot. The house burned because of a faulty chimney, caused by a tornado twisting the flue. Most of the pictures of Brad, his trophies, and his personal items vanished in the fire.

The trailer where Douglas Sims resided sat on the same lot for a time, until released to the family. David and Betty went into the trailer to clean it out and found "so many bottles of alcohol, we couldn't believe it." They removed it from the land and sold it to *Bob's Mobile Homes*. David sold the land to a local gentleman who owns much of the land in Sardinia. The space where the trailer once stood at 1270 South still remains empty of houses.

Douglas Sims' brown, 1982 Ford pickup stayed, after police processed it, for some time in the law enforcement lot. On March 26, 1990 David requested the truck's release after Sims' incarceration. David drove the truck as his own for some time afterward and then sold it.

Discussing the Maddux case, years later, still brings some officers to tears.
Jon Oldham retired from the Indiana State Police. From 1995-2002 he served as sheriff of Decatur County. During the writing of this book, he was receiving treatment for cancer. "You could not find a better officer than Jon Oldham," said a retired officer during interviews for this book; every officer and civilian interviewed echoed this

sentiment. Even those whom Oldham arrested spoke with awe and respect of the man who dedicated himself to keeping the law. Everyone in Westport seems to have a "Jonny Uh-oh" story.

Unfortunately, Jon Oldham met something bad he could not stop. He lost his long battle with cancer at the end of 2012. His funeral drew most of the county. "He was a hero around here," says one newspaper reporter. He is a loss to the community, law enforcement, and those who knew him. He continues to be a model for local law enforcement. Jon Oldham's daughter is writing a book at this time on her father's career. She is considering calling it "Jonny Uh-oh."

Charles Whitehead was on his way home from a Florida golf tournament in 1998 when a heart attack took his life. Many in Westport missed his presence and remember him as a good person and fine officer.

After twenty-one years of serving, Robert Klene is retired from law enforcement. He and his wife of forty-one years own a lovely farm near the Westport area, the same farm his dad purchased in 1961. He is a firm believer in continuing education, including grief counseling, for officers.

Sergeant Ed Lewis retired from the state police and is now a retired Crime Scene Investigator Lieutenant for the Dearborn County Sheriff's Office in Indiana. Dearborn County's population is a little over 50,000 and it spans 305 square miles. Lewis remains victim-oriented and explains, "We handled (Brad's) case as carefully as possible in an effort to ease the pain of the family." His family raises registered Texas Longhorn cattle as a hobby. He has logged over forty-five years in law enforcement.

After twenty-six years of service, Indiana State Trooper Terrill "Terry" Steed retired in 1997. He remains married to the "local girl," and in August of 2012 they celebrated forty-one years of marriage. Today he "is retired but works five days a week." He works in security.

Indiana State Trooper Greg Allen, Brad's little league coach, is now Decatur County Sheriff Greg Allen, as of 2010. He lives on several acres, which also belong to the animals for which he loves and cares. He is known to be fair and people-oriented.

In 2010, after six terms of office, Decatur County Prosecutor William O. Smith retired. He had served as the county's prosecuting attorney for twenty-four years. The longest serving prosecuting attorney in Decatur County's history attempted a different type of challenge: researching history. Smith had already published "A Brief History of the Underground for Escaping Slaves in Decatur County," a manuscript in 2007. The Greensburg Optimist Club elected Smith as Law Enforcement Officer of the Year in 2010.

Circuit Court Judge John Andrew Westhafer, the man who had sat on the bench for Douglas Sims' trial, retired from the Decatur County Circuit Court in December of 2012 after serving thirty-five years. He plans to spend time with grandchildren and to travel.
Indiana lost an incredible man of law when Justice Jon D. Krahulik died in September 2006. In a tribute to Krahulik, written in the 2006 Indiana Law Review, Indiana Supreme Court Justice Frank Sullivan wrote, "Justice Krahulik helped give new law that resolved unanswered questions and updated old rules to the needs of the 1990s." (Vol. 39, #4) In a public statement released after Krahulik's death, Chief Justice Randall T. Shepard stated, "He was a wonderful colleague whose presence was greatly enjoyed during his all too brief service on our bench."

Jack Hileman is deceased, as is "Grandpa" Dave. They went to their graves mourning the loss of Brad.

Ben Frost died in a motorcycle accident several years after Bradley Maddux's murder. A few of his friends wonder if it was suicide. Several vehicles were behind him, and the drivers witnessed the wreck, including the father of Summer Hobbs. Mr. Hobbs held Ben as he was dying on the roadside; Ben's last words were, "You were always like a father to me."

The Meadows family left the Westport area because the rumors never ceased. Mike Meadows said he left because, he said, he could not withstand the rumors regarding his relationship with Doug Sims. Being called "gay" is still the worst thing imaginable in Westport, Indiana.

Most of Brad's friends and fellow students continue to reside in the Westport area, raising families of their own.

There is still an indention in the earth at Mt. Olivet Cemetery where Douglas Sims hastily buried Brad. It remains despite the changing of the seasons, the weather, and time.

Douglas Sims' clemency was denied on March 11, 2011. He cannot apply again until 2016. Sims is currently one of the 1,143 inmates incarcerated at the Indiana Department of Correction's Correctional Industrial Facility. Established in 1985, it is a medium security institution, meaning Sims is not locked down in a cell for twenty-four hours. There are several programs Sims can participate in while incarcerated at CIF. There is a dog and cat rescue and rehabilitation program held in conjunction with local animal shelters, alcohol and drug rehabilitation programs, and on-site education opportunities where inmates may obtain Associate's or Bachelor's degrees. At the time of this writing, he has not taken part in any program that may shorten his sentence. Sims has a cat that his departing cellmate left, he brews his beloved tea on a hot plate in his room, he has a job, and he takes part in religious services within the prison walls. Sims' release into the public is scheduled for on March 9, 2020. He plans to return to Westport, Indiana to live with his family. Sims refused numerous requests for interviews for this book.

Because the prosecution could not pursue the sexual molestation charge, the court system does not require Sims to register as a sex offender upon his release from prison. He is only one of thousands of such inmates released in the United States: a legally unregistered child predator.

Doug Sims' parents continue to reside in the same home as they did at the time of his arrest. They visit him when they can. Mr. Sims underwent two open-heart surgeries. In 2012, they celebrated sixty years of marriage. "I think we're handling it all right," Mrs. Sims says of her son's arrest and incarceration.

13 HELP IN PREVENTING CRIMES AGAINST CHILDREN

I spent several years of my career in law enforcement working around criminals in the county jail and the penal system. I was a private investigator who worked her share of cases where in which child sexual assault occurred. I have interviewed both the criminal and the victims of crimes against children. I attended some of the most prestigious law enforcement schools and training. With what I learned from the perpetrators and from my ongoing education, I created personal safety classes for senior citizens, adults, special interest groups, and children. I have lectured, taught, and made a living of studying crime. Once upon a time, I was a model with a well-known firm, dreaming of Los Angeles and performing on stage. Today I am far from that career path, and criminology is as much a part of me as being left-handed or female. They say it chooses you, but I believe the opposite is true.

Only 5% of child sexual abusers will admit guilt. Only one in ten victims will report the harassment, with 90% carrying the secret into adulthood. The Bureau of Justice Statistics report less than half of the cases go to trial due to weak or inadmissible evidence or lack of evidence. Thus, the crime will continue to be difficult to prosecute. Rather than chasing these cases years later and hoping the perpetrator gets what they deserve for harming a child, we need to arm the child with resources to repel the offender. Reactive versus proactive—why rearrange the deck chairs on *RMS Titanic?*

Brad was a trusting, innocent, and naïve twelve-year-old little boy seduced by a professional predator. Brad's alcohol consumption is not the important issue. Brad, his family, nor his friends deserve blame for his murder. Douglas Sims' parents do not warrant culpability for Brad's murder. Society, law enforcement, and Westport are not responsible. Douglas Sims is the sole recipient of the blame for the murder of Bradley Maddux.

We are a reactive society when it comes to being safe. We put up security lights after someone is hurt in a certain area. We worry about burglaries in a neighborhood after a home is broken into. We buy alarms for a business after we lose money in a robbery. And we say the worst things we can say:

It will not happen here.
It will not happen to me.
It is too terrifying to talk about, so I will not talk about it.

Once people dismiss those three lies out of their life, their thought process, and their world, only then can they truly begin to educate themselves and live *without fear*.

Children do not need to live in fear any more than adults need to live in fear. Living in fear is not possible if a person wishes to remain sane. There are neurotic people who literally live in states of constant fear and paranoia; their body degrades quickly because of all of the stress. A Chiclets-colored warning system was created for airports shortly after September 11, 2001, when red means "high alert." We cannot constantly live in red. This is why it always remained in yellow; it kept us alert and reminded us of the need to be wary and compliant. Our bodies and minds are not geared for living in red. We cannot survive or function in that continual hyper-extended state of awareness. But there is one thing the body does naturally, and does well. It has instinct, which it reacts to unconsciously and immediately.

Instinct is millions of years of training, available in a millisecond, and it happens when you do not even know it and when you need it most. It says *NO; something is wrong, do not go there, danger, warning, look out!* Sometimes we verbalize it as "hinky," or "the hair stood up on the back of my neck," or, "He was just weird." We are born with instinct All humans, like animals, possess inherited instinct, but society often represses these reactions. We are told to stop feeling suspicious of people or situations that make us apprehensive. Cops possess good instincts because their training requires them the recall and use the feelings their instincts bring. Someone told them in their adulthood that it is okay—even important—to evoke these memories.

Children have wonderful instincts because it has not been

beaten out of them—which really means that no one yet told them that they are silly, girly, overreacting, or suspicious. A child's instinct is that little warning bell that says, "Something is wrong." It rings when there is a "bad secret." One way to help develop instinct and safe behavior is to teach a child the difference between a "good" secret and a "bad" secret. A "good" secret practice is, "what is inside that pretty wrapped box under the Christmas tree? How does it make you feel to guess?" Discuss, then, what a "bad" secret would be – the opposite. "How does that make you feel?" And the warning bell rings. Children will be able to tell you because they know. They are already living it on the playground, in the classroom, and socially; there are bad secrets somewhere. Parents also must promise to never be angry if the child shares a "bad" secret. This is a part of creating communication between parents and children. Smash that weapon the molester has: the weapon of silence. Keep talking. Keep communicating. Let the child talk. Build that trust. And keep the promises.

There are ways to teach a child safety rules without creating paranoia or fear. These are techniques to ensure a child is aware without being scared of the world.

It sounds so basic, but teach at an early age: never, never get into a car with a stranger. Never approach the car of a stranger, no matter how nice they may seem. Discuss "stranger" because the word is so ambiguous to a child. The coach, the Priest, the man next door—who is a "stranger"? The car is usually the transport to crime scene #2, so instill this important rule.

Create a special "code word." Establish an agreement with the child that they should not get into a car to leave school / class / ball practice, etc. with anyone but a parent, guardian, or someone with the "code word." Make the code word simple, like the pet's name, a color, or a favored team. Ensure the school officials are aware of this as well (without giving the code word). Practice this as if it were a fire drill.

Here is an example:

(The code word is the child's favorite color, "Orange")

238

A parent is late due to a meeting, so they ask a neighbor to pick up their child from school. They tell the neighbor the code word: "orange."

The neighbor goes to school and picks up the child, who asks before getting into the car, "What's the code word?"

"Orange," the neighbor replies.

If the child does not ask, the neighbor should ask them, "What's the code word?" before allowing them into the vehicle.

Now the child understands it is safe to go with this person. Be sure to reward this behavior later on the same date.

Do not say something like, "You could have been killed if they did not know the code word!" Make it positive and fun: "I am so proud of you! You did a good job remembering that code word."

Every child, at some point, becomes lost in a public place. Teach children to seek out women when they cannot find their guardian in a public place. Small children should be told to look for female legs, as this is their height level. Females are less likely to harm a child. If it is in an area of retail, such as a mall, teach them to go to someone behind a counter. These people are more likely to assist and be safe to approach.

Teach a child to dial 911 at an early age. Have them memorize their address and phone number and make the latter a game. Show the child that police and firefighters are their friends. It angers officers to hear an adult tell a child, "You better behave or that policeman will come take you away!" when they see an officer in public. Abductors sometimes use uniforms and fake badges as a ruse, so teach the child that if they are told to go somewhere with an officer, take another adult with them.
The above information is not just for children, but for adolescents and teens as well. I would also add: parents

239

need to teach their children their workplace name and business number. In my classes of high school kids, nine out of ten did not know where their parents worked or what their parents did for a living. The only reason they knew their parent's work number was because it was programmed into their cell phones. When asked, "Where does your mom work?" the most they could answer was, "Some office."

People cannot constantly rely on cell phones. Children must memorize emergency contact phone numbers and addresses should be memorized.

When I worked as a private investigator, an agency hired me to interview witnesses for the defense in a child molestation case. They believed it was a false charge based on confusion—a child blaming an innocent person for a family member's actions. The outcry (charge) came from a little girl who was in a third grade classroom. I'll call the accused "Mr. Teachum" for "Teacher" because this is what he did for a living; he taught in an elementary school in a fairly large city. The children I interviewed were typical kids: sweet, open, and bright. I sat on the floor with them, on their level, casually asking them questions and letting them ramble. After my first few interviews, I telephoned the lead investigator. "We have an issue."

"Why?" they asked.

"Our client," I said firmly. "I have reason to believe he's guilty."

Silence. We were both children's advocates. Finally they said, "Keep going with it and let's see what happens."

Teaching is a noble profession. The hours are long, the job conditions are not ideal, and the benefits are not the best. You teach for the love of education and the love of creating the future. It is akin to law enforcement in that sometimes it seems to be you against the world. To mar the good name is not only disrespectful to the millions out there who carry the badge nobly, but it is also a travesty.

The outcry was this: during story time, certain children were privileged to sit on Mr. Teachum's lap while the others sprawled on the carpet near his chair. It was during this time that he touched a young girl in her vaginal area. The outcry came from a troublemaker, a child who seemed to always be in the principal's office for reasons that were not good news. No other complaints or accusations emerged about Mr. Teachum. Parents praised him; the teachers I spoke to all said lovely things about Mr. Teachum. The students, however, in little ways, told different stories.

Only girls got to sit in Mr. Teachum 's lap during story time. Only girls were asked to hold Mr. Teachum's hand when they walked down the hall. "That Mr. Teachum, I'll tell you, he looooves the girls," one male student told me, as if speaking of a juvenile high school male crush on the cheerleaders. I learned the victim had been warned, "If you tell, I can't be your teacher anymore"—a sophisticated threat for such a young child to create.

I never led the children on with my questions; I never put ideas into their heads. I asked open-ended questions. They said other things that made me delve deeper, interviewing more children. My casual questions ("Tell me about story time") brought forth interesting answers and I remained pokerfaced as we sat on the living room floors of their homes or on the couches and talked about school. I had no doubt the students loved Mr. Teachum, but by the end of this assignment, I had no doubt Mr. Teachum was guilty.

Child molesters do not have pointy tails or horns—I wish they did—but if people open themselves to learning about the warning signs, they take their first step towards keeping children safe from these devils. Too many people want to keep the secret and say, "I don't want to talk about it." This is the molester's tool, and he/she will use it to full advantage.

The parents of Mr. Teachum 's victim told me they were not interested in prosecuting. "She's been through enough," said her mother, "and he'll lose his job, his security. We can't do that. He has kids. We're just going to pray for him and his family."

Prayers do a lot of things, but they do not stop a child molester.

I will never forget a presentation I planned to do for a group of new parents on Crime Prevention for Children. Minutes before going onstage, the hostess asked a favor: "Please don't talk about child molestation," she stage-whispered. "Or rape, or murder. Those things are just too scary."

After introductions I explained (after reviewing my now-

241

useless notes) that I thought we should begin by opening up with questions from the floor. Immediately the audience began. "How can you make sure someone's not a sexual predator?" I began that part of my previously planned presentation. Then someone asked me about rape prevention for adolescents. Another person asked me about a local child who had recently been found murdered. I snuck a glance at my hostess, who sat looking very pale and nervous. After a few more questions, I completed the original planned presentation and finished it to a great applause. I should have applauded my audience, for they asked the questions. Knowledge, in the case of child safety, is a great, great power.

Kids are sponges with feet; they soak up everything. They hear, see, and smell everything we do. They are not stupid, and they figure things out very quickly. Adults teach children not just by words, but also by actions. The majority of communication is unspoken. Kids learn fear and prejudice from adults, whose words have an impact on them. The quieter we are, the better they hear us. "We don't argue in front of the children," one of my audience members told me once. "We go in the garage where they can't hear." That is a joke. And children may not hear the words, but they can feel the anger. Remember, their instinct is very well-tuned. People say, "We stay together for the children," but they hate each other, so the kids are stuck in an environment of loathing, perhaps domestic violence. In a violent home, a baby in a crib, as young as three months, will teach itself not to cry because it associates crying with violent actions and loud, scary noises. So this baby will lay in its own body fluids, hungry and thirsty, and it won't make a sound.

So, what does *not* work well in regards to the safety of children?

"Stranger Danger" misleads many people because the majority of predators know their victims.

The "fingerprinting program" creates false security. What good does it do? It helps to identify a body when it's too late to keep the child safe from harm.

Teaching a child martial arts or to fight for the purpose of self-defense also lacks in efficiency. Again, most children know their attackers. The large majority of molesters do not snatch up a child from the playground and run. There is no eight year old who can fight off a determined thirty-year-old man by kicking and punching.

Single parents who go on dates should know someone before introducing him or her to the children and preferably even perform complete background checks on potential serious relationships. This is not paranoia—it is being careful, and a good, honest person should understand.

Do not try to be a "Rescue Ranger"—offering a loving relationship to an adult because they had a horrible childhood or were abusive in their last relationship. Understand that survivors of child violence will most likely abuse their own families. Studies show, time and time again, a person who abuses their spouse or significant other will also abuse their child.

Society cannot keep a glass box around children, refusing to let them live their lives because of danger. A life lived in fear is not truly living. Teaching them basic safety and open communication is the first step. Some of these safety tips can be turned into a game. Children can learn other safety advice without realizing they are learning—a hug, self-esteem, and love are free and easy to give and create trust, communication, and help self-esteem. I have made a life of crime prevention, but I cannot guarantee safety. No one can. But I can suggest skills to teach safety.

Picture a classroom of giggling, wriggling third grade kids. The teacher raps the desk and asks for silence, but whispers and muffled giggles still continue. It is a typical third grade class in a typical third grade room; it could be in New York City, Houston, Texas, or Westport, Indiana. No matter where it is located, experts on crimes against children estimate that three out of five girls in that classroom and two out of five boys in the same room are molestation victims. The statistics are astonishing. Those sweet faces, their innocence already gone by the time they leave elementary school. What can we do? The best defense is education.

Oftentimes molesters intimidate their victims by threatening to ostracize them from their peers, to destroy their relationships, to remove the gifting, or harm their parents. Parents must tell their children: "If anyone threatens you, you need to tell me," and talk about the definition of "threaten." Parents should ask the child for their input: "What do you think 'threaten' means?" This is a crucial part of creating communication.

Adults should promise they would never punish them for honesty. At six years old, I foolishly threw a ball where I was told not to play and broke a window in my grandfather's boat. I went to him to confess, offering my full piggy bank with shaking hands and trembling lip. Because I was honest about it, I was not punished. I had to give up a portion of my allowance to help pay for the damages, but I was not punished for being dishonest. Had I covered my crime or lied about the broken window, I am sure grounding or even a spanking (my parents were old school!) would have occurred. Do you see the difference? Use your own childhood examples to explain it to the child—they will understand it as well.

Parents should be wary of adults whose social circles consist of children or childless people whose homes are made for children: lots of toys, gifts, candy, few or no rules, etc. If the adult has children, watch for toys that are not age-related. I worked a child molestation case where the perpetrator had a wife and three-year-old boy, but his home was filled with pinball machines, video games, and movies that were aimed at the preteen crowd—the age of the girls he molested. By the time he went to prison, we counted at least fifteen victims—every female adolescent in the neighborhood. I am sure there were more. Remember, the average molester has over 100 victims.

Everyone needs to follow his or her instinct. A "strange vibe" about something happens for a good reason. An officer I worked with listened at her family dinner conversation as her four boys spoke enthusiastically of spending after school time at "Nick's house." Nick's house was where all of the neighborhood boys congregated for video games, ice cream, candy, soft drinks, and games. Their mother asked, "What do Nick's parents say about all of this?" When she discovered Nick was in his thirties and lived alone, she took action: forbidding her children to go visit, and notifying other parents.

Websites like www.criminalwatchdog.com list predators in neighborhoods. Parents should check local and state police departments for listings of sex offenders' addresses in their area. It is a great idea to be aware and be involved in Neighborhood Watch, PTA, etc. Adults should also notify other parents of any concerns they have.

It is healthy for a parent to be suspicious of adults who give children multiple gifts without reason. These are called "unsolicited gifts." Molesters buy silence with food, presents, and time (baseball tickets, movies, etc). Parents must be wary of adults who also try to "buy" parents. In a case I worked, the perpetrator paid for the cheerleader outfits, braces for their teeth, swim classes, baseball team dues, and other extracurricular activities for the neighborhood kids, his victims—particularly if their parents were single mothers. He tried to appear as if he were "helping out hardworking moms." His wife stood by him and proclaimed he was innocent despite many testimonies.

Parents should do secret spot checks of a child's Internet use. They ought to get to know the parents of the child's friends and as well as the child. One of my students came to me with a printout of her daughter's best friend's Myspace page. The friend, who was thirteen, had listed herself as being "21 ... . . . sexy, hot, and horny ... . . . single, love guys." I advised my student to notify the parents.

"My husband says to mind my own business and let her parents deal with it," my student admitted.

I asked her, "if this girl becomes a missing child, how will you feel that you did not step in? What if this girl was your own?"

My student went to the parents, who were mortified at what they read, and the Myspace page was removed.

If an adult finds children presenting themselves as over-age and using this kind of language, it is important that they refrain from anger. Talk! Ask them why they are doing these things—what makes them think they have to behave this way to meet someone? DO NOT accept the answer "It's just a joke." Young people today are more sexually active, far more exploratory, and way more curious than their parents' generation. Get to the bottom of it and find out.

Don't just assume babysitters are good because someone recommends them. Interview them like you would an employee. After all, this is a job, and they are working with a most precious commodity. Ask pointed questions; do not be afraid to ask, "Have you ever harmed a child?" Watch their reaction. Replies such as "Why?" or "What do you mean 'harm?'" are red flags. Ask pointedly, "When have you invited friends over to the house where you are sitting and the homeowners are gone?" Take note of their reactions and listen to the their answer. Watch their eye contact, throats (swallowing, pulse quickening, redness in the neck), and look for other nervous ticks. Then ask, "Why not?" and evaluate that answer. The reply of "It's not right" is a better answer than "I'm not dating right now." Open-ended questions prompt a better answer— and the body language and eye contact will tell about the person's character. Gavin de Becker's timeless book "The Gift of Fear" is an excellent resource with questions for parents to ask the school and information on how to interview sitters and caregivers.

Sandy Jones insists her child's babysitters know infant CPR and the correct way to burp, feed, and clean a child. Sandy asks them pointedly for demonstrations and certifications. She leaves emergency numbers and instructions, both written and verbal, in an easy-to-find location. She is being safe, not sorry. She also uses open-ended questions during interviews ("Why do you like to babysit?" instead of "Do you like children?") and chooses her sitters from college students specializing in nursing or prenatal care. Sandy, who is in her forties, noted as a teen that she made $10 *a night* as a sitter when today's sitters ask for $15 *an hour* but have no particular skills. Sandy asked one potential sitter, "What if my baby needed changing?" The girl replied, "I call my mom and she comes over." The mother lived three blocks away! No one else had ever asked the girl that question before Sandy; they assumed she was a competent caregiver—at twenty dollars an hour.

Teenagers, of course, know everything, and adults, of course, know nothing. Having taught in high school, I assure you, they consider us geriatric after hitting twenty-five, useless at thirty. But it is up to the adults to fight for date rape prevention training in these schools. On average, date rape occurs when both victim and perpetrator are between the ages of eighteen and twenty-five. Teens are much more physical now in high school—constantly hugging and laying on each other; they are like boa constrictors on rubber tree limbs. They are needy, seeking love and attention. If they do not get it from home, they will try to get it elsewhere. Parents and caregivers need to talk to teenagers—boys and girls—about limitations. I read their high school notes; some of them wrote some bold, highly sexual things to one another ("let's fuck in the stairwell during the assembly like we did last time" suggested one fifteen-year-old girl to a boy). It is no longer, "Do you like me, check yes or no." Society needs to stop saying, "Not my child." Adults need to put limitations on texting, computer time, and phone use. Parents should not become angry upon discovering a child is promiscuous, having online chats one would read about in *Penthouse* or using language that makes your gums bleed. Use questions instead: Why? Who?

- Why would you do this?
- Why would someone want you to do this?
- Who would ask you to act this way?
- Who else behaves this way at your age?

Questions like these lead to discussions, which are incredibly important because shouting, "I forbid you to use the computer!" or "No more cell phone for you!" makes the kid more rebellious and invent new workarounds. I was a teacher; I saw what they did. I listened to them. I watched one sweet-faced white girl pull more than the wool over her wealthy parent's eyes during a parent-teacher conference. That same girl had a penchant for sex in the bathroom with boys who were non-white, drug users, and in a street gang. As an instructor, I could not discuss that with her parents unless she was caught in the actual act; just overhearing her talk about her exploits meant nothing. I was the enemy camp as far as her parents were concerned, a person who made up mean stories because I "just did not like their child." Listen to your child's instructors!

Date rape prevention should be taught to girls, and boys

should be in the audience as well. Parents need to ask a child's school about such a program, and if they refuse to hold such a program, contact a YMCA or YWCA. Young people will be more honest and open to these types of programs without a parent in the room. I have watched some amazing things happen in these classes, where young ladies gain personal strength they did not know they had and young men see things in a different light. The Y holds excellent programs and is unafraid to talk about these issues. Public schools fear addressing certain issues because they fear legal problems. Schools tend to be reactive to trouble. The Y is proactive with prevention and education.

The majority of date rapes occur under the influence of drugs and/or alcohol. Young people need education about alcohol use and drug use/abuse. Rather than a "Just Say No" presentation, students should listen to a speaker from an amazing organization, MADD, Mothers Against Drunk Driving. These are people who have lost a loved one to someone driving under the influence, and they give educational, heartfelt presentations about how someone intoxicated got behind the wheel of a car and made a bad decision that took a life. Standing in front of a teen or tween and lecturing does not work, but having them listen to a stranger and hear their story is more likely to hit a nerve—in the heart. MADD is an amazing organization.

Parents need to know the protocol for background checks on teachers and staff at the child's school. It should not be assumed that private or more expensive schools have better systems in place for crime prevention. Parents should ask if there is a reporting system for children who are victimized. They should ask about the protocol if a child goes missing. Caregivers should ask school officials about school safety programs. How often are fire drill and emergency plans carried out? Is there an anti-bully program? Are teachers trained to report bullying? How and when? People should never be afraid to ask. This is the welfare of a child.

Using our votes and our voices, we all must insist schools address safety issues. Part of the reason I left the high school system was the archaic way of thinking. When I tried to introduce a Domestic Violence Education program for students, a principal told me, "We don't have any students here with that problem, and neither do their parents." My "Stop Bullying" project was also turned down. My students, who were the ones spearheading the projects, were crestfallen. Young ladies as young as thirteen, fearful of abusive boyfriends or violent family members, came to instructors. Parents must insist that their child's school provides some sort of counseling opportunity, hotline number, or literature—if not for their own child, then for others.

Teach children to "tell someone" and to "keep telling" if something bad happens, until they get a response of belief. Children do not lie about molestation unless coached, and this is very, very rare. Child services personnel are trained professionals who can immediately spot a false confession. These cases do not even make it to trial.

If a child does report abuse, it is imperative that adults keep their anger in check. Listen to them and assure the child they did the right thing by reporting the crime. Assure the child you believe them and they are safe. Molesters will threaten everything from loss of gifting to family harm, so you must give assurance of safety and security. Report it to authorities as soon as possible.

Worry over the Halloween "poison candy" story has now forced a nation to adopt "safe Halloween" parties. A 1985 study conducted by Sociology Professor Joel Best of California State University reported that the "razor blade in the candy" scare is an urban legend. There have been only two dangerous candy incidents. A Texas father attempted to murder his own son by hiding the weapon in the boy's Halloween candy. A family in Detroit used the "poison candy scare" to cover up a child's accidental overdose when trying the uncle's illegal drugs. It is interesting how the "dangerous candy" story has taken hold of us as a people. When I explain this to my friends who are parents, they say, "I know but..." and continue to search their child's candy for razors and poison, "just in case." Or they "only go where it is safe." One incident, years ago, to this day have created a countrywide scare.

Do molesters wait for Halloween as their national holiday to prey? A 2009 study was conducted by South Carolina psychology professor Elizabeth Letourneau called, "How Safe Are Trick-or-Treaters? An Analysis of Child Sex

Crime Rates on Halloween." Over 67,000 sex crimes were studied; Letourneau and collaborators discovered that, even before the U.S. began warning parents and law enforcement began focusing on sexual predators for October 31, "Halloween has long been one of the safest nights of the year from sexual abuse."

Consider that children need discipline, but they also need assurance and love. Perpetrators of crimes against children often seek lonely children with low self-esteem, those whose parents are going through a divorce, who are lonely, who need a friend or a parent. Perpetrators will either seek out these children in advance—or they find a child alone at the right time by accident. And they make an art form out of this.

I observed a parent in a shopping mall grab their child who wandered about twenty feet away. The parent shouted into the little face, "Are you crazy! Do you want someone to steal you!" *This* is crazy—it is not educating. A television program had an ex-law enforcement officer "teaching" children safety. He kneeled down and said into the kids' faces with a grave demeanor, "Someone will grab you and try to shove you into a car! You fight! Scream and fight!" As if a six year old can fight off an adult. The poor kids! Their faces blanched and their little eyes became widened in terror. This clown makes a lot of money inducing fear.

We can create a safe world for children through education without causing paranoia and fear. Our first step is to educate ourselves and take off the blinders. Yes, molestation, rape, and abduction are scary—which is why we must teach ourselves about the devils lurking amongst our little angels. This is akin to a war. You do not win a war without educating your army about the enemy.

Every prison in the United States is overflowing right now. From super-max, where inmates are locked down twenty-four hours a day, to camp, where inmates can wear their own (carefully monitored) clothing and leave the unit for outside jobs, every U.S. prison is at capacity or higher. This includes federal, state, and local. Ninety eight percent of incarcerated persons will be released in the United States. Because of the current state of our prison systems, experts predict that percentage will rise in the next few years.

It has been proven sexual predators do not stop. Again, by the time they are arrested the average molester has at least 100 victims by the time of their arrest. If a football stadium were filled with children every day for a month, it would not equal the number of estimated sexually abused children in the United States every year. This equation is based on the number of adult survivors—those who have been victimized—for whom it is often too late to recover.

"Lock them all up and throw away the key" is not an answer to our incarceration issue. Neither is "Kill them all," branding offenders, or some sort of cinematic-invented idea about islands consisting of only inmate populations, car races that murder the losers, or simply instant death. The Founding Fathers created the Constitution for a reason, and there is no such thing as a quick fix. However, the country does need to revisit sentencing guidelines and definitions in regards to crimes against children.

Ignoring the issue is akin to child abuse itself. If legislation and law makers continue to ignore the weak laws and sentencing, they are just as guilty as Douglas Sims and the other thousands of other perpetrators who are out there now, as I write this, sizing up the next Bradley Maddux. If you disagree or think this is someone else's problem, then look at the family photos on your wall, in your photo album, on your Facebook page or on your desk. Any of those children could be the next Bradley.

There are aggravating factors for capital punishment and they vary from state to state. One of the factors in Indiana is: "(8) The victim of the murder was less than 12 years of age." In Connecticut, it is: "(8) Murder of a person under 16 years of age." In Delaware: "(9) The victim was a child 14 years of age or younger, and the murder was committed by an individual who is at least 4 years older than the victim." New Hampshire is a bit more ambiguous: "(9) The victim was particularly vulnerable due to old age, youth, or infirmity."

There should be an adoption of one aggravating factor for capital punishment for all states: "The victim was younger than the age of that of a legal adult." In some states, an adult is eighteen; in others, an adult is considered to have had their seventeenth birthday. This is the state's adopted standard for the definition of "adult." Therefore, a person who has sexually *assaulted* someone younger than seventeen, in a state where seventeen is considered an adult, should legally be charged as a child molester.

"Sex offender" does not necessarily mean "sexual predator." A sex *offender* may be someone who, at nineteen, had engaged in consensual sex with a sixteen-year-old and charges were pressed. A sex offender may also be someone who sexually harassed a victim or was involved in pornography. Some of these people have the possibility of rehabilitation. A sexual *predator* is someone who preys, who assaults more than one victim, and who does not stop. The crime is so entrenched in them, they cannot stop, no matter the consequences.

The U.S. Department of Justice conducted an interesting study on the Recidivism of Sex Offenders Released from Prison in 1994, and it included the results on 4,295 released male offenders. These offenders were incarcerated for child molestation. The offenders studied came from various prisons across the United States, from Texas to New York. The study revealed:

The study showed that the released child molesters were all men who were arrested, convicted, and sentenced to prison for a sex crime against a child. When they committed their imprisonment offense, most (62.9%) were age thirty and older, and most (60.3%) of them molested a child who was age thirteen or younger. Some of the victims were below age seven. Nearly half of the men (48.4%) were twenty or more years older than the child they molested.

Released inmates with more than one prior arrest for child molestation were more likely to be rearrested for child molestation (7.3%) than released child molesters with no more than one such prior arrest (2.4%).

On average, child molesters return to society after serving nearly three years (33.7 months) of a nearly seventy-year sentence (81.1 months). Upon release, almost half of the child molesters still had at least three years of their sentence remaining to be served.

The 4,295 child molesters had at least one arrest for child molesting (the arrest that led to their imprisonment). For 3,509 (81.7%) of them, that arrest was their first ever arrest for child molestation. For the other 786 men (18.3% of the 4,295), it was not their first. Some had one prior arrest for a sex offense against a child, some had two, and others had three or more.

Among those with three or more priors was a man whose first arrest for the molestation of a child was in 1966, when he was age twenty. When released in 1994, he was serving an eleven-year sentence for molesting a child under the age of fourteen. The prior criminal record of this serial pedophile spanned three decades, with arrests for child molesting in the 1970's, the 1980's, and the 1990's.

Of the 4,295 released child molesters, 1,693 (39.4%) returned to prison during the three-year follow-up period. The majority of those charged (approximately 982 of the 1,693, or 58%) offenses occurred in the first twelve months after their release.

Among the men imprisoned for molesting a child aged thirteen or younger and who gained release in 1994 for that crime, 2.8% were returned to prison for repeating the act on another child. Of those whose imprisonment offense was against a fourteen- or fifteen-year-old child, 3.7% had a new arrest for child molesting after their release. Of the men who were in prison for molesting a sixteen- or seventeen-year-old child, 1.2% were arrested for molesting another child after leaving prison in 1994.

When sex offenders were arrested for new sex crimes against children after their release, the new arrest typically occurs in the same state that released them.

This study reveals typical facts about sexual predators:

- They have committed the same crime prior to the incarceration
- They will be released early

- They will commit the crime again

Of course, this is only a single study, and studies are not perfect. But it represents the results of what most studies of predatory behavior reveal. It reveals what some of the offenders themselves will tell you.

The sentencing for child molestation varies state to state, but now it is time; every state needs to adopt one sentence: mandatory life without the possibility of parole for the first conviction of child molestation—what some in the business call "L-WOPPED."
Mandatory life without parole for sexual predators is a discussion amongst lawmakers in several states. It could solve the issue in one stroke of a judge's pen. It will not solve everything, for there are thousands of predators not arrested, even more who are not caught, and still more not even reported. But for every predator put behind bars, that's 100 future children who may not be victimized, assuming each predator has 100 victims. Lock up two predators and that is 200 potentially safe kids. Do the math: If five predators are sentenced to mandatory life without parole, that means at least 500 children—an entire school—are safe from molestation.
Aside from the safety of children, organizations and institutions are also at stake. Child predators utilize positions of trust, or obtain a position of trust, in order to prey on their victim. Teachers, coaches, or religious leaders are in such positions. When the predator destroys the child's trust in people, they also destroy the trust in the institution.
Consider the anger toward the Catholic Church some years ago when multiple religious leaders within the church were found to be sexual predators and high-ranking members of the clergy covered it up. Unfortunately, Catholicism received horrific press and was labeled as the church of pedophiles. Abusers come in all faiths. The Catholic Church has literally thousands of people in its ministry, but the actions of probably less than 100 tainted the institution. A coach who abuses their students gives a bad name to education, which is already struggling, in this country; it is difficult to keep students in school and

educate them to the best of the abilities on so little.

Little league members who abuse their team members make parents think twice about signing up their children for sports. If these sexual predators suffered imprisonment for life, institutions and organizations would have better reputations and legal support. Rather than just dismiss or move the predator, now they would have state sentencing guidelines behind the decision to prosecute. The "Why prosecute, nothing will happen" attitude potentially disappears.

Crime has what is called a "ripple effect." It is akin to throwing a rock in a still pool. There is the initial splash, which causes a ripple, which results a bigger ripple, which culminates in the next outer ripple, and so on, The waters take a long time to calm again. Picture the rock as the crime and each ripple as a section of the population: the home, the neighborhood, the community, the town, the state, the section of the United States... No one remains untouched. Remember the urban legend of the poisoned Halloween candy? One man's attempt at murder has made a nation stop or change its trick-or-treating tradition. Consider this ripple effect: When Brad was murdered it hurt his family, then his friends, then his neighbors—suddenly an entire town began locking their doors at night, realizing they were not as immune to evil as they thought. By creating a mandatory life without parole sentence for sexual predators, the system keeps potential victims safe from the perpetrators and creates a safe environment—effectively stopping those ripples in society. Not only are the kids safe, but also the communities. No more parents, families, and friends missing their loved ones or having to live through the dynamics of assisting a molested child. Will it stop all crimes? No—nothing will. Will it lower the crime rate? Taking away one criminal lowers the crime rate in any community.

Molestation victims have a high risk of dropout, suicide, and drug/alcohol abuse. They often victimize others. Many molesters admit they were molested as children. By placing child molesters away for life, there is the potential to stop creating future molesters. It could stop future addicts and possibly lower prison numbers because those who do not attend school and or who succumb to substance abuse often turn to crime. Yes, it sounds simplistic and no, it does not hold all of the answers. But is it not worth the attempt?

Many cases have gone public where a person on parole or probation has harmed or killed another child; the incident makes the news and people are upset, then it becomes old news. A child goes missing, a bawdy and loud talk show hostess shouts down special guests, and it is entertainment. For every missing or murdered child on television, there are a hundred Brad Maddux's who do not make national news. But society shakes heads and lives in denial, saying, "It doesn't happen here." We have to start caring. This is our country; these are our kids, our future, our lives.

But until we change the laws, we change almost nothing.

Douglas Sims has never discussed what happened on March 10-11, 1990 when he left with Brad Maddux. All he has said was, "He wouldn't do what I wanted him to do," meaning Brad would not go to North Vernon with Sims to obtain more alcohol. We know this is not true. Brad would have happily driven with Doug to North Vernon, or Doug's house, or anywhere.

Several people involved in this case believe Doug Sims had assistance in cleaning up his trailer, where many believed he killed Brad Maddux. Another officer has a contrary opinion, one that has not been divulged until this time, and it is a theory with which this writer agrees. It is more probable that Sims did not murder Brad in the residence but in the back of the pickup truck. Blood evidence of that magnitude is almost impossible to clean up in any amount of time. Blood, particularly when watered down, is difficult to control. Even standing or lying Brad in the tub to bleed out, then transporting him to the truck, would leave a blood trail, and the timeline demanded for this—between the murder and the time officers contacted Sims—does not fit.

A dead body is difficult to manage, more so than people realize. All muscles relax, meaning urine, excrement, and other body fluids release. Carrying a sleeping person or someone passed out cannot be compared to lifting the actual deceased. This is what is meant, literally, by the phrase "dead weight." Sims was a strong man, but Brad

256

was a husky boy. Sims used what he knew, which is what murderers do. He knew Brad and he had a semblance of feeling for him; he did not want to throw him out like garbage. But he had to hide evidence. His feelings for taking life were diminished by working on the kill floor in a slaughterhouse, for this is a brutal job, and he had also possessed the self-discipline taught by the military. Doug Sims simply shut himself down and performed a duty that had to be done in order to save himself.

What happened that horrific night? After all of the rumors, gossip, and evidence has came forth, following thousands of hours of interviews and research, casual discussions with law enforcement officers—some of whom wept openly about this case—here is what most likely took place that night:

After the fight in the street with his friends, Brad returned to the truck to tell Sims that he decided not to go for more alcohol; Brad wanted to stay with Junior and Rob. However, Brad was intoxicated, and Sims used the ability a child molester has to woo Brad back into the truck; perhaps he told him, "Oh, come on. We'll be right back." Regardless of what was said, they left together.

They returned to Sims' trailer home and Sims plied Brad with more alcohol, then brought out the handcuffs and placed them on Brad. Once Brad was handcuffed in another "handcuff game," Sims either made a pass or alluded to such and Brad said, "I'll tell." Brad was a relative to Sims, not a stranger. Brad was close to his family and more likely to tell them. Lastly, Brad was a sweet boy, but he had a tough side.

Remember, Sims did not have time to cultivate Brad like he may have done with other boys.

Panicked, Sims started bargaining with him. "Don't tell. It was an accident." Sensing his fear, or perhaps anger, Brad began trying to get out of the handcuffs. Most people think the way to escape handcuffs is to fight against them. Perhaps Brad was thinking of the last words his best friends had said to him. Brad struggled enough to leave marks on his wrists. Then he started shouting, angry.

Sims then grabbed the first thing he could reach—a sock—and gagged Brad. Now the crime has escalated.

257

Sims knows what releasing Brad could lead to: shame, name-calling, and worse. This is where the future splits and the offender makes the choice. Release Brad and become…? Or take away the problem?

Sims walked Brad out of the house, probably making more promises, placed him in the truck, and then put the necessary gear into his truck: knife, sharpener, and shovel. He drove out to a secluded spot where he knew they would have privacy. Perhaps he went there before, seeking privacy. Nonetheless, it was a cemetery, and this way Brad would at least have a burial. More proper than, say, the woods, or some secluded area. Sims could come visit; people would place flowers, unknowingly, but they do put flowers here on or near his makeshift grave.

Doug Sims cut the boy's throat in the back of his truck, which he could easily clean and no one would see it as he drove. He removed the handcuffs and then pulled off Brad's clothes. He didn't bother with his socks; there was no need. Pulling off the shirt and hoodie could have caused the head to tear off the body slightly. He was not going to touch that bloodied gag—too nasty. Doug Sims hastily buried the body, but not too deep because it would have taken too long. Somewhat panicked now, he just tossed the items into the woods. People threw trash out here all the time. He kept the bloodiest items: blue jeans, jacket, and grey sweatshirt. Because the ground was soft and the truck had sat idling for a moment, he had to gun the accelerator to fishtail the truck out of there. He drove to the car wash, washed out the blood, and returned home. Once at the house, Doug Sims quickly burned at least three items of Brad's clothing, then he stashed his own on the neighbor's property with the plan of returning for the items later. They were away, and he could retrieve them without suspicion soon. He "over-cleaned" his own home, but in his haste he left the blood drops on the bathroom door and tub. Return the now clean handcuffs to the drawer, and it was only a bad dream. No evidence, no record, and no one to tell on him.

This is only a supposition, of course, but it makes sense in criminal theory, in logic, and based on evidence. "Making sense out of a senseless crime," as one investigating officer said. Perhaps this is as close as we can come.

"It should've been us that night Brad was murdered," Junior Armstrong says today.

"Could've been," Rob Nugent tells Junior.

"Should've been," Junior corrects him. "We were so drunk and passed out cold in that tent. Sims could have come back and got us, too."

It is a lovely evening and a visitor is sharing it with Betty Sims, sitting on rocking chairs on the front porch of the home where her son, Douglas, grew up—where he lived most of his life. When she discusses "Doug," she looks out over the horizon, then right into the visitor's eyes. When she listens, she leans slightly forward. Her arms stay crossed over her too-thin body. Doug's crime and subsequent incarceration has affected her and her husband's health severely.

She believes it is alcohol that led to Doug Sims' demise, but she listens carefully to other theories, nodding. She is an intelligent, likable woman. She and the visitor discuss choices made at the last moment, at the wrong moment, which can lead to a person's downfall.

Suddenly she says, "Doug made a very poor choice, and now he is paying for it. Now he must pay for it. He has to do his time."

The visitor explains how a homophobic community can cause a person to hide their true self, how sexuality has nothing to do with child abuse. Doug Sims carried a lot of baggage, but he had no reason to harm children. Betty understands this clearly, more clearly than many people.

"I don't think Doug wants out of prison," Betty surmises. "He has what he wants. His tea, he has a cat, and he watches his sports on T.V. He likes the job they gave him." Her visitor wonders if it is because he feels safe. Like the military, prison leaves few choices for people, and some need that constant discipline to survive. Betty wonders about this herself.

Later Betty folds her arms tightly around herself and stares out across the horizon. "I never knew he liked little boys," she says suddenly of her son, Doug. Tears fill her eyes. "I never knew."

On March 10, 2013 a friend speaks with Daryl Maddux on the phone. Daryl's voice is strong, but the friend can tell he is trying to be brave. "It's hard, because this is when we lost him," Daryl admits. He sighs deeply. "It's just ... never easy."

Beware the devil you know more than the devil you don't...

14 ACKNOWLEDGEMENTS

One night while working feverishly on this manuscript, I suddenly felt Brad Maddux standing over my shoulder and leaning over to read the screen. I kept writing. Brad wore a dark T-shirt, blue jeans, and scuffed sneakers; the look on his face was of interest, and his lips moved slightly as he read. I could see the glow from the computer screen lighting up his face, highlighting his freckles and blue eyes. I did not look up and he faded away. He was whole, his usual boyish self, curious about what I was writing and why. He was not afraid or in danger; he was not sad or lost. He was a twelve-year-old boy who wondered why he was the focal point of such a story.

Thank you St. Michael, who has shielded me probably more than I know (it is a job, believe me).

Thank you to Katherine Johnston, who first alerted me about the Brad Maddux case and the petition to keep Douglas Sims behind bars. Sometimes the most extraordinary of events occur in the simplest of things: a phone call when someone says, "Hey, listen..."

One article on Brad led to another, thanks to my readers at *Examiner.com/Nashville*. And thanks to my readers who signed the petition to keep Douglas Sims from being granted clemency in 2011.

Thanks to my long-time true friend and sometimes co-worker, Police Psychic Gale Carrier (*PsychicOfNashville.com*), who kept saying, "You should write a book." Well, here it is, my friend.

Thanks to my students, past and present, who burn with

261

the desire to question and to change the criminal justice system.

The system needs changing. Our children need protection. Thanks to the warriors who do this daily, in no particular order: The best PI in the US, Karen Hewitt of Hewitt & Cowden Investigations (Texas); Chief Sandy Green and Four Rivers Search & Rescue; Metro Police Department of Nashville; the Davidson County Sheriff's Department's Sheriff Daron Hall & Bill Hampton; Judge Andrei Lee; Crystal Wagoner (one of the best former investigators and instructors out there), my friends & coworkers who are foster parents; Rene Whiteman (Dallas County Constable's office); Mark Smouse (Mansfield Police Dept); Sheryl DeMott (Tennessee State Prison); K9 Search & Rescue (Stewart County, TN); Phillip Barber (Metro Fire Dept.); Steve Heim (Metro Nashville Airport Public Safety); MADD/Mothers Against Drunk Driving; Ralph Richardson of NAACP; Ed Butler; John Waide, Ph.D.; LCSW (Nashville, TN); PFLAG/Parents, ; Families, & Friends of Lesbians & Gays; Officer Ken Hardy; Attorney Katherine Sketo; Officer Jon Stephens; Officer Joseph Blair; Captain Randy Hickerson (Metro PD); Attorney Jennifer Wade; Officer Gene Martin (Metro PD); Lynne Albright (Dallas Police Dept., Ret.); Lisa Warfield, Paralegal; Attorney Leslie Bloomberg (AL); Attorney Connie Johnson (TN.); Officer Stephen Hale; Probation Officer Lamenta Poe; the team at the Tennessee Bureau of Investigations; the YWCA & YMCA; Carolyn Jenkins; Kevin Cook (Volunteer State University Criminal Justice Department); C.D. (Cool Dude) Holman (Davidson County Juvenile Court); Clemmie Greenlee (Peacemakers & Magdalene House, Nashville, TN); and of course: The Indiana State Police Department; Decatur County (Indiana) Sheriff's Department & Westport Police Department.

A special word of thanks to the *Greensburg Daily News*, as well as *The Republic*, whose coverage of the Maddux case was factual without taking advantage of the victims. The Indiana State Parole Board department was always polite. The employees in the office of County Clerk Janet Chadwell (Indiana) were friendly and assisted in record retrieval, and they were a blessing to people not completely familiar with the court system records. Thank you for your assistance and concern. The Indiana Prison System was always quick to answer questions and was so professional.

Thank you to the City of Westport, Indiana for your hospitality and graciousness. You were so friendly to a stranger with a camera asking a bunch of questions, whose cell phone never had service!

Thank you to the best attorney you could have, Ron Vrablik (Nashville, TN) who always has my back, and a seat at the lunch table for exchanging great stories. (*www.svnash.com/*)

Huge thanks to Paralegal Laura Locke (Nashville, TN) who knows her business, and is a blessing as a friend.

Thank you to Esther Loeb, Holocaust survivor and my adopted grandmother, who taught me that one can overcome any odds and laugh too. I wish I could share this with you. I miss you so much that my heart aches. *Shalom.*

Thank you to my family who supported me. Thank you to my forever friends: Barb, Shirley, Pat Smith, Pat Stone, Lise, Alex, LaDonna, Dad and Wanda Hetzel, Nelda Byrom, "Nurse" J. Schweizer, My FB family, insert your name here for thanks: _____. Thank you to my mother who instilled in me the burning desire to read and then write: "richer than I you can never be; I had a mother who read to me" (Strickland Gillilan). For Zan, what would I do without you? I do not want to know.

To Mary Gardner, always loving, supportive, and strong, who listened and suggested, who said, "Go for it." For this I love you even more.

To my grandmother. I miss you every moment.

To Kuki Gallmann, who said to me in her most passionate Italian voice, "You must write!" *Kwa heri*, my friend.

Thank you to Jon Oldham, a real police officer and a true

263

investigator. I thank you for opening up the door to me and never hesitating once in your trust. If I could do it all over again, I would have worked with you.

Special thanks to the employees and officers of case #42-8321: I made the calls, and you immediately invited me in. Thank you for the time you took to talk with me and then to proofread, to ensure I got it right. Each of you showed the dedication, concern, and professionalism all officers should have in their daily jobs while working this case. I wish I could have worked with each of you. Thank you for doing your best for Brad, and thank you for working with me.

Thank you to the friends and family of Douglas Sims. Thank you for trusting me with your stories, for telling me things no one else has heard, for letting me in. There were sides to Doug that defined him, both good and bad. Thank you for understanding we have to see both sides in order to prevent future horrific events.

Special thanks to Brad's friends, who shared with me the stories and the information, telling me things no one else knew. I thank you for your trust and confidence. In his short life, he touched so many people. Bradley had very special friends. He is smiling down at you.

Special thanks to Rob Nugent, who painfully took me through that horrific night, ensuring no detail was spared to make certain the truth was told. You are a blessing. "If it can save one child, it's worth it," he told me. Rob is truly a good man.

Special thanks to Ernest "Junior" Armstrong, who also excruciatingly led me through that night and the days that followed—despite the nightmares and flashbacks it would cost him. Junior is one of those rare breeds: a good guy with angel's wings.

Finally, mostly, thanks to the Maddux family, who I respect beyond the stars: A simple written thank you is not enough for opening your hearts and homes to me. You trusted me with Brad's story and your words and thoughts. Each and every one of you is a blessing to this world. I hope this book helps you find some semblance of peace. It is my hope we will educate others, help make children safe, and keep the perpetrators behind bars. Then we have done justice. Brad's finest traits are in all of you.

20% of book sales are donated to a non-profit charity called Living Beyond Breast Cancer (www.lbbc.org) which provide cancer prevention & education, in Brad Maddux's name, as chosen by his family.

15: APPENDIX & RESOURCES

Studies cited and suggested reading:

Abel, G.G. & Harlow, N. (April 2002). The Abel & Harlow stop child molestation prevention study. Retrieved from http://www.yellodyno.com/pdf/Child_Molestation_Prev ention_Study.pdf.

Allen, B. & Bosta, D. (1981). Games criminals play. Ra John Publishers: Sacramento, CA.

Best, J. Halloween sadism: the evidence. Retrieved April 1, 2013
from
http://www.udel.edu/soc/faculty/best/site/halloween.ht ml.

Chaffin, M., Letourneau, E., Levenson, J., & Stern, P. (2009). *How safe are trick-or-treaters? An analysis of child sex crime rates on Halloween. "Sexual Abuse: A Journal of Research & Treatment."* Vol. 21 no. 3 363-374 Retrieved April 1, 2013
from: http://sax.sagepub.com/content/21/3/363.abstract

de Becker, G. (1997). The gift of fear, Little, Brown, & Company: New York.

Durose, M. R.; Langan, P.A., & Schmitt, E.L. (November 2003). The U.S. Department of Justice study on the Recidivism of Sex Offenders Released from Prison in 1994. Retrieved from
http://bjs.ojp.usdoj.gov/content/pub/ascii/rsorp94.txt.

Finkelhor, D., Hammer, H. & Sedlak, A.J. (2002). Nonfamily Abducted Children: National Estimates and

Characteristics. *Juvenile Justice Bulletin–NCJ196467, 1-16.*
Order #MC19. Retrieved November 1, 2011 from
http://www.unh.edu/ccrc/Missing_Kids_Papers_pubs.ht
ml.

Finkelhor, D., Hammer, H. & Sedlak, A.J. (2002).
Nonfamily Abducted Children: National Estimates and
Characteristics. *Juvenile Justice Bulletin–NCJ196469, 1-16.*
Order #MC19. Retrieved November 5, 2011 from
https://www.ncjrs.gov/html/ojjdp/nismart/04/.

Greenfield, L. (1996, March 1). Bureau of Justice Statistics.
Child Victimizers: Violent offenders and their victims.
Retrieved November 10, 2011 from
http://bjs.ojp.usdoj.gov/index.cfm?ty=gsearch.

Helmstetter, F.J., Jarome, T., Kim, J.J., Lee, T., Li, S-J.
(2009, November 25). *Chronic stress selectively reduces
hippocampal volume in rats: a longitudinal MRI study.* National
Institute of Health Peer Reviewed Journal on the Internet
(20) 17. Retrieved February 17, 2012
fromhttp://www.ncbi.nlm.nih.gov/pmc/articles/PMC278
3199/.

ABOUT THE AUTHOR

Judith A. Yates is an award winning true crime author and criminologist. She is a True Crime and National Crime & Courts Examiner for examiner.com/Nashville. She contributes to corrections.com and Serial Killer Magazine. Her collegiate work appeared in national journals. Her nonfiction has appeared in several newspapers. Ms. Yates has taught crime prevention & education since 1991 and is an expert on domestic violence education. She holds a Master of Science in Criminal Justice; she was recognized for her thesis on school violence. She is currently completing her PhD in Criminal Justice.

Ms. Yates has been employed in corrections, loss prevention, private investigations, and as a professor of criminal justice. Ms. Yates has attended law enforcement schools & training across the country, to include Texas, New Mexico, Tennessee, and Maryland.

She performs guest speaker presentations and training across the country for various organizations, to include the Texas Association of Legal Investigators, Dallas, Texas Police Department, Mansfield, Texas Police Department & Sheriff's Office, National Parents, Families, & Friends of Lesbians & Gays (PFLAG), The International Association for Identification, The Federal Bureau of Prisons, Dayton-Hudson Loss Prevention Departments, and the Tennessee Correctional Association.

Ms. Yates volunteers with animal rescue groups. She volunteers for several nonprofit organizations to prevent crime and educate the public on crime.

Ms. Yates shares her home in Tennessee with horses, dogs, cats, and snakes. Her hobbies include photography and found objects artwork.

This is her second book. See www.Judithayates.com.

CPSIA information can be obtained
at www.ICGtesting.com
Printed in the USA
LVHW101038210722
724055LV00027B/51